A Philosophical Examination of Social Justice and
Child Poverty

A Philosophical Examination of Social Justice and Child Poverty

Gottfried Schweiger
Paris Lodron University of Salzburg, Austria

and

Gunter Graf
Paris Lodron University of Salzburg, Austria
International Research Centre for Social and Ethical Questions, Salzburg, Austria

Except where otherwise noted, this work is licensed under a Creative Commons Attribution 3.0 Unported License. To view a copy of this license, visit http://creativecommons.org/licenses/by/3.0/

© Gottfried Schweiger and Gunter Graf 2015

Softcover reprint of the hardcover 1st editon 2015 978-1-137-42601-7

The authors have asserted their rights to be identified as the authors of this work in accordance with the Copyright, Designs and Patents Act 1988.

Open access:

 Except where otherwise noted, this work is licensed under a Creative Commons Attribution 3.0 Unported License. To view a copy of this license, visit http://creativecommons.org/licenses/by/3.0/

Published with the support of the Austrian Science Fund (FWF): PUB 296-Z22

 Der Wissenschaftsfonds.

First published 2015 by
PALGRAVE MACMILLAN

Palgrave Macmillan in the UK is an imprint of Macmillan Publishers Limited, registered in England, company number 785998, of Houndmills, Basingstoke, Hampshire RG21 6XS.

Palgrave Macmillan in the US is a division of St Martin's Press LLC, 175 Fifth Avenue, New York, NY 10010.

Palgrave Macmillan is the global academic imprint of the above companies and has companies and representatives throughout the world.

Palgrave® and Macmillan® are registered trademarks in the United States, the United Kingdom, Europe and other countries

ISBN 978-1-349-49067-7   ISBN 978-1-137-42602-4 (eBook)

DOI 10.1007/978-1-137-42602-4

A catalogue record for this book is available from the British Library.

Library of Congress Cataloging-in-Publication Data

Schweiger, Gottfried.
   A philosophical examination of social justice and child poverty / Gottfried Schweiger and Gunter Graf.
   pages cm
   Includes bibliographical references.

   1. Child welfare. 2. Poor children – Social conditions. 3. Poverty. 4. Social justice. I. Graf, Gunter, 1983– II. Title.

HV713.S373 2015
362.7086'942—dc23   2015002672

Contents

List of Tables	vi
Acknowledgments	vii
Introduction: Philosophy and Child Poverty	**1**
1 Social Justice for Children – A Capability Approach	**15**
1.1 The currency of justice	16
1.2 Selecting functionings and capabilities for children	37
1.3 Sufficiency and equality	51
1.4 Conclusions	64
2 The Injustice of Child Poverty	**67**
2.1 Concepts and measures of child poverty	70
2.2 The Ill-Being and Ill-Becoming of child poverty: physical and mental health	85
2.3 The Ill-Being and Ill-Becoming of child poverty: social inclusion and education	93
2.4 The subjective experience of child poverty	104
2.5 Conclusions	115
3 Responsibilities for Children in Poverty	**118**
3.1 Attributing responsibilities to agents of justice	122
3.2 Important agents of justice and their responsibilities	139
3.3 The family and the state	148
3.4 Conclusions	160
4 Advancing Our Approach to Global Justice for Children	**162**
4.1 Conclusions	174
References	176
Index	193

List of Tables

2.1	Poverty thresholds for 2013 by size of family and number of related children under 18 years	73
2.2	Poverty in the USA	74
2.3	Poverty status of related children under 6 years of age in the USA	75
2.4	Rate of material deprivation and at-risk-of poverty rate in Europe	79
2.5	At-risk-of-poverty rate in Europe	80
2.6	Number of people in severe material deprivation in Europe	81
2.7	Child well-being in rich countries	84
2.8	Education, unemployment and earning in the USA	103

Acknowledgments

This book is the product of some hard work over a long period of time. We thank the colleagues with whom we discussed our ideas and arguments; they helped us write a better book. In particular we want to thank our home institutions, the Centre for Ethics and Poverty Research at the University of Salzburg and the International Research Center for Social and Ethical Questions (ifz), and their director, Clemens Sedmak. We also thank the Austrian Science Fund (FWF) for funding our research project Social Justice and Child Poverty (P 26480); the fund provided us with the opportunity to realize this book. We hope that our work not only contributes to the philosophical discussion but also helps to make the world a better place for children.

OPEN

Introduction: Philosophy and Child Poverty

Child poverty is surely one of the most severe problems in today's world and undoubtedly an ethical issue that needs to be tackled. It is hard to find anyone who argues against the claim that children should not be poor and that we should do something about that. But if we go beyond these obvious truths and dig deeper, we will find many unanswered questions spanning different disciplines, including conceptual, empirical and – as we will particularly argue in this book – normative questions. Child poverty is first and foremost an issue of social sciences, and most publications and studies on this topic belong to that field. But due to its wide-ranging consequences, disciplines such as medicine and psychology are also concerned with it, and more and more researchers acknowledge that such a complex phenomenon must be investigated based on a multidisciplinary approach. Furthermore, it is a highly relevant political topic, and the fight against child poverty is part of the agenda of national and international politicians alike. The reduction of child poverty was part of the Millennium Goals, it will certainly be a goal in the post-2015 agenda, and it is included in the Europe 2020 strategy of the European Union, as well as in countless national action plans or policies.

If one looks at the current state of research and what is done to help children in poverty, it is not easy get the full picture. There are many different conceptions of child poverty, different methods to measure it and no consensus on how best to alleviate it. Philosophy is currently only marginally involved in these debates, but the fields of poverty research and poverty alleviation are implicitly deeply entangled with philosophical issues – most importantly, from our point of view at least, with normative and ethical ones. We would like to briefly name four of them here, before going on to argue for the importance of a deeper philosophical look into child poverty and show how we will develop our argument in the course of this book.

The first issue is conceptualizing poverty and child poverty. Two ideas are well suited to illustrate that: firstly, poverty is an 'essentially contested' concept, which means that there will presumably never be a consensus on how to understand it properly; secondly, it is a 'thick concept', in the sense that it combines both descriptive and normative dimensions (Schweiger 2012). Every concept of poverty is more than just an empirical description, including a normative dimension, which unfolds in two directions. On the one hand, poverty is evaluative. Describing an adult or child as poor is in most cases also meant to describe the living condition of this person as bad and, to some extent, morally wrong. Entailed in almost all definitions found in poverty research, in policy contexts and in the public and media discourse is that being poor is not good, not something that should be aspired to. On the other hand – and this follows from the judgment that it is something bad – poverty has a certain appellative character. It is used to trigger actions of other people or institutions. Due to this normative dimension, poverty is in a way an 'essentially contested' concept: reaching a consensus on its definition and measurement is very unlikely. Paul Spicker, for example, has distinguished twenty-four concepts of poverty in sociological research alone (Spicker 2007). What it means for a person to be poor is highly unclear, simply because we need to have some kind of normative theory in the background to tell us what aspects of human life or of life in a particular society are important enough to determine poverty. Are resources or capabilities what matter, or is it life satisfaction? What are the important things that we can and should use to measure and track poverty? Naturally, various normative theories can be used for that purpose, and they will most certainly produce different results. We will introduce and discuss many of the relevant concepts in the course of this book. What is important at this stage is to realize that normative considerations have an important place already in the conceptualization of poverty and that it is not possible to grasp it descriptively only.

The second issue is poverty measurement. There are many ethical issues about conducting poverty research itself, especially with children (Bostock 2002; Sime 2008). Poverty is a sensitive issue; it runs deep, making the poor vulnerable. Qualitative research in particular often demands that people talk about private matters. It happens very close to the lives and experiences of poor people, and it touches upon sensitive issues, which are connected to feelings of anger, shame and humiliation. Furthermore, there is an almost unavoidable imbalance in power and knowledge between the poverty researcher and the poor person; this has to be dealt with.

The third issue is fighting poverty and the question of moral responsibilities of researchers. Poverty research is done not only to gather more knowledge about the poor, to count them and to describe their lives, but because this knowledge should be also used to a large extent to change something and to help end poverty. Many poverty researchers claim with Else Øyen that helping the poor is one of the major drivers to engage in research in the first place (Øyen 2009), but it is highly unclear what kind of obligation is triggered by describing and defining a person as being poor and towards what persons it is directed. Some sort of obligation is almost always implicitly inherent, and so many studies about poverty conclude with some sort of policy advice or name institutions that could make a difference. In the case of national or international poverty surveys that count and monitor the poor, those who are obliged to change the situation are often directly named: the particular state whose official offices track poverty, the European Union or the World Bank and its member states. Poverty research is therefore not only needed to guide policymaking; the definitions and measures employed have power (Ruggeri Laderchi, Saith and Stewart 2006) – if one is not counted as being poor, it can mean that one does not receive benefits or other forms of support by the state. Alice O'Connor has described this issue from a different perspective and argued that poverty research that focuses too much on counting the poor and on refining methods to 'intrude' in their lives and to monitor them is in danger of losing its connection to economic and political issues. Rather, it is necessary to combine poverty research with inquiry and criticism of the economic, social and political environment in which poverty is produced and reproduced and how the national and international institutions have to change to get down to the roots of the problem.

> Although liberal in origins, poverty knowledge rests on an ethos of political and ideological neutrality that has sustained it through a period of vast political change. Very much for this reason, it can also be distinguished by what it is not: contemporary poverty knowledge does not define itself as an inquiry into the political economy and culture of late twentieth-century capitalism; it is knowledge about the characteristics and behaviour and, especially in recent years, about the welfare status of the poor. (O'Connor 2001, 4)

The fourth issue is the inclusion of the poor themselves in theorizing poverty. This raises deep questions related to power: Who decides or should decide what poverty is and who is characterized as poor? Who has or should have the power to help and change the living conditions of the poor? In short, whether one is counted as poor or not is usually not dependent on whether one views herself as poor. Poverty measures focus mostly – and for good reason – on objective indicators such as income, wealth, goods and capabilities, but there is a growing concern that this focus might be a major shortcoming and that the multidimensionality of poverty and social exclusion demands *the inclusion of the view of the poor themselves* (Brock 1999; Norton 2001). The rise of the debate about subjective well-being, which obviously cannot be determined objectively without reference to the interior view, and its use for poverty research is also an indicator for this (Kingdon and Knight 2006). Finally, the *role of poor people themselves* in the *conceptualization, measurement and evaluation of poverty* is in question. Do they know best, maybe better than poverty researchers, what poverty means or should mean? Neither poverty research nor normative philosophy is situated outside the real world, which is full of relations of power and domination, and it is a fact that some knowledge is privileged and a few have the power to shape the discourse about poverty. Robert Chambers, one of the pioneers of participatory work, writes about that issue:

> A question remains: whose analysis and categories are to be privileged? These are largely 'ours', those of professionals who are not ourselves poor, expressed in 'our' language. The words, concepts, categories and priorities of poor people, especially illustrated by the way they were elicited and expressed in the Voices of the Poor, were rich and varied with commonalities. There are trade-offs to be puzzled over: between 'their' realities and ours; between local participatory diversity and commensurability for purposes of aggregation; and between many categories representing poor people's realities and fewer categories more manageable for outsider professionals and for measurement. (Chambers 2007, 37)

We cannot tackle all of these issues in-depth in this book. They give, however, a first glimpse into the highly complex issues that surround any debate about poverty and the ways in which philosophical, in particular normative, questions, arise. This is not breaking news, neither to poverty researchers and policymakers nor to philosophers. However, today philosophy and poverty research still usually work separately and hence miss out on the benefits of a certainly needed interdisciplinarity. There are, of course, a few exceptions; for example, Monique Deveaux's

(Deveaux 2013) attempt to include the poor as agents of justice (we will comment more on that in the last chapter) or Thomas Pogge's discussion about the flaws in the poverty measures of the World Bank (Reddy and Pogge 2010). But more needs to be done, and it is a shame that philosophy is not a part of most interdisciplinary discussions about poverty. Such collaborations demand much from both sides: social scientists working empirically have to become aware of what they can actually profit from the highly sophisticated debates in philosophy about justice and morality, and philosophers need to acknowledge that the reality of poverty is much fuzzier than we often assume it to be and that constructing valuable theories about poverty and its alleviation implies doing justice to the empirical basis.

Let us now speak more about the aims and scope of this book. It is important to make clear from the beginning that we will be first and foremost concerned with child poverty as it typically occurs in developed countries with welfare systems, as in most member states of the European Union, the USA, Australia and Canada. There are many differences between these countries and systems, and it would be wrong to suggest uniformity here, but they usually manage to avoid, at least to a large degree, extreme or absolute forms of poverty in which children miss the resources for survival and basics such as shelter and access to the most important health care services. Nevertheless, studies show that child poverty is also a big issue in these countries and that most of them are far from giving all their children a fair start in life. The reason for our focus on child poverty as it appears within relatively wealthy states is threefold: First, it is to a certain extent a pragmatic decision. It is not possible to discuss all ethically relevant facets connected to child poverty in this book; we had to narrow down the topics of investigation for the sake of simplicity. Furthermore, data from developed countries are more extensive and more easily available. We know more about how poverty shapes children's lives and the opportunities they get, and a moral theory can be developed in regard to a richer and more substantive material. Second, the injustices of child poverty are more difficult and philosophically challenging to grasp when relative forms of poverty are at stake. As we have already stated, in the countries we take as points of reference, children usually do not die because of poverty, and state support as well as welfare benefits damp the worst consequences of their situation. In some sense, they are better off than their peers in developing countries or failed states; a moral evaluation of child poverty needs to go deeper than pointing to the fact that even the most basic elements of their lives are missing. Finally, our focus on the concept of *social justice*, which we consider very useful and rich for evaluating child poverty, quite naturally leads to a focus on developed countries with functioning democracies and institutions which, despite all their problems and weaknesses, (still) provide a solid social structure for large parts of their citizenry, especially if they are compared to states where almost no infrastructure and only minimal state support is available. Most philosophers in the field developed their theories in regard to such contexts, and many discussions still relate to nation states and 'internal' distributions of goods, isolated from relationships between countries. We agree that it is important to extend these theories to the domain of global justice and world poverty, and attempts to do so have substantially enriched the theoretical landscape in the last years. In the last chapter, we will therefore briefly address some of the additional questions arising in relation to evaluating extreme forms of child poverty in the developing world.

Our book is located within a certain approach of normative reasoning and thinking about poverty: namely, the capability approach and its most influential representatives, Amartya Sen and Martha Nussbaum. The capability approach has many advocates and certainly also many critics, and we neither hope nor aim to defend it against all of them. Our goal in this book is to apply the approach to a specific topic. Therefore, we will not be able to scrutinize it on a general and fundamental level; we leave these intellectual battles to others. Still, we will say much about the capability approach, how it should be applied to children and what additional value it brings for the analysis and critique of child poverty. As a consequence, we will bring forward several arguments that speak in favor of the approach in general and support many of its assumptions. The capability approach seems a good starting point for our examination, not only because it can provide the normative underpinnings for our goals but also because it is widely used in a variety of academic disciplines as well as policymaking. When it comes to academia, it is extensively discussed, developed, applied and criticized not only in philosophy but also in economics, social policy, political science and development studies, which confirms its interdisciplinary usefulness. A no less influential document than the Human Development Report, which is published annually by the United Nations and monitors human development on a global level, explicitly draws on the capability approach, even if some have questioned how accurately the report represents its theoretical and normative background (Pogge 2002). On the national level, too, governments are interested in the approach and apply it for diverse purposes; the reports on poverty and wealth in Germany (Arndt and Volkert 2006) and the reports of the United Kingdom's National

Equalities Commission, for example, apply the capability approach as part of their theoretical background for their respective concerns (Burchardt and Vizard 2011). And last but not least, it has been inspiring and guiding the work of NGOs and local development initiatives in many different countries and cultural contexts (Deneulin and Shahani 2009). This richness is an asset for our examination of child poverty and social justice, and we will draw not only on the philosophical writings of Nussbaum and Sen but also on the research done in other disciplines which have applied the capability approach to children and to poverty.

Any application of the capability approach faces some challenges that should be made clear at the outset. To begin with, there is no full consensus in the literature on which set of claims and postulates are constitutive of the capability approach. In fact, different authors work on it, and each of them has introduced some new elements or focus points, something that is, inter alia, documented through a constant rise in academic publications on the subject. Furthermore, the capability approach can be characterized not only as a theory in political philosophy but as an 'intellectual movement and programme for action' (Venkatapuram 2011, 114) involving many different agents on the theoretical and practical level. This fact also introduces a certain internal variety and complicates its representation as a clear-cut theoretical concept. In the formulations of Nussbaum and Sen, there is no uniformity to be found, either. While Sen is considered the founder of the approach, Nussbaum joined in early on and over the years developed her own account, which is, in some aspects at least, different from Sen's ideas. In the end, our suggestion will be to work with a kind of 'hybrid', combining elements of both theories, a strategy which has itself proven valuable in other contexts (see, e.g., Wolff and de-Shalit 2007; Venkatapuram 2011).

Besides the capability approach, another major influence on our examination of child poverty comes from the multidisciplinary research on children's well-being and well-becoming. We will argue that these concepts should have a central role in a theory of justice for children, claiming that a just society is one in which each and every child develops and achieves functionings and capabilities that are necessary for her well-being and well-becoming. This introduction of well-being into the capability approach might seem odd, because of the rivalry between capabilities and subjective welfare as possible metrics of justice (a topic which we will discuss in more detail in the first chapter). Let us be clear from the beginning what we understand as well-being and well-becoming. They are not the same as subjective welfare or happiness or satisfaction; in our view, well-being is a multidimensional concept encompassing a wide range of important features of children's lives: health, education, social inclusion and participation, access to material goods and shelter and the like. A concept of justice for children that is oriented towards children's well-being and well-becoming is primarily concerned not with them being happy but with providing them with the full range of capabilities and functionings that they are entitled to reach comprehensive well-being. Such an objectivist understanding of well-being, as an actual state of being well, and of well-becoming, as the change from one state of being to a state of being well, is now common in much research on children and guiding policies. The capability approach is itself such an objectivist approach towards well-being; for example, Mario Biggeri and his colleagues understand children's well-being as the combination of important capabilities and functionings (Biggeri and Mehrotra 2011). It is also possible to interpret the ten central capabilities of Nussbaum as being a formulation of a concept of well-being. This perspective has been articulated by Alexander Bagattini:

> According to the capability approach, the well-being of persons is identified with a bundle of capabilities that are essential for human nature. (This is seen in analogy with other beings in nature, like plants that need photosynthesis or predators that need to be quick and silent when hunting.) In her recent book, *Creating Capabilities*, Martha Nussbaum gives a list of ten basic capabilities that are supposed to be constitutive for the well-being of human beings: life; bodily integrity; bodily health; senses, imagination, and thought; emotions; practical reason; affiliation; concern for animals and plants; play; and control over one's environment (Nussbaum 2011, p. 33f). Due to its objective account of well-being, the capability approach is very attractive for a conception of child well-being. (Bagattini 2014, 175)

Let us say something about the concept of well-being then. First, we suggest that well-being in childhood matters for its own sake. While it is true that most political philosophers evaluate childhood only insofar it contributes to the genesis of the characteristics necessary for the good life of an adult, this conclusion seems wrong, as a thought experiment by Harry Brighouse powerfully shows (Brighouse 2003): Imagine a tragic world in which happiness in childhood – even though no necessary condition – is a serious barrier to flourishing in adulthood. Under such circumstances, it is obvious that we would consider the scarce individuals who managed to have both a happy childhood and adulthood to be privileged. The standard and more reliable route to get to a flourishing adulthood via a dreary childhood is an inferior option. Furthermore, let's assume with Brighouse that in such a tragic world there is a reliable correlation between the degree of dreariness in childhood and the level of flourishing in adulthood. Would we really judge parents who impose enormous amounts of dreariness on their children compared to those who allow moments of enjoyment, even knowing that it affects the child's future negatively, as the better ones? We agree that the answer to this question is not an obvious one; there is the strong intuition that the well-being of children seems to matter for its own sake, independently of its contribution to life as an adult. It is simply a good thing that a child lives a flourishing life, exercising and developing her capacities (Macleod 2010). Accordingly, we assume, in line with most theorists in the field, that childhood is intrinsically valuable and that children as the subjects of moral concern have a right to a good life.

Second, the child's condition, which includes a particular vulnerability, immaturity and dependency on others, makes her well-being an especially salient normative category. Children cannot be held responsible for their life choices as adults can, and therefore any harm to their well-being is particularly problematic from a moral point of view. Hence, a society that does not manage to sustain a certain level of well-being for its children cannot be a just one. This does not mean, of course, that the well-being of children is the *only* thing that matters for justice. The child's future as an autonomous and thriving citizen – her becoming – is of importance as well, as is the well-being and well-becoming of all other members of society. However, since it often gets completely neglected in theories of justice, we want to stress clearly the importance that the well-being of children, qua children, should have for normative reasoning.

Third, a comprehensive understanding of children's lives must include a multitude of information. It just is not enough to know, for example, the economic situation of a child or her family in order to judge if she is indeed well off. There is more to disadvantage than can be expressed in monetary terms. In many approaches to the measurement of child poverty, this insight is well established. There, the well-being of children is judged in different dimensions, which are also set into relation with each other. When looking at the lives of children explicitly from a *normative* perspective, such a multidimensional approach is also requested. This is the case for the following reasons: First, if philosophy wants to develop an understanding of justice that is applicable in the real world and its non-ideal circumstances, it must work with a realistic picture of well-being. It should reflect our intuitive judgments about the subject and allow plausible assessments of the social position of an individual (Wolff and de-Shalit 2007, 21). It is obvious that different aspects of children's lives matter; it would be a theoretical distortion to reduce them to a single good or source and to suggest that being privileged in one dimension compensates the difficulties a child experiences in another. Suppose, for example, that a child with superior academic achievements has serious difficulties socializing and finding friends. The argument that the success in one area is a good reason for neglecting the problems in the other does not, from a commonsensical perspective, do justice to the child's situation and misses important aspects of her wellbeing. Second, only a pluralist view of the well-being of children allows a differentiated look at what kinds of disadvantages are especially harmful or, to approach it from a different angle, which aspects of a child's life can have a comprehensive and sustainable positive effect on her general situation. Evaluations from a social justice perspective must be sensitive to such differences. Of course, many empirical questions concerning the identification of the most important dimensions of a child's life emerge here, and philosophy cannot answer them a priori. However, its theories must be able to grasp and conceptualize them adequately.

With our focus on children's well-being we strongly agree that it is wrong to look at children *only* as 'human becomings' (Qvortrup 1994; Lee 2001), meaning that they are conceptualized primarily as the future adults they will become. There are very good reasons to take their well-being per se into account and to give it normative weight. In fact, this already follows from a very basic and commonsensical assumption about the moral status of children: namely, that they are entitled to the same moral consideration as adults. This means that their moral claims count equally to those of adult members of a society and that it is morally wrong to discount them with the argument that they are 'only children' (Brennan and Noggle 1997). However, we would also like to stress that considerations concerning justice for children cannot exclusively focus on children qua children. As important as it is to recognize the 'being' child as a social actor in her own right participating in and constructing her own childhood (Uprichard 2008, 304), there is also a need to allow for a life course perspective which recognizes that children usually become adults and that childhood is the most formative period of human life, influencing profoundly the level of well-being one experiences later on, from adulthood to old age. The overemphasis on the child's future and the child's becoming, which is prevalent in large parts of political philosophy, should not be replaced by an overemphasis on childhood itself as is, at least partly, currently the case in the blooming field of childhood studies (Uprichard 2008, 305; Qvortrup 2004, 269). Rather, the being and the becoming aspects of childhood have to be brought together, and a child-sensitive concept of justice has to operate within the tension between a present- and a future-centered perspective on children's lives. This does not mean a return to an oversimplifying and misleading notion of children as incomplete or innocent incompetents (Archard 2004) who stand in sharp contrast to fully developed and capable adults. Competency depends on both context and task, and in many aspects and situations, children can in fact be more competent than adults (Alanen and Mayall 2001); in addition, it must be acknowledged that development and change are processes at work during the whole life cycle, including adulthood and old age. Still, we suggest that the child's future and her *well-becoming*, that is, her development to a state of well-being over time, is a particularly important normative category; justice should be concerned with human life as a whole and not just with sections of it. Well-being in adulthood and old age is also morally relevant, and therefore one should not underestimate well-becoming considerations, especially since they can get into conflict with claims to a child's well-being. And while childhood is intrinsically valuable and should not be subordinated to adulthood or seen as a mere preparatory phase, it is reasonable to say that children (normally) lack morally relevant characteristics that are of great importance for adulthood and that can be certainly fostered – but also inhibited – by the way children are raised and educated. In particular, we want to argue that the ability to live a self-determined and autonomous life according to a mature conception of the good is generally a valuable achievement in human life (Rawls 1971; Nussbaum 2000; Sen 1999). Now, to act on one's own judgment and to live a life one has reason to value presupposes knowledge, experience, stability of character, the ability to assess the consequences of one's actions and to relate them with one's identity in time, as well as a certain level of emotional health. These abilities, skills and facets of life have to be trained and nurtured – if not, the well-being in adulthood, which crucially includes the ability to act on one's own judgments, is seriously jeopardized. However, sometimes trade-offs are necessary, and so the way children are treated and reared should also include a developmental perspective (Noggle 2002; Brighouse 2003; Adams 2008). Indeed, it is very plausible to claim that children have a right to an adequate development of their capacities, especially those relevant for exercising autonomy broadly construed. Accordingly, injustices for children can be comprehensively grasped only when the effects certain treatments in childhood have on the whole life course are considered.

Before we present a brief outline of the chapters in this book, we want to say something about two issues that we do not deal with but that are related to the topic at hand. The first issue is the question of the moral status of children, in particular toddlers and newborns, compared to that of (some) animals. There is some philosophical debate about why we should treat such young children differently compared to bonobos or other apes, and this debate is centered on issues of rationality, autonomy and the ability to experience harm. We do not have a clear-cut answer and we also do not engage with this question in this book. Our premise is to say that human children have a moral status which implies that we should treat them with respect and be concerned about their well-being and well-becoming. We will later on explicate what this means in terms of responsibilities of different agents of justice towards children. Whether this moral status should also be applied to other non-human children is not our concern; we leave it to others to debate whether or not a just society would also require us to battle child poverty among non-human animals.

Closely connected to that issue is the second question: the status of children not yet born. This question has two aspects, both of which are connected to a rich as well as controversial philosophical and political debate. On the one hand a society which wants to realize justice for all its children has to take a stance on abortion and also on what it owes to children during pregnancy. We also do not give a answer here, although we will briefly touch upon the issue that it can have harmful consequences if the mother is poor during pregnancy and that this health risk for the baby has to be taken seriously. It is a very delicate question whether or not the right answer here is mandatory prenatal care, based on evidence that being poor influences reproductive health and that girls living in poverty more often get pregnant (voluntarily and involuntarily) than their non-poor peers. On the other hand we focus in this book more or less exclusively on children already born, and we do engage with questions of intergenerational justice. Poverty reduction and alleviation, also during childhood, fight an injustice that should not exist from the start, and intergenerational justice is part of the larger question of how we can make sure that each and every child that is born is free of poverty.

This book is organized in four chapters. Chapter 1 develops a concept of social justice for children. We will argue that the capability approach provides a good framework and discuss some issues that arise when applying this approach to children. Neither Sen nor Nussbaum have written much about children, how a capability-oriented concept of justice for children should be constructed and in what ways it differs from a concept for adults. The most important modification we want to make is to have a more dynamic understanding of functionings and capabilities, since childhood is a phase of development. Furthermore, an initial focus on achieved functionings seems advisable, since children lack some of the conditions, like autonomy and rationality, to enjoy capabilities in the genuine sense of the term. We will also tackle the issues of selecting relevant functionings and capabilities for children and will specify which distributional rule is best suited for our purposes. We will suggest that a sufficiency-based rule is the most adequate one and explain how it should be interpreted in the context of modern welfare states. Nussbaum and other capability theorists present the capability approach as a concept of minimal justice, which focuses on severe injustices as they typically appear in global poverty in poorer countries. This feature of the approach poses some problems for our case, since we will criticize child poverty in affluent countries, where poverty is usually less severe and harmful. We will conclude the first chapter by claiming that children are entitled to a set of functionings and, as they grow older, capabilities that are important for their well-being and well-becoming. It is a question of justice that they enjoy these functionings and capabilities up to a certain threshold as far as the states in which they live can secure. Furthermore, every child is, within reasonable limits, entitled to develop and achieve well-being as adults. We want to catch this aspect with the term 'equality of opportunity to well-being', which, again, can be expressed on the basis of important functionings and capabilities.

In Chapter 2, we will, based on these normative considerations, examine child poverty and investigate how it affects certain important functionings and capabilities related to both the well-being and well-becoming of children. We will focus particularly on mental and physical health, education and social inclusion, which we consider rather uncontroversial aspects of the well-being and well-becoming of children. We develop our argument in close dialogue with the results of empirical research and show that there is overwhelming evidence that child poverty has detrimental effects on all of them. This finding will lead to the conclusion that child poverty has to be understood as a corrosive disadvantage. It negatively affects more than one important functioning or capability, both horizontally and temporally: child poverty is corrosive during childhood, throughout the whole future life course of the children and to their chances for well-being as adults.

In Chapter 3, we will focus on 'agents of justice'; that is, persons or institutions responsible for securing justice for children in poverty. We will develop a model of responsibilities, using and further advancing a suggestion of Iris Young as presented in her book *Responsibilities for Justice*. There, she distinguishes different grounds or parameters that can be used to attribute agents of justice with various kinds and weights of responsibilities. The grounds that will be at the heart of our model are causation (being responsible for that injustice in the first place), power (being able to help the victims of that injustice), privilege (having benefited from the existence of that injustice) and interest (having an interest in overcoming that injustice). We will then distinguish eight potential groups of agents of justice (the poor child, the family and close caregivers, the neighborhood and close social environment, the state and its institutions, the community of citizens, the economy, the international institutions, the global community) and give a first ranking of the weight of their responsibilities in the context of child poverty. Our model is still vague, but this reflects both the complexity of the issue and the limits of philosophical inquiry. Attributing concrete responsibilities to the groups of agents we named based on the criteria we presented requires deeper empirical knowledge than we can bring to bear in this book, and to some extent it will never be possible to disentangle all of the relations and interferences. We will then take a closer look at two highly influential agents: the family and the state. We will argue that families in poverty are limited in their power and that their parenting behavior is shaped and influenced by how these parents grew up and how they have lived in poverty. It is not possible to disaggregate exactly how much of the behaviors that are actually harming their children can be attributed to this circumstance, for which they are not responsible themselves, and how much responsibility they have to shoulder. Being poor comes with a restriction of freedom; this restriction, however, is not a total one, and it would be unjust to neglect poor parents completely as agents of justice. We will conclude that the state has high responsibilities to support the child and her family in order to overcome poverty and to secure that the child achieves the functionings and capabilities she is entitled to.

Finally, instead of summarizing the book, Chapter 4 will sketch how our concept could be advanced to cover issues of global justice and global child poverty, which we widely neglect in the other chapters. We will identify a few of the questions that need to be tackled and give an idea how they should be approached. Again, the great urgency and need to address child poverty as a global phenomenon should be obvious. Here too, however, the topic needs philosophical inquiries that clarify in detail the moral implications involved.

Except where otherwise noted, this work is licensed under a Creative Commons Attribution 3.0 Unported License. To view a copy of this license, visit http://creativecommons.org/licenses/by/3.0/

OPEN

1
Social Justice for Children – A Capability Approach

In this chapter, we will outline a concept of social justice for children based on the capability approach. So far, this issue has received much less attention than it deserves given the particular social and political status of children in today`s world. The capability approach, as well as most other theories of justice, has not dealt with children thoroughly, although more and more literature on important questions in this regard is being published. We seek to answer two important questions that every concept of justice has to deal with: what is the right currency of justice, and what is its right principle? To phrase the questions slightly differently: what kinds of things are children entitled to as a matter of justice, and how should they be distributed? Our answer to the first question is that children are entitled to the achievement of important functionings; only as they develop is it adequate to provide them with capabilities. Hence, the capability approach to justice for children we want to defend is in large part a functioning approach. In regard to the second question, we defend a sufficientarian approach. In a nutshell, each and every child is entitled to reach a certain threshold in all these important functionings, and failing to do so constitutes an injustice. Since the main target of this book is child poverty in affluent societies and welfare states, we will model our concept of justice on children living within these societies, although we believe that many of our claims hold universally and could serve as the basis for a concept of global justice. In the end, we argue, justice for children is about safeguarding their well-being and well-becoming, and the functionings and capabilities that matter for justice, as well as the thresholds for them, should be selected with reference to that. Hence, well-being and well-becoming are the guiding principles for our approach.

1.1 The currency of justice

The first question a concept of justice for children has to answer is, what is the adequate currency of justice? That is, what types of things are children entitled to as a matter of justice? The capability approach is first and foremost an answer to that question; it claims that the best available currency of justice is constituted by capabilities. In what follows, we will argue that the approach has something very valuable to offer to the conception of justice for children but that it must shift its sole focus from capabilities, which essentially incorporate the notion of freedom of choice, to functionings that are actually realized. Justice for children has to be thought of as a dynamic concept that starts with functionings as the right currency; as children grow up, capabilities become ever more important. In the end, for adults, capabilities are what matter most, and the state or any other agent of justice should refrain from imposing functionings upon people who do not wish to have them.

Let us begin by spelling out some of its central concepts and assumptions. The origin of the capability approach lies in Sen's criticism of utilitarianism and in his claim that human well-being cannot and should not be identified with subjective welfare or utility. There are several well-known objections to the traditional formulation of utilitarianism, and replicating and assessing all of them here would exceed the scope of this book. Instead, we would like to point to some of Sen's and Nussbaum's concerns directly related to the metric of justice employed by utilitarians (Crocker 2008, 126–129). First, subjective welfare 'does not adequately represent well-being' (Sen 1990, 47). In its standard interpretation, it reduces the diversity of human experience to one single measure and suggests that, in the end, all different types of pleasures or satisfactions are commensurable. But does it really make sense to compare the pleasure we feel eating ice cream to that we get from helping a friend in need or raising a child? From Sen's and Nussbaum's point of view, it does not; they argue that the theoretical simplicity gained by adopting such a monist understanding of human well-being comes at a high cost: it cannot integrate our commonsensical experiences of how we perceive our lives and the intuition that a variety of different aspects matter for our 'wellness'. To be clear, subjective welfare is highly valued in the capability approach, and indeed, Sen refers to it as a 'momentous functioning' (Sen 1985, 200). However, it should be seen as one aspect of a person's well-being and not, as utilitarians suggest, the only thing that matters.

Second – and this is connected to the first point – the phenomenon of 'adaptive preferences' also suggests that a focus on a subjective metric is misleading when conceptualizing the well-being of a person. To make his point, Sen refers to empirical evidence: human beings often adapt their assessment of their own situation, including their wishes, hopes and general psychological state, to the circumstances they find themselves in. On the one hand, this may have the effect that one can feel subjectively happy even when suffering considerable disadvantages:

> Our mental reactions to what we actually get and what we can sensibly expect to get may frequently involve compromises with a harsh reality. The destitute thrown into beggary, the vulnerable landless labourer precariously surviving at the edge of subsistence, the overworked domestic servant working round the clock, the subdued and subjugated housewife reconciled to her role and her fate, all tend to come to terms with their respective predicaments. The deprivations are suppressed and muffled in the scale of utilities (reflected by desire-fulfilment and happiness) by the necessity of endurance in uneventful survival. (Sen 1999a, 15)

On the other hand, some individuals might have 'expensive tastes', meaning that they feel satisfaction or subjective happiness only if they possess or consume costly goods, such as high-powered sports cars or Almas caviar. In such cases, unhappiness related to the nonavailability of such goods should hardly be taken as an indicator that their overall well-being is jeopardized. Again, these feelings are important to consider as an aspect but not as the only definitional feature of their well-being. Accordingly, the malleability of any mental metric counts against its adequacy.

Third, Sen argues that a focus on utility sees a person only as the 'site' in which pleasant or painful experiences take place; there is no further interest in any other information about her interests and objectives. Or as Sen and Williams once put it: 'Persons do not count as individuals in this [utilitarian approach] any more than individual petrol tanks do in the analysis of the national consumption of petroleum' (Sen and Williams 1992, 4). In other words, the informational space employed by utilitarianism neglects a person's agency; that is, her ability to act and bring about change in the world in line with her own values and goals (Sen 1999b, 19). According to Sen, being able to pursue a life she has reason to value is an immensely important feature of a person's agency. Sometimes realization of values can imply hardship and may jeopardize many forms of human welfare and well-being. Nonetheless, he claims that a person's freedom to follow her ideals must be considered in evaluative exercises.

The second position (or better, family of positions) Sen has extensively criticized regarding its informational space can be labeled 'resourcism'. Its central claim is that an individual's social position can best be judged by her possession of some set of external resources. It comes in different versions, but the arguably most influential account is defended by John Rawls, whose work on justice has had a profound impact on the development of the capability approach. For Rawls, external resources relevant for the evaluation of social position embrace both material ones (such as money and wealth) and immaterial ones (e.g., rights and liberties). What really matters about them, according to Rawls, is that they are useful for pursuing a wide range of conceptions of the good life while being neutral about what this goodness consists of. In Rawls's theory, it is up to the autonomous citizen to decide what kind of life she wants to lead. The state should provide only the means and the institutional settings needed for an ample variety of ways of life; it should have no right, however, to prescribe one doctrine (moral, religious or spiritual) that all its members have to follow. This skepticism stems from the conviction that even between completely reasonable and rational persons, there will be no full agreement about fundamental ethical and political matters. However, according to Rawls, a set of all-purpose means that are useful to all and therefore have to be distributed in a fair way can be agreed on. At the same time, they are useful for making interpersonal comparisons, since the same index of these resources (primary goods, in Rawls's terminology) can be used to evaluate the social position of every citizen – they express each person's level of advantage (Rawls 1982, 163). Surely, Rawls's theory of justice is complex, and his account of primary goods is but one of its aspects. Its critique should therefore not be taken as a critique of the whole theory, which has to include many more facets. Nevertheless, resourcism is arguably deeply entrenched in it and cannot be easily given up without a complete modification of his concept of justice (Nussbaum 2006).

Against resourcism – be it Rawls's or any other version – Sen has brought forward inter alia the following two worries: First, Sen argues that the possession of resources is a misleading indicator for the social position of an individual; a variety of factors influence a person's ability to use a bundle of resources for her objectives. In the societies we know, it is not generally the case, as a matter of empirical fact, that two individuals who possess the same (primary) goods are equally advantaged. Personal heterogeneities, environmental diversities, variations in social climate, differences in relational perspectives and distributional issues within the family influence a person's abilities to convert resources into valuable outcomes (Sen 1999b, 71-72). A person in a wheelchair, for example, has to invest considerable resources just to achieve a degree of mobility someone without the disability enjoys with no investment whatsoever. As a realistic notion of advantage, resources are therefore problematic and in fact lead to unfair judgments. At closer examination, their alleged neutrality fails, allowing for discrimination against the less fortunate, who are generally in a less favorable position to use their resources for the ends they value. Second, and entangled with the first objection, Sen argues that a focus on resources 'suffers from [a] fetishist handicap in being concerned with goods [...] rather than with what these good things *do* to human beings' (Sen 1980, 218). Resourcist theories are right, according to Sen, to stress human agency, and indeed, resources are often a good approximation of the freedoms one enjoys. However, they are only the *means* to achieve these freedoms and do not adequately represent a person's actual opportunities to achieve well-being or to find value in life, which are, according to Sen, the *ends* we should seek and therefore include in societal evaluations. There are also other forms of resourcism, and some of them broaden the notion of what counts as a resource considerably, bringing them, in fact, closer to the metric of justice of the capability approach, which we will argue for in the course of this chapter. Take, for example, Ronald Dworkin's influential position, which is typically discussed under the heading "equality of resources", where he advocates that individuals should, over their life span, have access to an equal share of resources These resources consist of two types, personal and impersonal ones:

> [A person's] personal resources are his physical and mental health and ability – his general fitness and capacities, including his wealth-talent, that is, his innate capacity to produce goods or services that others will pay to have. His impersonal resources are those resources that can be reassigned from one person to another – his wealth and the other property he commands, and the opportunities provided to him, under the reigning legal system, to use that property. (Dworkin 2000, 322–323)

In Dworkin's theory, therefore both external goods (income and wealth) and the internal features of a person (such as talent and ambition) are seen as resources relevant for justice. However, personal resources are to a large extent subject to the natural lottery, and their unequal distribution usually cannot be redistributed easily or without ethically problematic measures. But people can be compensated for their low share of personal resources with impersonal ones. The fairest way to do so, according to Dworkin, is determined by a hypothetical insurance market where people can be insured against being untalented, handicapped and the like. Here is not the place to discuss Dworkin's theory in detail, but there are two interrelated issues we would like to note. The first one is that Dworkin's resourcist metric of justice has to be distinguished from a capability-based theory, and the second is that his idea of equality of resources is connected to assumptions that are plausible in the context of ideal theory but lead to problematic consequences in nonideal circumstances (Pierik and Robeyns 2007). This book needs a theory that works within nonideal contexts, and this is a strong reason to reject the sophisticated form of resourcism put forward by Dworkin. We now treat these two issues in turn.

Taking up and extending a critique of Dworkin's theory first brought forward by Andrew Williams (Williams 2002), Roland Pierik and Ingrid Robeyns introduce the following example to show that there is a difference between equality of resources and equality of capability, which Dworkin explicitly denied; they argue that capabilities, in fact, can not be subsumed under his theory of resources (Pierik and Robeyns 2007; Dworkin 2000, 299–303; Dworkin 2002). Amy and Ben are twins and happen to have exactly the same personal and impersonal resources; both want to found a family with a member of the opposite sex. We do not know how they would like to divide care work and market work between them, but there are basically three categories of persons in this regard: homemakers (who are primarily in charge of domestic work and child rearing), ideal workers (who work to generate income and neglect domestic work) and coparents (who share different kinds of work roughly equally). We also know that half of the men in society prefer sharing coparent duties and that the other half prefer being ideal workers. With women, the distribution of preferences is as follows: Half are indifferent to being an ideal worker or a coparent, 40 percent want to be either a coparent or a home worker, and 10 percent prefer to be ideal workers. According to this distribution of preferences, Ben has a very high chance of becoming a coparent (90 percent) and a reasonable opportunity to be either a home worker (60 percent) or an ideal worker in his relationship. For Amy, the situation looks different. She has a 50 percent chance of becoming both a coparent and a home worker. But the option to become an ideal worker in her family is nonexistent because there are no men willing to do the domestic work on their own. Now, given that the preferences of the members of this society are authentic and not influenced by prejudice (two important conditions for a just background structure), Dworkin's theory leads to the conclusion that there are no morally relevant inequalities between the situations of Amy and Ben since they possess exactly the same resources. The actual distribution of (authentic) preferences and tastes is a matter of luck and should not be seen as triggering claims of justice (Dworkin 2000, 69–70). As will become clear in the following, a capability perspective would judge this example differently. There is a difference between the real freedoms of Amy and Ben. Their resources are the same, but what they can do with them is different. This aspect matters from the perspective of justice, expecially in nonideal circumstances, bringing us to the second reason why we reject Dworkin's resourcist approach for the purposes of our book. Dworkin's theory can best be classified as an ideal theory of justice that works with strong assumptions and idealizations. His principles of justice are derived from a thought experiment assuming that the people involved choose against a background of equality of opportunity and nondiscrimination the rules that should govern the institutional structure of their society. He abstracts from inequalities and power structures as they exist in virtually all societies and does not consider histories of subordination, be it in relation to gender, race or wealth, and simply assumes that the preferences of all people involved in his thought experiment are authentic. It is therefore not clear what the implications of his theory are for real-world contexts. He seems to assume that legal measures and economic redistribution (Dworkin 2000, 175) can effectively fight injustice, ignoring the widely established relevance of sociocultural inequalities, which are of the uttermost importance for studying, understanding and alleviating poverty. Here, a direct focus on how people effectively live their lives and the real freedoms they enjoy seems to provide a more feasible way than a focus on resources – even if understood in Dworkin's broad way. Looking again at the example of Amy and Ben, the difference in the opportunities they have within a social context because of sex should be alarming; downplaying the issues of justice involved by pointing to the fact that they have an equal share of resources just seems too easy an excuse.

With this we do not claim that Dworkin's approach cannot, in principle, be fruitfully used as a normative background theory for criticizing poverty. However, it seems to us that much more theoretical work needs to be done to apply it in this domain and that the capability approach provides more accessible tools to deal with injustices as they factually happen. It is true in part that it lacks the clarity of Dworkin's (also Rawls's) theory of justice, a clarity gained by idealization and abstraction. However, clarity is not very useful if it is too far from the social world's realities. Here, so we argue, the capability approach works much better.

Let us look at Sen's alternative account to well-being and advantage, which solves, or so he argues, the issues criticized on the other proposals. In doing so, he introduces the concepts of functionings and capabilities, which focus directly on an individual's life and which enable the conceptualization of her opportunities (e.g., Sen 1992, 39–42; Sen 1999b, 74–76; see also Alkire 2002, 4–11). Functionings are the activities and states that make up a person's life; they are the different 'beings' and 'doings' living consists in. And since human existence encompasses many different doings and beings, the category of functionings is a broad one and includes being healthy and educated, having a shelter and taking part in the life of the community, as well as being undernourished, killing animals and feeling emotional distress. In any case, it is essential to note two things: First, they have to be distinguished clearly from the resources employed to achieve these functionings, even if most of them depend heavily on some of their input. Second, the criticized mental metrics as used by utilitarians can be seen as a relevant subcategory of functionings (e.g., being happy), but they do not – by far – include all the necessary information about an individual's circumstances. For Sen, however, it is not enough to look only at the functionings realized by a person in order to compare his situation with that of others. As already indicated, he considers the freedom to lead a life one has reason to value as one of the most valuable features of human life. In order to express this idea, he introduces the notion of capabilities. They are defined as the functionings a person has actually access to and reflect the person's freedom to realize different achievements. To give an example: eating is a functioning, while the real opportunity to eat is its respective capability. Normally, it is important to look at capabilities not one by one but in combination with each other – usually, the realization of one specific functioning influences others, and only a holistic approach can retrieve all the relevant information. Notice that Sen in fact originally introduced the concept of a capability to refer to *a set of combinations of functionings*, each representing a feasible lifestyle (Sen 1980; Sen 1992). However, in his other writings, he uses the term 'capability', as introduced here, to refer to the freedom to achieve one particular functioning, a usage that is nowadays widespread in the literature. Take, for example, someone who has to make a choice between a job that gives him an income necessary for a decent living but that is so time-consuming that his personal relationships will be reduced drastically. It is this interconnectedness between different valuable achievements that must be considered for evaluating a person's situation comprehensively. If not, it might get overlooked that a good choice with respect to one domain was – all things considered – a tough or even tragic one. Since capabilities are a kind of freedom, it also becomes clear that the approach gives a high value to people's agency, which is, according to Sen, understood as the faculty to act and bring about change according to one's values and objectives (Sen 1999b, 19). In the end, people should be able to identify with their choices and actively shape their own lives; it is therefore decisive for a just society to provide the conditions to make this, in fact, possible.

It is crucial to understand that the notion of well-being as it is used in the capability approach must not be identified with what is typically termed 'welfare' in political philosophy or economics, where the term is understood exclusively in relation to individual preferences or happiness. As shown, this position was powerfully rejected by Sen. Or to put it differently, the notions of well-being, on the one hand, and functionings and capabilities, on the other, are closely related, and there is by now a vast literature confirming this diagnosis (Comim, Qizilbash and Alkire 2008; Deneulin and Shahani 2009; Biggeri, Ballet and Comim 2011). Welfare, on the other hand, in Sen's terminology, is only one aspect of the overall well-being of a person and must not be reduced to it.

A person's capabilities (but also achieved functionings) depend on many different factors. They are a product of a person's abilities and skills, as well as the political, social and economic context she finds herself in. They obviously usually depend on resources; without the necessary goods, it is simply not possible to live a self-determined life according to one's own conception of the good. However, what matters is the 'relationship between persons and goods' (Sen 1980, 216) and what the relationship allows us to do and be.

In this context, the term "conversion factors" is helpful. It was introduced by Sen to conceptualize the relation between resources and the realization of certain functionings, and it calls attention to the degree a person in fact can use the goods at her disposal for her purposes. At least three different kinds of such factors can be identified, all of which have to be taken into account when evaluating the real freedoms somebody has access to (Sen 1992, 19–21; Sen 1999b, 70–72; Robeyns 2005, 98–100). First, there are personal conversion factors. Our physical, psychological and emotional characteristics, as well as our achieved levels of skills, influence what we can 'get' out of the resources we command. If we are in good health, for example, we do not need a lot to achieve basic mobility. However, due to illnesses or impairments, moving around can be burdensome and only possible with the right assistance or technical tools (e.g., by using crutches or a wheelchair). We can observe that, in some cases, lower levels of well-being or freedom resulting from personal heterogeneities can be compensated by more or special kinds of resources. Sometimes, however, even the best support or the greatest wealth does not outweigh the respective disadvantages (Nussbaum 2006). Personal conversion factors highlight the many differences existing between people and their relevance for using the goods they possess for their ends. They can add much interesting information to evaluative exercises and detect inequalities relevant for ethical theories, but they also point out that during a person's life course, the characteristics decisive for her realization of valuable functionings vary greatly.

Second, there are environmental conversion factors relating, for example, to varieties of climates and geographical locations but also to pollution and the prevalence of diseases. All these aspects have a direct impact on the individual, her freedoms and level of well-being and must be considered in the conceptualization of a person's capabilities. Pure survival in a country with low temperatures depends on adequate clothing and shelter with heating facilities and the respective investments that are not necessary to make in milder regions of the world. Or, to give another example, the high levels of smog and problems in the water supply as experienced by some of the world's megacities directly bear on the quality of life of their inhabitants. These environmental circumstances restrict good human functioning in many ways, and even considerable wealth cannot outweigh them. The life of each person must therefore be examined in a variety of environmental dimensions to get a realistic picture of what can be achieved with a fixed set of goods.

Third, social conversion factors play a role in how an individual can benefit from resources or a certain amount of income. This category embraces public policies, power relations and social norms, for example, and emphasizes that every individual is embedded in a social context that is crucial for understanding her real freedoms. Educational and health programs run by the state might allow access to important functionings without demanding material wealth, and the absence of crime or violence contributes massively to the quality of life in the locations in question. If the streets are not safe, options of what can be done with one's possessions get restricted. A nice car is of no use if it is too dangerous to drive it on the streets. Discriminating practices, gender roles and societal hierarchies, too, must be taken into account when analyzing the relationship between persons and goods. If there are rules excluding girls from the educational system in a certain society, even having the best schools next door is not helpful for the capability to be educated; if a social norm forbids women to cycle, possessing a bike in combination with cycling skill does not lead – as is usually the case – to the result that a woman will consider cycling a real option; her actual possibility to use the respective good gets restricted by her social environment.

Summarizing, conversion factors point to the complex relationship between what a person has and what kind of life she in fact enjoys, and accordingly, we need to know many aspects of a person's situation in order to judge how well off she is. Resources, social institutions and norms, as well as the environmental context, all play an important role, and an analysis focusing on functionings and capabilities must take all of them into account while acknowledging that they matter primarily as means and not for their own sake. Two important points follow from these considerations: First, the capability approach entails a position called 'ethical individualism', which claims that the individual is the fundamental moral category. In the end, the quality of a society is judged by how well it manages to show respect and concern for each and every one of its members, taken one by one. As Nussbaum once put it:

> [...] the capabilities sought are sought for *each and every person*, not, in the first instance, for groups or families or states or other corporate bodies. Such bodies may be extremely important in promoting human capabilities, and in this way they may deservedly gain our support: but it is because of what they do for people that they are so worthy, and the ultimate political goal is always the promotion of the capabilities of *each person*. (Nussbaum 2000, 74)

Second, however, it must not be overlooked that this focus on the individual does not ignore the social nature of human life. On the contrary, what the discussion about conversion factors showed is that the capability approach stresses the social embedding of every person and that only against this background can her individuality come forward and her life be assessed adequately. This also means that the capability approach naturally goes hand in hand with a critique of social relations which hinder the social conditions of freedom for every citizen (Graf and Schweiger 2014). The evaluation of capabilities, therefore, has to recognize the many ways oppression and exploitation are present in a society and how these phenomena affect relations of equality between people (Anderson 1999).

We have outlined some of the criticisms capability scholars have brought forward against other informational spaces, and we have introduced the notions of functionings and capabilities and put them into the wider context of the concerns of the capability approach. From our point of view, they provide the best approach to a metric of individual advantage, and they should also therefore be used to make interpersonal comparisons that matter from a social justice perspective. They shift the focus from a mere provision of goods to the question of what these goods allow persons to be, do or achieve, recognizing variations in a person's ability to convert goods into valuable functionings. This characteristic, together with the explicit recognition of the multidimensional nature of a person's well-being and the central place attributed to human freedom, makes this metric of justice suggested by Sen preferable to other options, such as primary goods or utilities. Furthermore, they allow for a direct connection to the social scientific literature, where functionings and capabilities are used in issues of measurement and conceptualization. Does this conclusion also hold for children, with whom this book is concerned? Or do we need to adapt the capability approach somewhat? In what follows, we will discuss why the adequate currency of justice for children does not straightforwardly consist of capabilities, as is typically the case for adults.

Children are different in many important aspects, the two main ones being that children are not autonomous beings from the beginning but become autonomous over the course of childhood and that they are developing beings who change rapidly and whose development can be severely hurt by outside influences. Both imply that children are more vulnerable to certain forms of harm and that they are heavily dependent on others as well. We distinguish three kinds of vulnerability: physical, mental and social; the last can be further differentiated into legal, economic and political forms. These forms correlate with dimensions of powerlessness. It is evident that a child's body suffers more severely than an adult's from physical violence, such as shaking, and that certain hazards that are only a small problem for an adult can be a deadly threat for a newborn or toddler. It is also a fact that the physical and mental development of children can be severely distorted by external factors like toxic chemicals in the environment and that such influences on development can be irreversible (Landrigan and Goldman 2011). Various psychological research studies on the development of the self and personality and on socialization have examined the effects of outside surroundings on children. For instance, it has been shown that girls who suffer from maltreatment during childhood may develop a low perception of their own social power in relationship with others; this state may be predictive of a propensity for abusiveness in their relationships with their own children (Bugental and Grusex 2007). Another example includes the associations found between early attachment security and measures of emotional health, self-esteem, agency and self-confidence, positive affect, ego resiliency and social competence in interactions with peers, teachers, camp counselors, romantic partners and others (Thompson 2007). It is crucial always to be aware of the fact that there is only one chance for each child to develop and grow up, and distortions in early life cannot be taken back. Still, research like this should not be interpreted to mean that children are passive objects in their own development and that childhood predicts everything. Rather, it should help us understand that all humans are dependent and are shaped by interactions with others and the environment – interactions that greatly influence who we are and what we are able to be and do.

The social vulnerability of children partly stems from their limited capacities and their needs and partly from how childhood is framed in modern societies (Graf 2015). They are economically vulnerable because they cannot take care of themselves in the same sense as adults. Most importantly, they cannot (up to a certain age) work and are not allowed (again, up to a certain age) to work and be economic agents, and they have essentially no control over their income and other resources like housing and transportation. If their parents become unemployed, for example, children cannot substitute that lack of income or otherwise sufficiently support their parents to cope with this situation. They are, in fact, often victims of these situations and the high level of stress that they cause (Edwards, Gomes and Major 2013). Furthermore, they are legally subject to their parents and their decisions in many ways. If a child is neglected, it is often not in the child's power to claim proper treatment by her parents, and it can be very difficult for her to reach out and demand others to help and intervene (also because family relations are fueled by emotions). In many welfare states, parents have a wide range of rights to control and shape the lives of their children; in some of them even corporal punishment and with it many possible severe consequences for the child's development are allowed and tolerated (Durrant and Ensom 2012).

Children are politically vulnerable because they cannot effectively change their political position and they depend on the rights they are granted by others (Milne 2013). Children cannot fight for their rights in the way adults can, and they cannot organize themselves in a comparable manner that would gather them political influence. Their social vulnerability is hence also produced and sustained by their social powerlessness. Children have less power and fewer capacities and opportunities to alter their lives, and many opportunities they have are not good ones. The rare opportunities to acquire resources and funds to make a better living, for example, through work and labor, are limited, and there are very good reasons to ban children from working and laboring, not to speak of such illegal and evidently harmful ways as begging and stealing. In certain cases, it is better for children to leave their families and homes and live on their own (if they are old enough) or in other forms of care arrangements, but in general it is widely acknowledged that this is not good for either their well-being or well-becoming (Lawrence, Carlson and Egeland 2006).

The vulnerability and powerlessness of children reflect, thus, two dimensions of the specific moral and political status children can and should have due to the nature of their being. On the one hand, as we have argued so far, powerlessness increases and creates certain vulnerabilities in children; it is also socially created to an extent. On the other hand, to hold children powerless in some areas is not only permissible but an entitlement of justice and morality that children should be granted. It is important to note the crucial difference between children and women and other powerless subjugated social groups in large parts of this world. Being held powerless certainly does not protect women; they are oppressed, and justifications applied to children, like inferior competence and vulnerability, do not apply to women or minority groups (Nussbaum 2000).

Most theorists concerned with justice for children acknowledge that these vulnerabilities, together with their potential to develop into autonomous beings, constitute a particular 'nature' of children that grants them a different moral and political status (Archard and Macleod 2002; Brennan and Noggle 2007). It is also at this point, where the capability approach has been criticized for not being suitable as a normative theory for children. As Colin Macleod argues, the notion of capabilities is closely tied to an 'agency assumption', one that presupposes that the subject in question is able to make autonomous decisions. And since children – especially younger ones – miss this feature, the capability approach has problems to integrate them into his conceptual framework (Macleod 2010). We will argue later on that this problem is solvable and that the concepts of evolving capabilities and achieved functionings are of great value here. But before we do this, let us explore more deeply the question of autonomy and development, how children are 'special' and that it is very important to distinguish between different groups of them: Children are a very heterogeneous group, more so than a group of adults, when it comes to significant differences. A 'normal' two-year-old toddler's skills and capacities differ more from a 'normal' twelve-year-old teenager's than those of a 'normal' twenty-five-year-old differ from a 'normal' fifty-five-year-old's. Exceptions, such as people with severe disabilities, do no refute this assumption, because they are seen as just that: exceptions. Nor does this rest on a strong anthropological conception about what is human; it can be expressed only via a very shallow understanding of empirical facts about humans. A good comparison is provided by the concept and definition of health and disease: the fact that some people are born with severe cognitive disabilities does not lead to the conclusion that suffering from a head trauma that shows the same outcome is something 'normal' in the sense that it should not be seen as impairment to health. Humans can differ greatly in many aspects, but it is plausible to assume that children are particular in some of those and that these aspects change as children develop. A capability approach to children has to recognize these differences and changes and see them as morally relevant, a view supported by Nussbaum and Dixon in the context of children's rights:

> The idea of agency has a central role to play in the CA: the capability approach sees people as striving agents, and in contrast to approaches that aim only at the satisfaction of preferences, it aims at supporting the growth of agency and practical reason. This emphasis on agency, under a CA, further means that children should be afforded the maximum scope for decisional, freedom consistent with their actual – or potential – capacity for rational and reasoned forms of choice, or judgment. For adolescents in particular, this may mean recognizing a range of rights to sexual and reproductive choice, religious choice, and choices regarding custody. In many cases, it will also mean granting at least certain decisional rights to younger children. (Dixon and Nussbaum 2012, 559–560; footnotes omitted)

Childhood is a phase of rapid changes in all known mental, physical and social categories. So, when we write here about children, we should always be aware that the category of children is very vague and encompasses humans with great differences in skills, capacities and needs, which implies that a claim justified toward a toddler can be unjustified toward an adolescent. In fact, treating an adolescent like a toddler is denigrating and humiliating and certainly does not accord with treating her justly (Brighouse 2003).

What we can say, though, is that children lack the skills and capacities needed to make fully autonomous choices and decisions for themselves until they are grown up and are hence to be seen as adults. This does not mean that they cannot articulate their wishes and preferences or that they cannot decide anything for themselves from a certain age on, but a theory of justice for children cannot and should not assume that the subjects of this justice are fully autonomous beings. The same is probably true for many adults, but in a different sense, which does not hold as a general rule rooted in their 'natural' capacities. Many adults are restricted in their freedom because of external factors, but children are so because of what they are and what they can do and be, based on their still developing minds and bodies. This becomes obvious if one looks at very young children: A toddler cannot make any reasonable decision for herself and is dependent on adults to the extent that her life is in danger if she is abandoned. The lack of autonomy of children is surely based not only in human biology but also in the social arrangements constructed around childhood. The legal position of children, for example, restricts them in their autonomy even though it is unclear in the cases of some older children and adolescents whether they are really less capable of making their own choices than many adults, who are not equally restricted by the law. Such arrangements are in need of a close examination as to whether they really fit children, respect them and do justice to them, but in general, it is reasonable to claim not only that children are less autonomous but that there are good reasons to let them make only limited choices for themselves.

This refers both to their lack in competencies and to their nature as developing beings. All humans change throughout their entire life, but childhood is a phase of rapid and significant change like no other, and this development is highly influential for the whole future life course. Development does not simply happen to children; it must be fostered, and children's development is influenced by their environment and the people and institutions interacting with them. Children's development can be severely hurt and damaged, with sometimes lifelong consequences. We will soon introduce the concept of corrosive disadvantages, which is a suitable description of such damages with lifelong consequences. Children do not know what is best for their development, as well: A baby cannot know whether a vaccination helps prevent severe diseases, and she cannot know that the pain of getting a shot is outweighed by the lifelong protection from severe illness. Older children cannot know what learning is good for, even if they often enjoy learning, and that going to school is a crucial condition for their future well-being and for what they can do later on in their lives.

As a consequence, we wish to endorse the view that childhood should be a protective phase and that children have a right to have a childhood separated from the adult world in some features. Not having to make certain decisions and not being held responsible for one's actions to the full account also provide protection, and children would be overburdened if they were granted the full range of rights and duties as adults. Children lack the competencies and autonomy to make many decisions for themselves and to know what is best for them, their actual well-being and their future well-being. Such a justification of partial paternalism toward children, which decreases as they grow up and become more mature, is widely acknowledged, although there is significant disagreement about the justificatory bases of paternalism and how far it should go; for example, in regard to teenagers and adolescents who show (nearly) the same competences as most adults (Archard 2004; Franklin-Hall 2013; Anderson and Claassen 2012).

What such a developmental view of children, together with an acknowledgment of their agency, means for capability approach theory has already been fleshed out in some detail (Ballet, Biggeri and Comim 2011). In particular, the concept of evolving capabilities was introduced as a crucial conceptual extension to the prevalent terminology. Evolving capabilities include the dynamic aspect of the development of capabilities and explicitly link the person's abilities, achievements and circumstances at different points in time:

> The process of capability expansion or of evolving capabilities starts from an initial set of achieved functionings of the child at time tn. The process of resource conversion is very much affected by how different institutions, norms and cultures constrain or empower them, shaping the formation of a new set of functionings and capabilities that are inter-temporally distinct. The child's capability set (opportunity freedom, i.e. the vector of potential valuable and achievable functionings) is thus given by the resources/constraints, by his or her limited opportunities and by his or her own abilities. From the multidimensional capability set the choice will determine the vector of new achieved functionings at time t_{n+1}. The dynamic process is going to be influenced by feedback loops if seen as taking place in sequential periods of time. [...] The emotional and cognitive development of children goes through different stages in which their decision making and agency is shaped by their life experiences and mimicking behaviour. (Ballet, Biggeri and Comim 2011, 34)

The concept of evolving capabilities thus grasps the fact that capabilities change over time according to different factors. The already introduced notion of conversion factors is helpful to further clarify this point. If we look at internal factors, we realize that a child's opportunities typically broaden in childhood due to physical, psychological and emotional changes. Furthermore, children acquire skills that can be used to get more out of the commodities they have access to. This expansion of their capabilities is certainly related to biological facts about the way humans grow up, but it would be wrong to reduce human development to such a perspective – this is where social conversion factors come into play. On the one hand, they often relate directly to what is 'internal' to a person. The social context profoundly influences our psychological, emotional and even physical development, the skills we are able to learn and the aspirations we have. This shows that internal conversion factors, too, do not merely exist in a vacuum but must be interpreted over a certain social context. One can also mention here the close relationship between a child's capabilities and those of her parents or close caregivers (Ballet, Biggeri and Comim 2011, 30–31). As is well known from empirical research, disadvantages are often transferred from one generation to the next, and without improving the capabilities of a child's attachment figures, it is unlikely that her life chances will be comparable to those of her peers from a privileged background as understood in terms of the caregiver's capabilities (which do not equal their material wealth). On the other hand, social norms and institutions regulate our lives in many ways and our ability to use resources for our aims. The case of children in modern Western societies serves to illustrate this point: Often enough, their possibilities are constrained; for example, by the fact that they have to attend school, kindergarten or other educational facilities that entail a set of rules and restrictions that are, at least in some aspects, different from the regulations adults face. Furthermore, there are usually laws and social expectations in place, treating children and adults differently and granting them different degrees of authority over their own circumstances. As we have argued, such an approach is valid if it is applied sincerely and with care. But the point is that all these facets – and many more – have to be taken into account when analyzing the evolving capabilities of children and the effective freedoms they enjoy.

Analyzing the well-being and well-becoming of children in terms of evolving capabilities brings another aspect to the surface, which relates to the many interconnections between different functionings and capabilities, their synergies but also negative interactions. This point is worth emphasizing for several reasons and will provide a main point of reference for our argument about the injustice of child poverty, which we will develop in the next chapter.

First, it is likely that certain functionings and capabilities are valuable not only in themselves but also because their possession positively influences other functionings and capabilities. As we will argue in more detail in the next section, a clear case can be made that health, for example, fulfills such a function and that it therefore makes sense to have a special look at health, also in the case of social analyses and distributions of inequalities. This idea of particularly important dimensions of the life of a human being, which 'spread their good effects over several categories either directly or by reducing risk to the other functionings', was introduced by Jonathan Wolff and Avner de-Shalit in their book *Disadvantage*, connecting it explicitly with the capability approach. They term this category 'fertile functionings' (Wolff and de-Shalit 2007, 121) and suggest that their identification and promotion among the least advantaged members of society will lead to social change and a reduction of disadvantage. They are also very clear that social policy has to make sure that people in fact realize these functionings and that they not be defined as capabilities where freedom of choice plays a major role (Wolff and de-Shalit 2013). While this point has been controversially discussed for adults, for children the case is clearer; for them, the category of achieved functionings needs to have priority, especially when they can be proven to be fertile. However, since for children the differentiation between well-being and well-becoming is particularly important, the notion of 'fertile functionings' has to be understood from both perspectives, as well. On the one hand, they are important because they promote other dimensions of well-being. On the other hand, their positive effects might spread to a child's future and well-becoming. Certainly, both aspects are relevant and have to be included in the concept of fertile functionings. Which functionings play such a role is the subject of empirical studies, and a normative theory cannot develop its claims without considering such knowledge; it has to work with the best available evidence and must also acknowledge variations in different contexts. What is fertile in one case does not necessarily have this effect in another one, even if it is reasonable to assume that some functionings, health, for example, are likely to have a fertile effect almost universally.

Second, and very closely connected to the notion of fertile functionings, are 'corrosive disadvantages', which are also introduced and analyzed by Wolff and de-Shalit (Wolff and de-Shalit 2007, 121). Here the idea is that some disadvantages have negative impacts on many other aspects of life, leading to a variety of drawbacks. Again, such disadvantages might be relevant for the well-being of a child; for instance, when lack of decent living conditions directly translates into social problems. They also serve, however, as an important category for future-oriented analysis. Corrosive disadvantages have a middle- and long-term impact on a child's life, and their negative effects often become clear only when they are put into a life-course perspective. It is of great moral importance that children enter their lives as adults in a condition where enough significant life chances are still available for them. Consequently, moral harm is done not only insofar as children experience suffering and neglect in childhood but also when the way they live their childhoods reduces valuable options they find as adults. Take, for example, the case of physical abuse, experienced by many children. Its immediate damage is, of course, severe and its impact on the child's well-being disastrous. However, the full picture of its moral harm can be evaluated only if we take into account its impact on the child's future life, in relation, for instance, to health problems, social status, economic well-being and a range of psychiatric disorders (Lanius, Vermetten and Pain 2010; Widom et al. 2012; Currie and Widom 2010), all of which reduce a person's well-being, including the faculty of self-government and the effective pursuit of a life plan. In our argument about the injustice of child poverty, which we will develop in detail in the next chapter, it will therefore also be crucial to look at aspects of children's lives that have particularly positive or negative effects in the long run. Naturally, such an endeavor is connected to empirical knowledge, and indeed we will argue that philosophical theories about justice have to work closely with empirical analyses that add substance to purely theoretical considerations. As in the case of fertile functionings, finding out which disadvantages are indeed corrosive is not a purely philosophical matter. On the contrary, identifying and clarifying the causal relations between disadvantages is mainly an empirical task. The same is true for studying and understanding how patterns of disadvantage arise, why they persist and which factors contribute to the fact that they can even be transferred from one generation to another.

Fertile functionings and corrosive disadvantages are related in many ways. However, it is important to separate them on a conceptual level and to stress that there is more to the distinction than acknowledging that one and the same functioning can have good or bad effects, depending on its realization or absence (Wolff and de-Shalit 2007, 134). To illustrate this point, it suffices to note that, in many situations of disadvantage, it is not enough to eliminate the causes of the problem, including disadvantages considered corrosive. In many cases, something additional is needed to effectively overcome the difficult situation. Take, for instance, the case of someone who has an alcohol addiction. It is easy to imagine that this problem is a corrosive disadvantage, leading to many negative consequences; ending the addiction alone is not a guarantee that many of the experienced disadvantages disappear. It might be necessary for the person to develop a new sense of self-worth and self-efficacy – fertile functionings, which are not directly related to the experienced disadvantages – to succeed in life. On the other hand, the absence of many fertile functionings does not always lead to disadvantages. A sense of humor, to take Wolff and de-Shalit's example, is certainly of help in many ways to deal with difficult situations. But its absence probably has relatively few other negative effects and should not, in typical circumstances, be counted as corrosive.

Third, a look at the concept of evolving capabilities and the interrelation of different functionings and capabilities in their formation stresses the importance of *functionings*. As described by Ballet, Biggeri and Comim, the process of capability expansion always starts by an initial set of archived functionings and has to take into account which functionings will be realized during the development process, as well. Wolff and de-Shalit also deliberately write about fertile *functionings* (and not capabilities), characterizing corrosive disadvantages first and foremost in relation to achieved functionings. In their theory, they do not use the concept of evolving capabilities, and their focus is not mainly on children, but this observation is relevant nonetheless. The reason for this is that the ability to choose for oneself and to determine one's life is dependent on many preconditions, and a certain level of overall well-being typically has to be achieved so that choice in a meaningful sense can be exercised. In the terminology of the capability approach, this means that the category of functionings must not get neglected and that they provide valuable insights in the distribution of disadvantages in a society. We would like to emphasize that, in the case of children, it would be generally wrong to give them only the capabilities to achieve certain levels in different dimensions of well-being. What matters is that they actually lead good lives and not merely that they have the options to do so if they want to. In regard to children, Nussbaum prefers such a perspective as well:

> If we aim to produce adults who have all the capabilities on the list, this will frequently mean requiring certain types of functioning in children, since, as I have argued, exercising a function in childhood is frequently necessary to produce a mature adult capability. Thus it seems perfectly legitimate to require primary and secondary

education, given the role this plays in all the later choices of an adult life. Similarly, it seems legitimate to insist on the health, emotional well-being, bodily integrity, and dignity of children in a way that does not take their choices into account; some of this insisting will be done by parents, but the state has a legitimate role in preventing abuse and neglect. Again: functioning in childhood is necessary for capability in adulthood. The state's interest in adult capabilities gives it a very strong interest in any treatment of children that has a long-term impact on these capabilities [...]. (Nussbaum 2000, 89–90)

For children, however, functioning may be made the goal in many areas. Thus I have defended compulsory education, compulsory health care, and other aspects of compulsory functioning. (For example, I support an age of consent for sexual intercourse, so that children's bodily integrity is protected whether they like it or not.) Compulsory functioning is justified both by the child's cognitive immaturity and by the importance of such functioning in enabling adult capabilities. (Nussbaum 2006, 172)

Where does that leave us in the question of the right currency of justice for children? The restriction of children's autonomy is, as we see, not only a reaction to their limited competencies and skills but also justified by the need to protect them, their development and their future life chances (Noggle 2002; Archard 2003). It is hence a part of justice for children, and giving children too much autonomy over their lives too early would expose them to great risks. It is very likely that these children, once they have grown up, would make serious accusations and blame their parents and the state for having let them down by allowing them to quit school at the age of seven, by not getting healthy food because they preferred junk-food or by not going to the dentist and subsequently having serious health issues. Children cannot use capabilities in the way adults can, and they do not gain the same amount of value from having a choice when they are very young. A toddler does not have an increase in real freedom and does not see the value in being presented with many potentially valuable options – her needs are more focused. The risk of overburdening children by letting them decide is also to be considered. We see good arguments that claim that functionings, instead of capabilities, are to be preferred, but over the course of childhood and as children develop into more and more autonomous beings, capabilities become more important and finally take over. The developmental perspective of Nussbaum is only one important aspect, and the issue of autonomy and being protected as a child matter equally. We claim that functionings are the right currency of justice for children not solely because this will lead to the development of adults with certain capabilities but also because functionings represent what children need in order to have a good childhood, since they cannot make all decisions for themselves. One of the main reasons for preferring capabilities over resources is that people are given real freedoms, but for children real freedoms matter less, at least until a certain point in their development. This is not to say that freedoms do not matter at all for children, but they have to be interpreted in a suitable way, taking account of the fact that full autonomy is not the right category for thinking about children's choices. However, so far, we have described these concepts only as formal categories without specifying their exact content. In order to apply the capability to the problem of justice, something more must be said about this issue, and one needs to take a stand regarding (a) which functionings and capabilitities matter for social justice and (b) to what degree or threshold must they be secured in order to achieve social justice. In the next sections, we will address these questions in turn.

1.2 Selecting functionings and capabilities for children

The next task to further develop our concept of justice for children is to select functionings – for older children, capabilities – that are relevant for assessments of justice. Sen has never identified a comprehensive list of functionings and capabilities, either for adults or for children, that could be used as the basis for a theory of justice. On the contrary, he has brought forward some reasons why he is skeptical about such an endeavor (Sen 1993; Sen 2004b). He argues that a predefined list of what is valuable to human life ignores what people actually value and might be overly paternalistic. Furthermore, it goes against the ideal of public deliberation processes that Sen sees as the best and the legitimate way to answer value questions. Finally, he suggests that moral questions are notoriously difficult to answer and that this insight, too, speaks against the definition of a full list. Throughout his works, he frequently refers to some examples of capabilities he believes to be supported by a wide range of moral and political positions, which he terms 'basic capabilities'. However, his remarks on this subject remain only exemplary, and all in all, he refrains from substantial claims when it comes to value questions on an abstract and universal level detached from concrete contexts and socioeconomic circumstances. His version of the capability approach is therefore best understood as an 'analytical device' that can be used for different ends. In particular, Sen reminds us that evaluative exercises have to incorporate a variety of diverse concerns and dimensions. In doing so, he also explicitly stresses the many (causal) relationships between different functionings and capabilities and emphasizes how important empirical work is for the subject matter of political philosophy. From his point of view, the capability framework serves to clarify what is at stake in public reasoning, helping to make social evaluations open and transparent. However, it cannot, a priori, solve moral disagreements (Sen 2005, 157). Nonetheless, Sen is confident that there will always be enough intersections between different reasoned approaches, providing guidelines for actions that lead to the enhancement of justice (Sen 2009).

While Sen sees this 'undertheorization' of the capability approach as a specific strength, others have raised doubts about it. Most importantly, it has been argued that without some specifications of objectively valuable functionings and capabilities, the capability approach does not have any normative force, especially if one wants to apply the notion of social justice in a global and multicultural context (Nussbaum 2003; Arneson 2006; Nussbaum 2011, 69–75). In this line of thought, different lists have been proposed and discussed by philosophers and researchers who work empirically, but none of these lists seems to satisfy all critics. We agree that it will not be possible to have one list for all purposes and that it is important to specify the items according to certain goals and contexts. In addition, there will always be discussions about the adequacy of fully specified lists, if they include everything that is valuable or if they miss important information. However, a critique of child poverty needs to take up a position at least on some of the crucial elements for children's lives; only then will it be possible to inform and guide a society on the design of its institutions and on its policy decisions broadly construed. But fulfilling this task does not rely on an exhaustive and fully specified list of capabilities, be they deduced from philosophical argument or from the outcome of ideal deliberation processes. Much can be achieved with pragmatic and preliminary lists, and our treatment of the injustice of child poverty in the next chapter will be a good occasion to prove this point. But before we present the list we see as suitable for our purposes, let us briefly review two influential suggestions as to what such a list might look like in the case of adults.

The most prominent list is certainly Nussbaum's, which distinguishes ten central human capabilities. She argues that her list is grounded on the idea of a life worthy of human dignity, which in turn draws on the intuition that every person is a needy and social creature capable of reasoning. The central human capabilities are defended as universal and prepolitical entitlements, which every state has to guarantee for its citizens. According to Nussbaum, her list appeals to very fundamental values shared by many different moral and religious doctrines (although for different reasons), and it can be, over time, the object of an overlapping consensus in the Rawlsian sense. She is also very clear that in providing these capabilities to citizens, she does not mean to push them into a set of specific functionings. The choice to realize a specific life remains with each and every individual. Before presenting the list, it must also be noted that her understanding of capabilities is broader than Sen's. While Sen defines them as real opportunities, for Nussbaum they also include talents, internal powers and abilities. Sen's conversion factors are therefore already integrated in her concept of capability itself (Robeyns 2003, 75). In our view, this is more of a conceptual issue than one of substance, but it explains to some extent the ways they characterize and write about this concept – and these conceptual ambiguities have certainly provoked some misunderstandings in the literature. The list reads as follows (Nussbaum 2011, 33–34):

(1) *Life*. Being able to live to the end of a human life of normal length; not dying prematurely or before one's life is so reduced as to be not worth living.
(2) *Bodily Health*. Being able to have good health, including reproductive health, adequate nourishment and adequate shelter.
(3) *Bodily Integrity*. Being able to move freely from place to place; to be secure against violent assault, including sexual assault and domestic violence; to have opportunities for sexual satisfaction and choice in matters of reproduction.
(4) *Senses, Imagination and Thought*. Being able to use the senses, to imagine, think, and reason – and to do these things in a 'truly human' way, a way informed and cultivated by an adequate education, including but by no means limited to literacy and basic mathematical and scientific training. Being able to use imagination and thought in connection with experiencing and producing works and events of one's own choice, religious, literary, musical and so forth. Being able to use one's mind in ways protected by guarantees of freedom of expression with respect to both political and artistic speech and freedom of religious exercise. Being able to have pleasurable experiences and to avoid nonbeneficial pain.
(5) *Emotions*. Being able to have attachments to things and people outside ourselves; to love those who love and care for us, to grieve at their absence; in general, to love, to grieve, to experience longing,

gratitude and justified anger. Not having one's emotional development blighted by fear and anxiety. (Supporting this capability means supporting forms of human association that can be shown to be crucial in their development.)
(6) *Practical Reason.* Being able to form a conception of the good and to engage in critical reflection about the planning of one's life. (This entails protection for the liberty of conscience and religious observance.)
(7) *Affiliation.*
  A. Being able to live with and for others, to recognize and show concern for other human beings, to engage in various forms of social interaction, to imagine the situation of another. (Protecting this capability means protecting institutions that constitute and nourish such forms of affiliation and also protecting the freedom of assembly and political speech.)
  B. Having the social bases of self-respect and nonhumiliation; being able to be treated as a dignified being whose worth is equal to that of others. This entails provisions of nondiscrimination on the basis of race, sex, sexual orientation, ethnicity, caste, religion, national origin.
(8) *Other Species.* Being able to live with concern for and in relation to animals, plants and the world of nature.
(9) *Play.* Being able to laugh, to play, to enjoy recreational activities.
(10) *Control over One's Environment.*
  A. Political. Being able to participate effectively in political choices that govern one's life; having the right of political participation and the protections of free speech and association.
  B. Material. Being able to hold property (both land and movable goods) and having property rights on an equal basis with others; having the right to seek employment on an equal basis with others; having the freedom from unwarranted search and seizure. In work, being able to work as a human being, exercising practical reason and entering into meaningful relationships of mutual recognition with other workers.

Another example of a concrete list of valuable capabilities is the one offered by Ingrid Robeyns (Robeyns 2003), who distinguished fourteen dimensions for evaluating gender inequality. Her list is based on a methodology that involves four criteria: First, the selection process and the selected functionings or capabilities must be explicitly formulated so that they can be openly discussed, criticized, defended and, if needed, modified. Second, there is a criterion of methodological justification. The method used to generate the list must be clarified and scrutinized. Furthermore, it must be defended as to why it is appropriate for the issue at hand. Third, lists can be formulated at different levels of generalities, and an individual has to decide, according to the aims she pursues, at what level she works – reaching from ideal theory to pragmatic lists constrained by the given circumstances. Fourth, norms of exhaustion and nonreduction should be met: The capabilities on the list should include all elements that are important and should not be reducible to other elements. Her list is as follows:

(1) Life and physical health: being able to be physically healthy and enjoy a life of normal length.
(2) Mental well-being: being able to be mentally healthy.
(3) Bodily integrity and safety: being able to be protected from violence of any sort.
(4) Social relations: being able to be part of social networks and to give and receive social support.
(5) Political empowerment: being able to participate in and have a fair share of influence on political decision-making.
(6) Education and knowledge: being able to be educated and to use and produce knowledge.
(7) Domestic work and nonmarket care: being able to raise children and to take care of others.
(8) Paid work and other projects: being able to work in the labor market or to undertake projects, including artistic ones.
(9) Shelter and environment: being able to be sheltered and to live in a safe and pleasant environment.
(10) Mobility: being able to be mobile.
(11) Leisure activities: being able to engage in leisure activities.
(12) Time autonomy: being able to exercise autonomy in allocating one's time.
(13) Respect: being able to be respected and treated with dignity.
(14) Religion: being able to choose to live or not to live according to a religion.

As one can see, there are several similarities between Robeyns's and Nussbaum's lists, but that is not the point of interest for us. We are concerned with justice for children, and what is apparent is that neither Nussbaum's nor Robeyn's list is suited for them in every aspect. Let us discuss a few of the problematic cases: Nussbaum included the ability to move freely on her list, something that is, for good reasons, limited for children. It would be highly problematic if that capability would be granted to children at all ages, as it would put them at high risk. The same is true for the capability of practical reason and that children should be able to plan their own lives. This is certainly not possible in the same way as it is and should be for adults. Likewise, political participation, having the right to seek employment and to hold property are highly problematic for children, especially younger ones; these are not proper capabilities for them. If we think in terms of functionings instead of capabilities, which is more adequate for young children, these items on the list become even more problematic. Other capabilities are suitable for children, like health and education, but they should be interpreted in terms of functionings rather than capabilities, and they have to be adapted in regard to the actual development stage of the child. Basic competencies and knowledge in literacy, math and science are a good thing for a child of school age, but for the first months of life, children need to achieve other functionings first and have certainly other needs. The same inadequacies can be found in regard to Robeyn's list, but that is no wonder, since she drafted it not as a universal list but one with a particular topic in mind: namely, gender injustices; more specifically for adults, not young boys and girls. Being able to work in the labor market is for many children more a threat than a unit of justice; being able to raise children is a very problematic issue for teenagers, and there are many good reasons to assume that reproductive health during adolescence also includes family planning and being protected from unwanted pregnancy. What we would like to make clear is simply that a list for children has to look different than a list for adults, even though there are some very important overlaps. We now want to present and discuss six criteria for selecting functionings and capabilities that matter for children for the issue of social justice:

(1) A functioning or capability that is used for an analysis of injustice has to reflect a truly important dimension of a child's well-being or well-becoming; in this sense, it has to be child-specific. Justice for children is concerned with things that really matter for them and not with supplements or 'extras'. As we have seen, the category of functionings is at first a formal one, and in theory, one could make it a question of justice if a child is able to whistle or stand on her head. This would, however, be a distortion of the concept of justice, which should look at functionings that make a substantial difference to a child's well-being and well-becoming. The genuine importance

of a functioning for the well-becoming is best defined in relation to its contribution to the achievement of one or more other important capabilities as an adult. In our view, most approaches used to generate the lists found in literature (including the ones by Nussbaum and Robeyns) already incorporate in one way or another such 'significance criteria', and the dimensions they identify are typically truly important for a good human life; notwithstanding, they do not address the particularities arising when looking at children, and as a consequence and quite naturally, they do not tell anything specific about the well-being and well-becoming of children. In addition, we would like to emphasize that we see the notions of well-being and well-becoming as basic ones for normative reasoning. Hence, we deliberately depart here from Nussbaum, who suggests that her list can be justified based on the notion of human dignity and a life worthy of it. There are three reasons for this decision. Firstly, there is a certain ambiguity inherent to the notion of dignity: it is something all humans have and not something one can reach or fall short of. It is therefore nothing that can be a goal of justice in itself. Dignity can indeed be violated, and living conditions may be indecent, but the people whose dignity is violated and who have to live in such ways still have their dignity. By using the concepts of well-being and well-becoming, on the other hand, we want to highlight from the beginning that we are dealing with something aspired to, a goal that should be reached but that a lot of children are denied. Each and every child is born with equal dignity, but not all have the same chance to achieve well-being and well-becoming. Secondly, we understand dignity as a minimum concept, one that does not entail the full scope of justice. Justice encompasses a living in dignity but demands more. This is especially important if justice is applied in modern affluent societies and welfare states that have already reached a high level of development and welfare. It seems plausible that two children can both be treated with dignity but have a fairly unequal level of well-being and well-becoming, which should be criticized as unjust. Thirdly, well-being and well-becoming are developmental and dynamic concepts, while dignity is a more static concept. It is also obvious that well-being and well-becoming demand different things for children and adults, while it is less clear how to spell out the same using the notion of dignity. Justice for children is necessarily concerned with these issues of development and with the task to weigh the current and the future well-being of a child against each other.

Still it should be made very clear that human dignity is an important part of children's lives, of their well-being and well-becoming. Looking at what some researchers, including Nussbaum herself, have deduced from the concept of human dignity, many similarities can be observed, and it seems possible to interpret dignity and well-being in a way that they are more or less the same. Yet our shift to well-being and well-becoming is a signal that what matters for children is more than dignity, dignity being undoubtedly an important part.

(2) The selection of a functioning that matters for justice should be based on the best available (empirical) evidence. Research on the well-being and well-becoming of children is a multidisciplinary task involving a variety of perspectives, methodologies and research paradigms (Graf and Schweiger 2015). Specifying functionings for the purpose of social justice must necessarily involve a close dialogue with developments in the relevant fields and the knowledge of the physical, mental and social needs of children. This point entails that lists of functionings have to be adapted, modified and redefined if new evidence is available; indeed, results of the last decades show that the new knowledge coming up makes a substantial difference (Ben-Arieh 2010; McAuley and Rose 2010). In this regard, the list we will suggest does well, since it was generated with expert knowledge and specialists of different fields; nonetheless, it is clear that the list must be constantly scrutinized and connected to results gained by the scientific community. One final remark should be made in this context: While it is important to select functionings on the best evidence available, one should not expect a scientific method that will lead to a clear and uncontroversial result. In fact, the multidisciplinary approach we suggest is likely to lead to ongoing controversies about fundamental issues of children's well-being and well-becoming, which have to be confronted continuously and with the necessary intellectual honesty.

(3) Selecting functionings for the purpose of characterizing children's well-being and well-becoming in relation to social justice has to take into account if their (re)distribution is possible and feasible. In particular, their distribution must be influenceable by the institutional design of a society. In fact, this claim has to be at the heart of any approach that looks at distributions of well-being and well-becoming from a social justice perspective. Here, some difficult questions arise that are closely connected to a general critique of the capability approach as it was stated by some resourcists and that

we will mention later on in this chapter in our assessment of the sufficiency principle as defended within the capability approach. Some resourcists argue that functionings and capabilities are not the right metric for justice exactly because it is unclear what distributing them means and because it is not obvious that the basic structure of a society can have an influence on them. Functionings and capabilities, so the argument goes, might be a good metric for conceptualizing human well-being, but claims of *justice* have to rely on a different metric, and some sets of resources do, in their point of view, a better job in this regard (see Kelleher 2013). We agree that a theory of justice that operates within a functioning or capability metric has to face these distributional concerns and that there might be cases where a functioning is important for the well-being of a child but is not the subject of a justice-based claim. For instance, if a child has a serious accident and subsequently suffers permanent damage, for example, in cognitive and motor domains, it is likely that she will never be able to enjoy some of the functionings that other children can still reach without a problem. This fact is not, however, per se a problem of justice. Sometimes there are limits to what can be achieved, and there are limits to which kinds of support one is entitled to; we will address this point in the context of how a sufficiency principle should be interpreted so that both the demand side and the supply side are taken into account. Impairments and disabilities must be surely included in reasoning about justice as well, and it is certainly the duty of a just society to enable persons with disabilities the access to a broad range of functionings and capabilities as far as possible (Nussbaum 2006). In many cases, however, there are limitations to what is feasible – there are 'tragic fates' that have to be recognized by a theory of justice. But these distinctions and refinements should not lead us astray from the fact that many important functionings and capabilities are capable of being influenced by the way a society arranges its institutions. Social scientific evidence increasingly suggests that many aspects of human life are fundamentally shaped by the environment and social relations, as well as by the distribution of goods and rights. Hence, how a society is organized and how it regulates its institutions have an immediate impact on the functionings and capabilities of its members, and therefore many of them fulfill these criteria. Philosophy, too, has to work closely with other scientific disciplines, since this empirical work transcends its scope; the clear tendency is that certain aspects, such as health – which John Rawls, for example, still considered a natural primary good and hence not subject to social distribution – are now seen by many political philosophers as highly influenceable by social factors. Health justice is a blooming research field, and we agree that the evidence that great injustices are happening in this regard is overwhelming. These few considerations illustrate that a variety of functionings and capabilities are socially influenceable. Certainly, they are not distributable, as are money and other material goods, and in individual cases people will not be able to achieve them even with good institutions in place. However, a society can still provide the general framework for a just distribution, and it can do its best in order that its institutional design secures, at least to a very high degree, that every child can actually enjoy the functionings in question.

(4) The concept of justice demands that the functionings taken as the basis for the respective evaluations are, at least to some extent, objectively determinable and not merely subjective. They should not depend primarily on the assessments, experiences and evaluations of the subjects in question. In other words, what is important is not mainly that someone feels or thinks that she suffers from an injustice but that there are good external and intersubjectively comprehensible reasons that an injustice is happening. This set of criteria is relevant both for children and adults and connects to the arguments capability scholars usually bring forward to criticize subjective metrics of justice as defended, for example, by utilitarians. The subject's preferences are malleable and adapt to the circumstances it is used to, introducing distortions in its perception and evaluation of the situation. Claims of justice must therefore be aware of this danger and take these 'adaptive preferences' seriously. In the case of children, this aspect is of particular relevance and must not get neglected. For such reasons, happiness is not a good guide for justice for children, and it seems more suitable to take mental health as an indicator (Cabezas, Graf and Schweiger 2014). Furthermore, objectively determinable functionings allow comparing the well-being of children in a meaningful way, and they make changes and improvements traceable and perceivable by other members of society. Such information is indispensable for a concept of justice that can guide the design of institutions and policies. It needs 'hard' and accessible criteria for the evaluation of personal advantage. If not, measures for (re)distributing functionings and capabilities cannot be justified toward others, and it is unlikely that they are supported by the public. Objective measurability also limits

the possibility of cheating, which, again, has a positive effect on public acceptance of a just regime.
(5) The selection of functionings has to include children's own views. A concept of children's well-being and well-becoming cannot ignore what aspects are relevant to children themselves, how they perceive their lives and where they set their priorities. Respecting children and their agency is tantamount to choosing such an approach, and there is overwhelming evidence that children are capable of expressing their point of view if they are given appropriate opportunities to do so. Different settings and methodologies can be used, adapting them to specific age groups and cultural contexts (Lansdown and UNICEF Innocenti Research Centre 2001; Camfield, Woodhead and Streuli 2009; Percy-Smith and Thomas 2010). As a consequence, subjective experiences and the children's point of view are of great importance in the selection process of relevant functionings, although we want to stress that their consultative function has to be a priority. This point might seem to be in opposition to the one before, where the objective accessibility was emphasized. However, this is not the case because the selection process has to be separated from its outcome. Of course, subjective assessments are relevant for the process, but the fact remains that the functionings resulting from it have to be measurable – at least to a considerable part – objectively if they have a role to play in a concept of justice. Furthermore, taking seriously the child's point of view has a dimension that goes beyond the useful information if often generates. The respect a society owes its children entails that they have to be granted a 'right to be heard'. As we have argued above, it is generally not reasonable to give children full authority over their own circumstances. But they certainly have their own views from an early age on, and giving them the opportunity to express them is of value independently of any instrumental considerations (Archard and Skivenes 2009).
(6) Finally, the fertility or corrosiveness of a functioning – in the sense introduced earlier on – should be taken into account. According to their positive or negative effects on the development and achievement of other functionings and capabilities, different weights can be given to different functionings in the context of justice theory. Especially for children, these concepts have to be considered a priority because childhood is the phase of every human being's life where the foundation for well-being and well-becoming is laid and where the fertile or corrosive effect of a functioning (or its absence) has long-lasting consequences.

Finally, we will discuss a list that so far presents one of the best available approaches to children's well-being from a capability perspective. Mario Biggeri and his colleagues (Biggeri 2003; Biggeri and Mehrotra 2011; Biggeri and Libanora 2011; Biggeri and Santi 2012) proposed a pragmatic and empirically informed approach to selecting functionings and capabilities for children that are important to their well-being and well-becoming. They worked with two types of procedures, which we explain in what follows.

Biggeri and his colleagues took up Robeyn's suggestion and carried out a procedure to conceptualize a child-sensitive list of capabilities in the following way: In a first phase, a group of child experts (including UNICEF officers, psychologists, sociologists and NGO practitioners) selected, on the basis of their knowledge and experience, relevant capabilities for the evaluation of child well-being. Since the well-being of children is a concern for many stakeholders and different scientific disciplines, such an interdisciplinary and interprofessional approach seems to be required. There is a need to include theoretical and empirical as well as ethical reasoning to comprehensively grasp the different dimensions at stake, something that can be achieved only through a dialogue involving a broad range of experts. In the second phase, the reasons for the choices were explained and the inclusion of each capability was justified, relating them to other works on the capability approach, particularly those of Nussbaum and Robeyns, and to literature on children's issues as published by the UN Children's Fund (UNICEF), the UN Educational, Scientific and Cultural Organization (UNESCO), the International Labour Organization (ILO) and the United Nations (UN). Again, methodological concerns suggest this proceeding, taking into account the most important documents already developed in the field of the well-being of children, relating them conceptually to the capability approach and seeking valuable links and mutual improvements. In the third phase, an appropriate level of abstraction of the different items was chosen in order to make them generally applicable to children as a group while still including the uniqueness of each child. Finally, the list was rechecked both to include all relevant dimensions for analyzing the well-being of children and for nonreduction, meaning that none of the domains should be reducible to another. As a result, the following list emerged (Biggeri and Mehrotra 2011, 51):[1]

(1) Life and physical health: being able to be born, be physically healthy and enjoy a life of normal length

---

[1] The items marked with * have to be interpreted in accordance with the age and maturity of the child.

(2) Love and care: being able to love and be loved by those who care and being able to be protected*
(3) Mental well-being: being able to be mentally healthy
(4) Bodily integrity and safety: being able to be protected from violence of any sort
(5) Social relations: being able to be part of social networks and to give and receive social support*
(6) Participation: being able to participate in and have a fair share of influence and being able to receive objective information*
(7) Education: being able to be educated
(8) Freedom from economic and noneconomic exploitation: being able to be protected from economic and noneconomic exploitation*
(9) Shelter and environment: being able to be sheltered and to live in a healthy, safe and pleasant environment
(10) Leisure activities: being able to engage in leisure activities
(11) Respect: being able to be respected and treated with dignity
(12) Religion and identity: being able to choose to live according to a religion and identity or to choose not to do so*
(13) Time autonomy: being able to exercise autonomy in allocating one's time*
(14) Mobility: being able to move

We agree that this list in fact represents central aspects of the well-being of children on a general and abstract level. It represents many of the core elements also found in other approaches to this topic and brings together different fields of discourse. It also fulfills the six criteria we have proposed. All of these functionings and capabilities (according to the child's maturity and competence) are based on research, are objectively determinable (at least to some extent) and are highly influenced by social arrangements, and many of them are fertile. We believe this list is best understood as a pragmatic and empirically informed selection of the functionings and capabilities that matter for the well-being and well-becoming of children; it is based on broad consensus backed up by a wide range of experts from different fields (academic and nonacademic), giving the selection a high grade of credibility that extends beyond purely philosophical arguments. If it is in fact exhaustive, as Biggeri and his colleagues suggest, the question is certainly a disputed, not easily answered one. However, it does not seem to be necessary to have a clear and final stance on this issue in order to provide a theory of justice for children that is able to give a fundament for the evaluation of a society's practices and institutions and to guide its development for the better.

We therefore also disagree with Robeyns's fourth criterion (exhaustion and nonreduction), since it is too demanding and not necessary for all purposes and applications.

The identified functionings and capabilities are formulated at an abstract level and must subsequently be specified according to the relevant cultural and social contexts. Thus, they include both context-sensitive and context-transcending features alike: In order to give concrete meaning to them, they have to be related to existing norms and practices, taking a great deal of diversity into account. A child's social relations and friendships, for instance, cannot be conceived the same way in a rural region in western Africa, in a favela in Rio de Janeiro and in a wealthy region in London or Paris. There is, however, a universal core to them that reflects central features of how children can flourish, not leading to a complete relativism on what social relations of children should look like. Isolation or interactions based on physical or psychological violence or categorical subordination, for example, are wrong independent of context. Similar considerations are true for all the other dimensions, which always have to be interpreted in accordance with local beliefs and circumstances without losing sight of their defining features.

The composition of the list recognizes that functionings and capabilities usually develop over time, giving the well-becoming aspect an important role. In fact, many of the items have to be interpreted taking the age and maturity of the child into account in order to understand their concrete meanings, an insight that is intuitively plausible and a cornerstone of current thinking about childhood and children's participation. This also means that it is crucial to give children age-appropriate opportunities to exercise choices and to make use of freedoms, even if they should not be as ample as those of adults and controlled in a way that they do not jeopardize important functionings. Children are social agents from an early age on, and it is important for them to make their own decisions. Hence, freedom is also a central category for children, but it should be of course exercised in an adequate environment, conducive to the development of more and more rational and reasonable decision making, leading to a steady improvement in a person's global autonomy. Looking at children in this way and characterizing them as subjects of evolving capabilities (and not just as 'sites' where functionings get realized) fits well with a new ethical attitude toward children that sees them no longer exclusively as recipients of services or passive beneficiaries of adults' care or care of state institutions but as the subjects of rights and active participants in their development and in the life of the community (Lansdown and UNICEF Innocenti Research Centre 2001). Such an approach to children's development also makes clear that the concepts of functionings and capabilities, which are often clearly separated on a conceptual level, are in practice deeply entangled. Certain functionings have to be secured so that real choices can be made, and the situation of children illustrates this point further: as evolving agents, they rely on certain levels of health, education and social inclusion in exercising their choices – not only in terms of accessible opportunities but of actually realized functionings. Thus, for many social evaluations, it is reasonable to make functionings the most important category of analysis, especially when children are the target group. In the next chapter, we will also show that a focus on choice and freedom is often not the best way to scrutinize and evaluate the injustice of child poverty. Without downplaying their competencies, skills and agency, in many contexts it is basic to look at what has been effectively achieved and not at the options that are available to them. It matters, for instance, that children are in fact well nourished, not that they are capable of being so.

A few provisos are necessary: Firstly, we do not claim that this list is finished. It is open for discussion and further scrutiny, and other researchers using different methods or working on questions in a different context will produce slightly different lists. Secondly, the similarities to the lists of Nussbaum and Robeyns suggest, as we have stated before, that some functionings and capabilities are important for both children and adults. Thirdly, this list is still very vague and needs to be further specified in order to be able to be applied in different contexts. Nonetheless, it is a start, and we will use this list, more specifically some of the functionings and capabilities on it, to further examine the injustice of child poverty in the next chapter in more detail. We position ourselves therefore with a rather pragmatic approach within the mentioned discussions about adequate lists for theorizing justice. We do not aim for completeness; nevertheless, we are confident that on this basis we will be able to build a strong case that child poverty profoundly violates what social justice demands. Before we can do that, however, we have to discuss the issue of the rule or principle of justice we want to endorse.

1.3 Sufficiency and equality

In the last section, we have argued that functionings (and, if applicable, capabilities) should be seen as the best currency of justice for children.

In addition, we have proposed some criteria for selecting functionings and capabilities for children and presented a list that can give guidance for our purposes in this book. We have also discussed that justice should put priority on fertile functionings, which enable the development and achievement of other functionings and capabilities, and that the detection and alleviation of deprivations that constitute corrosive disadvantages should be prioritized. In this section we address the question of the rules and principles of justice and, hence, how these functionings and capabilities should be distributed among the children in a society and how much of these they are entitled to; that is to say, the question of putting a threshold on each functioning and capability below which a child is deemed to live in injustice. There is a long-running dispute between scholars about the right rule of justice, and the main options disputed are equality and sufficiency (or priority) or a mixture of these (Casal 2007). Some philosophers also advocate the use of more than one principle of justice; David Miller, for example, argues for a tripartite model of the principles of need (which can be interpreted in terms of sufficiency), desert and equality (Miller 1999). The capability approach is usually in the sufficiency camp (Arneson 2006; Anderson 2010), although Nussbaum recognizes the importance of equality, arguing that thresholds have to be specified in a way that does justice to the equal human dignity of every human being. This, she claims, leads to the conclusion that, for some capabilities, a sufficient level coincides with equality – for example, in voting rights. We do not want to recapitulate the whole debate here, for example, the criticism of Thomas Pogge (Pogge 2002; Oosterlaken 2012), but rather just jump in and argue for our version of sufficiency, which is not so far away from Nussbaum's although with a few alterations.

Nussbaum (Nussbaum 2011) demands that every human is entitled to all the central capabilities on her list up to certain thresholds, under which truly human functioning is no longer possible. Hence, the goal of justice, though not of the minimum justice Nussbaum has in mind, is not for everyone to have the same or the highest level of capabilities but for everyone to be secure in having enough for a decent living. Justice also forbids trade-offs between basic human capabilities; if a person falls below a threshold in one capability, it is not enough to compensate her by allowing a higher level in another dimension. Each capability on the list is of equal value, and a shortfall in one of them is enough to constitute an injustice. She also acknowledges, as we ourselves do, that the determination of the thresholds for her capabilities is not a purely philosophical task but involves empirical knowledge from other disciplines as well as public deliberation. The ten capabilities on her list should guide policies in each country, but it is the responsibility of each country to set an adequate threshold. Unfortunately, Nussbaum is rather vague and only arbitrarily discusses certain capabilities and their possible thresholds. In her view, for some capabilities, the threshold should be set in a way that leads to equality so that each human is basically entitled to the same level in that capability (e.g., liberal rights), while for other capabilities the threshold can be set lower and hence allows a certain degree of inequality (e.g., in housing and material living conditions). To her, granting each human each capability above this threshold level is a partial and minimal requirement of what justice demands, admitting that there are various ways a just society can deal with inequalities above the threshold. However, they have to be arranged in a way so that *equal respect and concern* are guaranteed for all citizens. According to Nussbaum, this implies that each and every capability must be secured up to a certain level and that they should never be assessed from a trade-off perspective:

> [...] *all ten of these plural and diverse ends are minimum requirements of justice*, at least up to the threshold level. In other words, the theory does *not* countenance intuitionistic balancing or trade-offs among them. The constitutional structure (once they are put into a constitution or some other similar set of basic understandings) demands that they *all* be secured to each and every citizen, up to some appropriate threshold level. In desperate circumstances, it may not be possible for a nation to secure them all up to the threshold level, but then it becomes a purely practical question what to do next, not a question of justice. (Nussbaum 2006, 175)

How can we, how should we interpret Nussbaum´s rule of sufficiency in regard to children in rich countries? She does not give a clear answer; it often seems as if she views the capability approach as mainly concerned with poverty in poor countries and the severe harm there. We wish to specify some important aspects.

(1) In rich countries, a higher level of well-being and well-becoming is obviously achieved for many children; the possibilities to realize a good life are much better than in most other countries in this world. Still, certainly not all children achieve the same level of well-being and well-becoming, and some even fall short of what justice demands in terms of minimal thresholds in these countries. Furthermore, we

agree with Nussbaum that it is important to focus on a particular problem in a particular context in order to be more specific about where thresholds should be set. For our approach in this book, this means that it is reasonable to first investigate the situation in rich countries in some detail before we extent our theory to global justice in the last chapter. The fact that rich countries have already reached high levels in many aspects and that welfare states do a partly good job to alleviate poverty and to secure a certain level of well-being and well-becoming for all children implies that we need to work with a different kind of threshold and minimal conditions of justice. Still, it is important to also have an absolute minimum in mind, since in rich countries, too, there are some cases in which we can find severe poverty and other forms of hardship like homelessness, exploitation, child trafficking, child hunger and prostitution. In general, however, we are concerned with 'relative' poverty, as we will discuss in the next chapter. The adequate thresholds under such circumstances can be set according to two principles: on the one hand, we have to ask what is possible in these states and what can they provide for children without violating other claims of justice. This speaks against too high standards for assessing justice for children, because we can never provide all children with a maximum in well-being and well-becoming for at least two reasons (Arneson and Shapiro 1996; Archard 2004, 62–63; Mills 2003): First, it is too demanding for those responsible for the upbringing of children. As important as it is to concentrate on children and to recognize them as equal sources of moral concern, we should not forget that we live in societies where everyone matters from a moral point of view. Maximizing the well-being and well-becoming of children in a strict sense would certainly lead to a disadvantage for other members of society and put unreasonably high burdens on them. Justice certainly does not imply the self-abandonment of all adult members in order to maximize the well-being and the life chances of children. Second, it is very difficult to understand what it even means to maximize the well-being and well-becoming of children. When it comes to well-being, it just seems unfeasible to say exactly what a perfectly good childhood looks like. There are just too many opinions about this, both in science and in commonsensical views, and any full definition will be ideologically charged. Regarding the well-becoming aspect, things are at least as difficult. Growing up is always connected to trade-offs, and some options to well-becoming can be held open only at the expense of denying others. Since there are definitely many valuable but noncommensurable options as to how to live one's life as an adult, maximizing well-becoming is probably not even a coherent idea. We see, therefore, that questions concerning the well-being and well-becoming of children are deeply entangled with general considerations about the good life. And since we agree with the diagnosis of political liberalism that there is no objective way to fully determine the nature of the good life (Nussbaum 2001; Rawls 2005), we also reject the mentioned ideas about maximization. On the other hand, we are always concerned with context-sensitive thresholds that are specified according to the living standards in that society. This reflects partly what is possible in a state but targets a different issue; namely, that it is important for justice for children that children do not fall behind for arbitrary reasons and that determining the adequate threshold by looking at the level that typically is achieved in that society is essential. For example, if most children in a society are able to acquire a certain level of knowledge and if that knowledge is used for further education or in the job market, it is reasonable and feasible to demand that all children be brought up to that level. This does not imply that each and every child should become a scientist but that each and every child should finish primary and secondary school and that all children that do so should be on more or less the same level. Finally, justice for children in modern welfare states always has a forward-looking perspective. As technology and livings standards grow and as we gain more knowledge on children's lives and health, we naturally can provide for them better; as a consequence, demands of justice also improve. In a historical perspective, this is quite obvious: the standards of justice for children 150 years ago were different; we did not know about many illnesses or about how they were transmitted and cured and we were still at the beginning of building public infrastructure like railroads, electricity and clean water in all places. Hence it was simply not possible to have all children grow up and live under the conditions we can easily secure for them nowadays and are seen as 'normal' today. Of course, the requirements for participating as an equal in the society one is part of have changed considerably, too. The knowledge and education needed for practicing full citizenship in a modern society today is different from what was necessary fifty or sixty years ago. And since this feature of political participation is usually given much weight by capability theorists (Anderson 2010; Nussbaum 2006; Sen 2009), the relevant thresholds have to be adapted accordingly. Another example would be life expectancy, something important and a good indicator for social inequality. Today life expectancy in all rich countries is much higher than it was a few decades ago; while we do not know whether it will further increase or not, it is clear now that, should it increase, it must do so for all and not just for a few – this will thus translate into claims of justice. If we know, for instance, that a new vaccination can increase the likelihood of getting older because it prevents several forms of cancer, then all children have a claim to get that vaccination (given that the medical knowledge is clear and that it really helps all without great risk of severe side effects). Justice for children is hence also a progressive concept.

(2) This leads us to the second point. The threshold levels demanded by justice in rich countries must always be specified by considering both the well-being and the well-becoming of children, which we would like to grasp via the concept of *equality of opportunity to well-being* in adulthood. Justice for children, as we stated before, is concerned not only with what actual functionings and capabilities a child has but also with what functionings and capabilities she can have as an adult and over her life course. That is why injustices during childhood are particularly severe; they influence a person's well-becoming negatively and violate the claim of these children to sufficient options for future well-being. We have not discussed what the well-being as an adult encompasses, but it would be possible to come up with a preliminary list using the same, although adapted, criteria we presented and assigning the idea of practical reason or autonomy a more important role; such a list would perhaps look the same as Nussbaum's or Robeyns's. In any case, some important functionings and capabilities we have showed to matter for both children and adults will be on that list, such as health, education and social relations. The state should have a strong interest to give each child the same chance to achieve functionings and capabilities that matter as an adult, which necessarily implies giving many functionings to children. If we want to secure health in adulthood, for example, we need to be concerned with health during childhood, and it is unjust that adults are impaired in their health because they suffered from health issues otherwise preventable or curable during childhood. Likewise, the state has a responsibility to provide each and every child with the education needed to achieve well-being as an adult. Without specifying in detail which capabilities and functionings are necessary for a concept of adult well-being, being able to find a decent job, to make reasonable political decisions and

to have a certain degree of health, literacy and knowledge of one's own body are certainly among them. Harry Adams's take on justice for children, for example, is oriented toward what children need in order to develop into autonomous adults (Adams 2008). We agree with most of his conclusions, particularly in regard to the importance of early childhood, but a sole focus on autonomy seems too narrow. Autonomy, as the capability approach is well aware of, is an important aspect of the well-being of adults, but it is not the only thing that matters, and justice for children must be concerned with many other aspects, as well.

(3) Our third point relates to Nussbaum's claim that equal respect has to be shown for each and every member of society – a category that obviously includes children. But whereas respecting an adult is to a large extent tantamount to respecting her choices and life plans, the situation for children is different. We suggest that showing equal respect and concern for children should mean that a society is equally concerned with every child's well-being and well-becoming. This does not mean supplying every child with the same set of resources but rather supporting them with the (material and immaterial) means required for achieving the necessary thresholds, a commitment lying at the heart of the capability approach:

> In defining the meaning of equal rights for different groups, a capability approach also insists that we start with an understanding of how groups and individuals differ in their requirements, given both physical and cognitive differences and also differences of social starting point. Indeed, it is precisely on account of the importance of context in determining what people are able to do and be that the capability approach has been defended as superior to resource-based approaches: two people may be given the same amount of some all-purpose resource such as wealth or income but differ in their real capabilities, whether because they have different physical needs or because they start from different social positions. Children, in many cases, will also be clearly different from adults in the support they require from the state in order to develop and enjoy their capabilities. (Dixon and Nussbaum 2012, 561; footnotes omitted)

We would also like to employ the distinction between demand-side and supply-side sufficiency here as proposed by David Kelleher (Kelleher 2013): So far sufficiency was presented in a way that exclusively looked at those whose functionings and capabilities lie below a certain threshold, and it was claimed that, as a consequence, they are entitled to treatment that raises them above the crucial level.

Such an account might suitably be called demand-side sufficiency view. One could also defend, however, a more differentiated '*supply-side* view' of sufficiency, which consists of two levels: First, bearers of justice-based entitlements must give reasonable consideration for those who suffer from capability failures (interpreted in terms of not reaching certain thresholds); second, they must take actions balancing the moral reasons to help and the 'other claims on the person's possible actions (involving other rights and freedoms, but also altogether different concerns that a person may, inter alia, sensibly have)' (Sen 2004a, 339–340). In other word, they must give *sufficient attention* to inequalities in the distribution of capabilities, and they have the duty of justice to intervene, taking into account their own circumstances and the other entitlements and obligations they have. This supply-side perspective is especially helpful for two reasons: it opens up possibilities of how extreme cases should be addressed from a capability perspective, and it explicitly introduces the issue of responsibilities, which has been rather neglected in the capability approach so far. Still, we would like to stress that a supply-side view has its dangers, and one must be careful to avoid misusing or instrumentalizing it in order to find excuses why the advantaged members of society do not have an immediate responsibility to act against poverty and inequality. In particular, it is important to note that the urgency to act attributed to the supply side is intertwined with the needs of the demand side. The stronger the suffering and injustices among the side of the disadvantaged, the stronger are the reasons for the supply side to neglect personal interests and to make sacrifices and efforts toward an improvement of the general situation. In this sense, the demand-side perspective remains an essential part of a capability approach to justice, even if there are clear and almost logically given limitations to it. On the one hand, it focuses on the victims of injustice and prioritizes their claims. This gives them the weight they deserve because, in the end, they are what matters. A supply-side view must be aware of the danger it poses; namely, being used by those better-off to avoid their responsibilities. In a public deliberation about how much is enough, victims of injustices are most likely in a weaker position to argue for the demand-side view, from which they will profit most in comparison with those in a more favorable position, who argue for the supply-side view. On the other hand and more importantly, how much those who are better-off can be reasonably demanded to give, that is the determination of the extent of the supply-side responsibilities, cannot be separated from the demand side, but is rather to be conceived as the just answer to it. Only the demand-side view can provide the necessary information for the supply-side view, and not the other way around. If a child is severely deprived, then the justified demands are higher than if that child needs fewer resources to reach the just minimum in capabilities and functionings. On the basis of this demand-side information, the supply side view can be brought in. This means that the state and other agents of justice are responsible for putting efforts into each child according to what she needs in order to achieve functionings and capabilities important for well-being and well-becoming. The state has to show equal concern for all children's needs and the particular conversion factors they require, whether it be providing public transportation to schools in rural areas, securing accessibility to education for children with disabilities, or giving ill children the necessary treatment and allowing their parents to care for them, for example, via a paid leave from work.

(4) The issue of setting an adequate threshold must also be discussed. It is important to see that the distinction between selecting functionings and capabilities and setting thresholds for them is not always so clear and that it is best to conceptualize the latter as a form of specification of functionings and capabilities. Setting a threshold is the task to replace one general description of a functioning or capability by a more specified one but also in terms of functionings and capabilities. For example, the threshold for being politically included and being able to participate can be specified in terms of being allowed to vote and to be voted into office. This threshold is nothing more than a specification that also uses the terminology and the underlying concept of functionings and capabilities. All thresholds discussed by capability theorists are, in fact, such specifications; in some empirical research, this also means the translation of a functioning or capability into a functioning of having certain goods. In such cases, the capability approach in practice gets very close to resourcist approaches, since it uses resources or rather the functioning to have certain resources as thresholds and specifications. It is more accurate to think of setting a threshold that can be specified using different functionings and capabilities. The threshold for being educated can then, for example, be going to school for a certain number of years, learning certain skills and knowledge determined by experts, being allowed to pursue further education on the basis of educational

achievements, for instance, and being allowed to pursue certain occupations based on that education. All these different functionings and capabilities can be used together to specify what the general functioning and capability of education encompasses and thus which level children should reach. Such specifications are necessary to put justice to work in policies. To state that each and every child is entitled to be educated is a phrase that might read well in a constitution, but it is not possible to evaluate the success of a certain policy or to criticize a state for failing its children on the basis of such a general statement. One has to know what it means to be educated and what the thresholds are. Here again, it is clear why the concepts of well-being and well-becoming are more suited for the task than the concept of dignity – a failure to educate all or some the children in a state can violate their well-being and in particular their well-becoming without being a violation of their dignity.

What becomes clear when setting a threshold in this way is that another distinction gets blurry; namely, that between functionings and capabilities, on the one hand, and the conversion factors needed to achieve them, on the other hand. In the case of education, for example, it is very plausible to assume that compulsory schooling for a certain number of years is a conversion factor for being educated and not the functioning itself. Nussbaum seems to understand it in such a way herself, as she writes that it is up to debate whether compulsory education should last for twelve years, claiming that under the given circumstances, nine years of schooling is not enough. In our view, this reflects pragmatic issues and the fact that many conversion factors have some value in themselves and are not to be used only instrumentally. To finish school is important because it implies that the children have gained certain knowledge and skills and because the official degree itself is of value in the labor market or in the pursuit of higher education. For pragmatic reasons, it is sometimes easier to determine conversion factors, which, again, are often resources. In regard to health, for instance, most empirical research uses thresholds like a child receiving certain vaccinations, which is surely not a specification of health itself but a means to achieve and sustain health. It is simply easier to measure than health itself, and it is also easier to design a policy based on the claim that each and every child should get certain vaccinations.

One more thing is extremely important: If setting a threshold always implies specifying a general functioning or capability into a set of more concrete functionings and capabilities, then this also implies at least three more important insights. First, not each and every child will be able to reach these thresholds. If we take education as an example, it is likely that we can grant each and every child certain years of schooling and that we can help them to acquire some knowledge and skills as well, but we can never make sure that all children reach the same level in all skills and knowledge. This does not mean, however, that the threshold has to be a different one for children with or without disabilities, for example. If the threshold embraces that each and every child should acquire a certain level in reading, writing and mathematics, including a certain set of knowledge about a range of topics, then this threshold will not be reached by many children with cognitive disabilities. This does not imply that we should lower the threshold for children with disabilities, but it rather signals that justice is limited with respect to tragic differences between humans we cannot alter – an argument that Nussbaum has developed in more detail (Nussbaum 2006). Second, it is evident that thresholds have to be sensitive to subjects and, to some extent, to the contexts they are applied to, as well. We have just denied that thresholds should be different for children with severe disabilities and for those without, but it is still important to have different thresholds for different age groups based on the general level of competence and skills. Hence, the thresholds should allow us to monitor the development of the child adequately. Consider health: Pediatrics need to define what can be considered a normal development and what are distortions that need to be treated, a major health issue for young children (Gardner 2015). If there is one general threshold for all children, such development issues cannot be detected because it is unclear which level of development should be reached at the age of two and which at the age of eight. The health threshold must be, on the contrary, set and specified in a way that is sensitive to what level a child should reach at what age (with certain room for individuality for sure). Otherwise, the threshold cannot be used in any meaningful way in the design of health policies. Such issues of setting adequate thresholds are certainly a task for which philosophers without an extra expertise are not suited; what we can do is emphasize that such tasks are essential and, at the same time, intertwined with normative and political issues. A third insight is that the capability approach suggests a step-by-step procedure for social justice assessments: in a first step, general functionings and capabilities have to be selected, and in the next step, they have to be specified, choosing adequate thresholds that then allow the implementation and evaluation of concrete policies. It is possible to evaluate certain living conditions of children as unjust solely on the basis of this second step, since the standard of evaluation and the respective benchmark would be otherwise too blurry. This also gives a first methodological answer to the question that Nussbaum leaves open; namely, how to choose thresholds in particular contexts.

(5) We also want to combine the sufficiency rule with a priority view in regard to children in general and, in particular, in relation to child poverty. In a joint article with Rosalind Dixon, Martha Nussbaum discusses two reasons for such a priority view in respect to all children (Dixon and Nussbaum 2012): cost-efficacy and vulnerability. By vulnerability they refer to the dependency of children on adults, and by cost-efficacy they mean that investing in children saves huge costs the state would have to invest in adults; for example, a vaccination that costs only a few cents can prevent the development of a disease that demands hundreds of thousands of dollars to be treated. The vulnerability of children, which we already discussed in length, implies that the state has the responsibility to step in if parents or other caregivers cannot provide for children because they cannot do it for themselves. Cost efficacy, Nussbaum argues, is also relevant in regard to fertile functionings and corrosive disadvantages. The capability approach demands that each and every human is entitled to develop and realize certain important functionings (in the case of young children) and capabilities (in the case of adolescents and adults) and to invest in a fertile functioning that helps to do what can save huge costs later on. The same is true for corrosive disadvantages, which undermine the development and achievement of these important functionings and capabilities. Nussbaum and Dixon cite nutrition, children's health and education as examples of such an investment in fertile functionings (or to avoid corrosive disadvantages), which should be prioritized by the state. That provides a good reason to tackle child poverty with a high priority. We want to move from the idea of a priority view toward children in general to the idea of prioritizing certain functionings and capabilities on the same grounds, or, to put it differently, of prioritizing the alleviation of particular injustices. Such a prioritizing has three elements: it asks how important a certain functioning or capability is; how severe and widespread its deprivation is; and how it can be overcome and what means are needed to secure justice in relation to that dimension. As we will show over the course of the next chapters, child poverty fulfills these three criteria (it affects functionings and

capabilities with a high priority, is widespread and can be overcome without unfeasible efforts) and hence should be tackled with a very high priority. This view is compatible with the idea of a moderate-sufficiency view that was developed by Richard Arneson (Arneson 2006). This view implies (a) prioritizing the gains in well-being of those who are below the threshold, (b) that those who are further below the threshold are to be prioritized and (c) that losses or gains in well-being above the threshold are important but that losses or gains below the threshold are to be prioritized. For children living in poverty, this has four implications worth stressing: First, children in poverty should be prioritized over children not in poverty, and the state or other agents of justice should provide them with the conversion factors they need, giving them priority over those that children need to achieve well-being higher than the threshold. For example, if the state can either make some elite universities better or remake the education system so as to enable poor, disadvantaged children to reach a level of educational sufficiency (in welfare states this could mean producing more or less equally educated children after the designated years of compulsory schooling), the state should prioritize the latter. Second, the moderate sufficiency view also implies that children are to be prioritized over adults due to the long-lasting consequences of injustices suffered during childhood. For this argument it is necessary to include a temporal dimension in the concept of well-being. The gains in well-being for children will be higher than the gains of older adults because the children will live longer. Also the losses below the threshold are more likely to be higher if children are not prioritized. As we will argue in the next chapter in more detail, poverty during childhood is very likely to heavily affect the whole life course in a negative way; if sufficiency is concerned with securing a certain level of well-being, not at a single point in time but over the life course, then it has to give priority to dealing with injustices that have longer-lasting effects on well-being. A third conclusion based on the priority view is important for global justice, but we want to mention it here also: severe child poverty in poorer countries should be tackled with a higher priority than less severe child poverty in welfare states, but not primarily at the expense of the children in poverty in welfare states but – if any expense is necessary at all – at the expense of adults who have a high well-being above the threshold. This follows from the rule to prioritize more severe child poverty over less severe and to prioritize children before adults.

These five points illustrate what justice for children in rich countries demands. We will not be able to set a specific threshold for all the important functionings and capabilities that matter for the well-being and well-becoming of children, but the thin concept employed by us revolves around giving all children equal opportunity to later well-being and making sure that they reach the highest level of well-being possible given the state's level of development. In modern welfare states, we have seen unprecedented progress over the last 150 years, partly with severely damaging side effects (climate change and resource exploitation) and at the cost of other countries. These issues should not be downplayed, and global justice should indeed be concerned with them and what consequences they should have for the design of justice in rich countries. It is perhaps necessary to adjust some dimensions of well-being, fundamentally rethinking the current consumerist orientation that requires ever more products at a cheaper price. In general, we assume that the functionings and capabilities we presented as important will hold even if the thresholds within them, hence the specified functionings and capabilities into which we translate them in a specific context, should vary; we certainly allow for the possibility that due to the demands of global justice, thresholds will have to decrease in rich countries in order to increase around the globe. Unfortunately, dealing with real-life justice and problems encountered along the way is sometimes messy and blurry (this is an accusation Nussbaum has often had to face). For our case, the case of child poverty in modern welfare states, we argue that we cannot come up with a definite list or definite thresholds for the items on that list, but this is not needed in order to fulfill an important philosophical duty; namely, to criticize this injustice. We will discuss this final point before moving on to examine child poverty and its effects on the well-being and well-becoming of children.

1.4 Conclusions

How can we criticize any injustice based on the concept of justice we have outlined so far? We have a preliminary list of functionings and capabilities and an underdetermined distributional rule for specifying the thresholds children are entitled to a as a matter of justice. This rule is underdetermined because the setting of thresholds of functionings and capabilities demands not only a high amount of interdisciplinary knowledge and expertise but the in-depth examination of particular issues and contexts; both aspects are highly complex, and we will not be able to sufficiently deal with them in this book. One could assume that, with these tools, we are not very well equipped to examine child poverty and to criticize it as unjust, an objection we would like to counter on four grounds, which get support from other applications of the capability approach for different purposes, for example, the one by Robeyns mentioned above (Robeyns 2003): Firstly, in order to criticize an injustice, we do not need a fully comprehensive concept of justice with a definite list and fully specified thresholds. Knowing that some functionings and capabilities are of high value for children is enough to judge it as unjust if they fall short of them for arbitrary and changeable reasons. Hence, a critique of child poverty can already start and be of value if it can be shown that child poverty interferes with the entitlements of the affected children to even just one important functioning or capability. Furthermore, it is enough to argue that children fall short either in one or more functionings or capabilities that matter for their well-being as children or in those that matter for their well-becoming and well-being as adults. Child poverty or any other injustice is unjust as soon as it interferes with either well-being or well-becoming, and it does not have to affect both, although the case is stronger if it does. In fact, we will argue that child poverty is a corrosive disadvantage because it usually deprives children not only of important elements of their well-being but also of their well-becoming.

Secondly, thresholds can already be applied for criticizing child poverty if they are only partially specified. We have argued that setting a threshold in a dimension means to determine functionings or capabilities on a less general level. How concrete this description must be depends, as Robeyns argued, on the task at hand. For our purposes, we do not think that it is useful to examine, for example, a particular part of the education system in a particular country, say the primary school in the United Kingdom. We are more concerned with the injustice of child poverty on a more general level that spans across all modern welfare states and abstracts from the many differences that clearly exist between these countries. For that general level, we do not need to specify the functionings and capabilities we will use on a highly detailed level, acknowledging that they cannot cover all important aspects. As we will show in the next chapter, these thresholds already serve to detect important violations of justice.

Finally, the specification of a threshold is relative to what is possible in a given country. In the next chapter, we will use a negative approach and concern ourselves with how child poverty affects the well-being and well-becoming of children in regard to important functionings and capabilities, using as a benchmark how they fare in comparison with other nonpoor children in that country. It is possible, although not plausible, that we miss an important aspect of injustice by this approach, because it could be the case that all children, poor and nonpoor, are below the threshold of what is possible and hence live in injustice. In order to determine that, we would need a different approach than the one we use and to pursue another inquiry. For our goal of criticizing child poverty, we are content with showing that it fulfills the criteria of not bringing these children up to the threshold that is possible in that state, and that level is well displayed by the fact that the majority of children reach it. It is hence for arbitrary reasons, namely for being poor, that some children do not reach that threshold in some important functionings and capabilities, which qualifies as unjust. The goal of the next chapter will be to build that case based on a close examination of empirical knowledge regarding three functionings: health, education and social inclusion. This empirical work does not show us that these three are so important that each and every child is entitled to reach a sufficient level of them; this work was done in this chapter. We will simply show that under the assumption that these three, health, education and social inclusion, are relevant for justice, empirical research indicates that child poverty is unjust – both in relation to the well-being and the well-becoming of children.

The fourth ground is that we are concerned with a group-based injustice when we criticize child poverty. We will make clear in the next chapter that we are not claiming that each and every child in poverty suffers from the deprivations we examine. Rather, we are concerned with these children as a particular social group in which many individuals are suffering from deprivations that can be traced back to their shared feature, namely being poor, which they cannot be held responsible for and cannot change themselves. Robeyns has criticized gender inequalities in many functionings because they cannot be plausibly attributed to different preferences (Robeyns 2003). For children this is even more obvious: poor children seldom wish to be in ill health or less educated, and more strikingly, it is certain that they lack a capacity to realize a preference for good health or education unless other persons and institutions provide them with care and other conversion factors.

Except where otherwise noted, this work is licensed under a Creative Commons Attribution 3.0 Unported License. To view a copy of this license, visit http://creativecommons.org/licenses/by/3.0/

OPEN

2
The Injustice of Child Poverty

In the previous chapter, we sketched a theory of social justice for children based within the capability approach. We argued that, as a matter of social justice, each and every child is entitled to reach a minimum threshold of certain important functionings and capabilities, which are essential to her well-being and well-becoming. Furthermore, we have suggested that in the case of children, a focus on achieved functionings is often more adequate from a social justice perspective than a focus on capabilities. However, this assumption has to be understood in relation to the age and competence of the child, respecting her agency from an early age on. As children move through childhood, as they mature and develop, choice and autonomy become more and more important, and social justice reflects this by shifting its focus from achieved functionings to capabilities.

Our aim in this chapter is to analyze the detrimental effects of child poverty on some important functionings (and capabilities for older and more competent children). On the one hand, we will use the concept of ill-being, which we define as the complete lack of achievement or insufficient achievement of at least one functioning that is essential to the well-being of children. On the other hand, we will describe the injustice of child poverty by referring to ill-becoming, which means that child poverty hinders the sufficient achievement of at least one of the important capabilities that define adult well-being. This means that we have two separate arguments to justify why child poverty is unjust: (a) it violates the justified claims of children to well-being and (b) it violates the justified claims of children to well-becoming. Even if we claim that the injustice of child poverty is proven sufficiently as far as it affects one important functioning or capability, we will show that, in fact, child poverty is best understood as having multiple and interrelated effects.

This chapter explores the ill-being and ill-becoming of child poverty in regard to physical and mental health, social inclusion and education. It will show that all these functionings can reasonably be taken for evaluations regarding social justice since they fulfill the criteria necessary for such an endeavor, as developed in Chapter 1. With our focus on these functionings, we claim neither that they are more important than others nor that child poverty affects them alone nor even that child poverty affects them primarily. On the contrary, our choice is a pragmatic one, and we hope to find broad agreement that these functionings are suitable for an examination of the injustices related to child poverty. We do not have a definite list; the one we presented and discussed in the previous chapter is just a first suggestion and an example of how such a list can be developed; since we claim that the injustice of child poverty is sufficiently shown if one important functioning cannot be achieved, it is also not necessary to provide a fully comprehensive examination of child poverty and its effects on all functionings to which children are entitled as a matter of justice. Nonetheless health, inclusion and education are all part of the list of Biggeri and his colleagues, and they are also included in many other lists of functionings and capabilities, for example, the ones of Nussbaum and Robeyns, as well as other conceptualizations of well-being of children (Amerijckx and Humblet 2014). Furthermore, they are relevant for both children and adults. They are not 'intrinsic goods of childhood' that would be of value only to children, but their particular form and the thresholds that should be used differ between children and adults. To be able to read and write sufficiently will be a good threshold for a child, but if an adult only reaches the same level of education, she will certainly be disadvantaged in many other areas of her life. In particular, health and education are also good examples for evolving capabilities and fertile functionings, and their achievement is essential to a person's future well-being in terms of functionings and capabilities. We will show that health (including both a physical and mental dimension), social inclusion and education are affected by child poverty in a way that the entitlement of children to well-being and well-becoming is violated. We will also show that these functionings are entangled and influence each other. For the most part our examination will be concerned with the functioning of these four and not the capability to be healthy, educated and included. We have argued at length why a focus on functionings is necessary in regard to children; another reason is the difficulty in measuring them in terms of capabilities. The studies we will present are all concerned with functionings and do not show if these children, also older ones, lack health, education or inclusion because of their own choices. Rather they show us the social determination of these functionings, which cannot be captured by referring to choice and autonomy, especially not for children and adolescents.

Before we address these claims, we would like to note two things. First, our argument is not that each and every child affected by poverty experiences it in the same way and suffers, for example, from ill health due to poverty or lacks education because of it. What we do claim instead is that in most – nearly all – cases, children living in poverty suffer from negative effects on at least one functioning they are entitled to as a matter of justice, and that this overwhelming majority is enough to justify evaluating it as unjust. We are concerned that children living in poverty suffer disadvantages compared with nonpoor children, and for this inequality there is no sufficient justification. Children, poor or not poor, cannot choose their parents or where they grow up and live, and they cannot choose to realize health, education or inclusion or other functionings and capabilities without being supported by others. It is also not plausible to assume that poor parents would prefer their children to suffer from these deprivations if they could choose differently. Again, our approach claims that well-being and well-becoming can be defined to a large extent objectively, with the consequence that we evaluate child poverty in a first step regardless of how it is subjectively experienced by those children themselves. In a subsequent step, we will come back to that issue and show how such subjective evaluations and the articulation of the subjective experiences of child poverty can further expand our critique. For the time being, we will focus on what can be said from a third-person standpoint using objective measures.

Second, we do not make strong claims about causal relations on child poverty and its connection to the functionings we explore in detail. We rely here on the available evidence brought forward by poverty research in other disciplines such as sociology, economics, psychology and medical research. For our claim, it is sufficient that poverty plays some substantial role in causing these deprivations regardless if other causes are also involved. Here, one can also point to the many studies confirming a relationship between poverty and child neglect as well as child abuse (Besharov and Laumann 1997; Gilbert et al. 2009), which obviously have very bad consequences for the children affected. But also here the causal relationships are difficult to grasp, a fact that also poses a challenge to the important issue of identifying the most important agents of justice for children in poverty, a subject we will address in a later chapter. We do acknowledge that from a policy perspective, it is important to untangle these causal relations in order to prioritize the effort on those that have the most detrimental effects. We are confident that the literature we will discuss here points in the direction that child poverty is in fact an important cause for the suffering of children in many other dimensions as well.

We are primarily interested in the injustice of child poverty, not in exactly how many children are affected by it or how best to count them. This implies necessarily that we are not much interested in how many children actually suffer the deprivation of one or more important functionings – for example, health – due to their poverty. It is enough for our argument that more children in poverty suffer these deprivations than their nonpoor peers for the reason that they are poor. Even if just a few children live in poverty and hence do not get what they are entitled to as a matter of justice, it is an injustice that deserves criticism and needs to be tackled. However, we still hold that it is valuable to take the breadth and depth of an injustice into account in order to prioritize it. We also acknowledge that it is possible to reach this same conclusion from many different perspectives; for example, on the basis of the costs that child poverty creates for society, which has been estimated in the USA to be as high as 500 billion dollars each year (Holzer et al. 2008).

2.1 Concepts and measures of child poverty

Before we examine the injustice of child poverty, we must discuss at least some aspects of the concept of poverty itself and present some data on how many children in welfare states are living in poverty. We do not and cannot aim to give a full overview of all the different debates in the different disciplines concerned with child poverty, but rather we aim to develop a basic understanding of the main aspects of child poverty. Because child poverty is mainly an issue of social sciences and not philosophy, we will need to focus on what is of significance for the purpose of our book and the following questions of social justice. Many questions that arise in poverty research are similar to those we discussed in regard to defining the functionings and capabilities that should be objects of justice. All approaches to child poverty need to define some goods, resources, activities or capabilities and functionings. They also need to define thresholds for these items, and then they need to determine who is counted: the individual child or the household. The last point is of particular importance because children usually live with adults and are heavily dependent on them (and their resources), and so, attempting to reflect this fact, child poverty is often measured on the household level. Moreover, the most commonly used indicator for child poverty is still income, and because children themselves do not have any relevant income in modern welfare states due to their not working, child poverty is measured using the family or household income. Before sketching the relevant measures in the USA and the European Union (EU) and the concept of social exclusion, we wish to outline the concept of poverty in general.

Poverty research has come to agree mostly that poverty has to be defined differently and measured according to the welfare and development level of the state that is researched. For this reason, the distinction between absolute and relative poverty has been often used in order to mark that relative poverty reflects things that persons need in a particular society (to live a normal or decent live), while absolute poverty refers to minimum standards necessary to survive or under which life is at least severely impaired (Alcock 2006). This distinction is, indeed, of some use, but it is also one of the key features of the capability approach that the same amount of basic goods and resources can yield different outcomes in different environments and for different persons depending on their needs and capacities. This applies to both relative and absolute measures. And even if there is some consensus about the goods, activities or capabilities and functionings that should be used to define relative and absolute poverty, the question of what thresholds for absolute and relative poverty should be set remains unanswered. We will see that in welfare states, setting the poverty line at 50 or 60 percent of the equivalent median income or understanding material deprivation as the enforced lack of two, three or four essential goods is often an arbitrary decision.

Another problematic issue in all poverty research in modern welfare states is whether thresholds are based on the median income or on deprivation measures defined according to what is seen as normal in a society: one criticism is that poverty is mixed with (mere) inequality and so thresholds are not able to capture poverty's essence. For example, Amartya Sen has criticized Peter Townsend, stating that, according to his relative measure, in a society where everyone has two Cadillacs, those able to afford but one Cadillac would be counted as poor (Sen 1983). Sen considers this a dissolving of the concept of poverty, which should be kept to cover those cases where people are really suffering from the deprivation of basic goods or capabilities and functionings that can and need to be defined in an absolute way. We agree with Ruth Lister that much of the debate between Sen and Townsend was not fruitful, but its core is still a challenge for poverty research in welfare states and, indeed, any philosophical examination of poverty in rich and highly developed contexts (Lister 2004, ch. 1). Sen's criticism has some merit and, if approved, would lead to acknowledging that child poverty in such an absolute sense is fortunately a rare thing in modern welfare states. Most children have at least some basic form of shelter, access to health care and nutrition and are protected from hunger. Opinions that relativize poverty as not being 'real' poverty are also not uncommon in the public and among poor people themselves (Beresford et al. 1999). Our answer to this challenge is twofold but in no way new.

On the one hand, we stress that every definition of poverty is always dependent on a normative background theory about what is needed for a decent or minimum life, something we will never be able to capture from empirical research alone. It is obvious that all human beings have certain biological needs, but it is also obvious that these alone are not enough to determine poverty (in fact, the concept of poverty would more or less coincide with the concept of health as it is often understood). One is able to survive for a long time in pain and hunger and without shelter or any social relations; should we claim that such a life is not deemed a life in poverty, it would say a lot about the moral status of our world. As we said, relative measures are not simply arbitrary and not solely interested in inequality, either; they are based on some kind of reasoning about what is a decent or 'normal' life in a particular society or state. On the other hand, it is not an either-or situation. To care about relative poverty does not imply that one should not care about absolute poverty and vice versa. An interest in absolute poverty does not make relative poverty less severe for those who suffer from it, even if we do know that many more severe forms of poverty exist in this world. We do acknowledge that there are questions of priority, which are also relevant for global justice and policy decisions, but this does not mean that we should not care about relative poverty and that it is not necessary to research what kinds of hardship and poverty exist in affluent societies and modern welfare states.

With these thoughts in mind, we will now discuss the official poverty measures in the USA and in the European Union. We will see that the issues of definition, determining indicators and setting thresholds are present and that no measure is and maybe never will be perfect and able to provide us with all the information about the breadth and depth of poverty.

The poverty thresholds used by the US Census Bureau are money income thresholds based on the minimal cost of food needs and adjusted for family size and age (DeNavas-Walt and Proctor 2014). It uses income before taxes; capital gains and noncash benefits (such as public housing, Medicaid and food stamps) are not included. The poverty thresholds were developed in 1963 and 1964 by Mollie Orshansky, using US Department of Agriculture food budgets designed for families under economic stress and data about what portion of a family's income was spent on food (Fisher 2002). The thresholds are annually modified using the consumer price index, but they do not reflect the level of welfare or income in the USA. In that sense, the official poverty line in the USA is absolute. The relevant annual thresholds in 2013 were $11,888 for a single person and $16,057 for a household with one adult under sixty-five and one related child under eighteen (see Table 2.1 for all the thresholds for 2013). There is no distinct measure for children; child poverty rates are determined

Table 2.1 Poverty thresholds for 2013 by size of family and number of related children under 18 years

Size of family unit	Weighted average thresholds	Related children under 18 years								
		None	One	Two	Three	Four	Five	Six	Seven	Eight or more
1 person (unrelated individual)	11,888									
Under 65 years	12,119	12,119								
65 years and over	11,173	11,173								
2 people	15,142									
Householder under 65 years	15,679	15,600	16,057							
Householder 65 years and over	14,095	14,081	15,996							
3 people	18,552	18,222	18,751	18,769						
4 people	23,834	24,028	24,421	23,624	23,707					
5 people	28,265	28,977	29,398	28,498	27,801	27,376				
6 people	31,925	33,329	33,461	32,771	32,110	31,128	30,545			
7 people	36,384	38,349	38,588	37,763	37,187	36,115	34,865	33,493		
8 people	40,484	42,890	43,269	42,490	41,807	40,839	39,610	38,331	38,006	
9 or more people	48,065	51,594	51,844	51,154	50,575	49,625	48,317	47,134	46,842	45,037

Source: US Census Bureau, www.census.gov/

Table 2.2 Poverty in the USA, by age

Year and characteristic	Under 18 years						18 to 64 years			65 years and over		
	All people			Related children in families				Below poverty level			Below poverty level	
	Total	Below poverty level		Total	Below poverty level		Total	Number	Percent	Total	Number	Percent
		Number	Percent		Number	Percent						
All races												
2013	73,625	14,659	19.9	72,573	14,142	19.5	194,833	26,429	13.6	44,508	4,231	9.5
2010	73,873	16,286	22.0	72,581	15,598	21.5	192,481	26,499	13.8	39,777	3,558	8.9
2005	73,285	12,896	17.6	72,095	12,335	17.1	184,345	20,450	11.1	35,505	3,603	10.1
2000	71,741	11,587	16.2	70,538	11,005	15.6	173,638	16,671	9.6	33,566	3,323	9.9
1995	70,566	14,665	20.8	69,425	13,999	20.2	161,508	18,442	11.4	31,658	3,318	10.5
1990	65,049	13,431	20.6	63,908	12,715	19.9	153,502	16,496	10.7	30,093	3,658	12.2
1980	62,914	11,543	18.3	62,168	11,114	17.9	137,428	13,858	10.1	24,686	3,871	15.7
1970	69,159	10,440	15.1	68,815	10,235	14.9	113,554	10,187	9.0	19,470	4,793	24.6
1960	65,601	17,634	26.9	65,275	17,288	26.5	(NA)	(NA)	(NA)	(NA)	(NA)	(NA)

Note: Numbers in thousands. People as of March of the following year.
Source: US Census Bureau, www.census.gov/

by counting how many children live in poor households. The poverty thresholds do not account for the differences in housing and living costs between areas but are applied nationally. That is of importance because, with the exact same amount of money, a family in a cheaper area can be much better off than a family with more income but living in a more expensive area.

Based on this calculation, there were about 45.3 million poor people in the USA in 2013 – about 14.5 percent of the population. This is one of the highest numbers in the fifty years that poverty has been measured in the USA, although the situation stabilized after sharp increases in the years 2007 to 2011, and the poverty rate went down in 2013 for the first time since 2006. Young people and children are more affected by poverty (for details, see Table 2.2); the poverty rate for children under eighteen was 19.9 percent (or 14.7 million children), while the poverty rate for people aged between eighteen and sixty-four was 13.6 percent and for persons older than sixty-five it was 9.5 percent. The poverty rate for children younger than six years old is even higher, reaching 22.2 percent (down from 25.3% in 2010), which accounts for 5.2 million young children living in poverty (Table 2.3). People living in institutional group quarters (such as prisons and nursing homes), college dormitories and military barracks and those without conventional housing (who are not in shelters) are not included in these numbers. Neither are unrelated children under the age of fifteen included, which means that children in foster care are not surveyed.

The European Union uses two different measures for poverty in general that also apply to children (Atkinson and Marlier 2010). On the one hand, it employs a relative at-risk-of-poverty threshold, which is set at 60 percent of the equivalent median income in a country. This threshold is relative and changes according to the average income. As

Table 2.3 Poverty status of related children under 6 years of age in the USA

Year	Poor	Percent
2013	5,231	22.2
2010	6,037	25.3
2005	4,784	20.0
2000	4,066	17.8
1995	5,670	23.7
1990	5,198	23.0
1980	3,986	20.3
1970	3,561	16.6

Note: Numbers in thousands
Source: US Census Bureau, www.census.gov

a result, the poverty threshold for a single person living in Austria, for instance, has increased over the years from an annual income of €10,200 in 2005 to €12,791 in 2011; for a household with two adults and two children under fourteen, the poverty threshold was an annual income of €22,681 in 2005 and €26,861 in 2011. In Greece, on the other hand, where the average income has decreased due to the economic crisis, the poverty line has decreased from an annual income of €7,178 in 2010 to €5,708 in 2012. If a household disposes of less income than that, all of its members are described as 'at risk of poverty'. These poverty thresholds are also relative in another sense; since they are national poverty thresholds benchmarked against the median income in a specific country, the at-risk-of-poverty thresholds are very different in each member state of the European Union. Just to give a few examples, for 2011 the at-risk-of poverty threshold was as high as €12,186 annual income in the Netherlands, while in Greece it was €6,591, in Bulgaria only €1,749 and in Slovakia €3,784. This means that a person with €10,000 annual income living in Vienna (Austria) is counted as being at risk of poverty, but if this person moves a hundred kilometers to live in Slovakia, she is no longer counted as poor unless her disposable income has changed. Using such national poverty thresholds obviously has certain advantages, because they are sensitive to the different income levels and to that extent also reflect differences in the living costs in the member states of the European Union. These different poverty thresholds also show the existing inequality in these dimensions.

On the other hand, the EU also measures poverty as material deprivation by referring to a list of goods and services that are deemed essential. The background idea for such a list was developed by Peter Townsend, who argued that poverty is an issue of being unable to do and have what is normal or standard in a society (Townsend 1979). He claimed, however, that poverty is always context-sensitive: there is no useful measure that applies to all contexts. Still, he also insisted that poverty is not only about survival and basic goods or capabilities and functionings but also about doing and having what a given society considers standard. Although Townsend asserted that he wanted to separate poverty and inequality, he ended up, as can be seen, connecting them more closely. As we will discuss, material deprivation is also close to concepts of social exclusion, whose wider focus tries to capture the important dimensions of what it means to be part of a particular society (Nolan and Whelan 2010).

> Individuals, families and groups in the population can be said to be in poverty when they lack the resources to obtain the type of

diet, participate in the activities and have the living conditions and amenities which are customary, or are at least widely encouraged or approved, in the societies to which they belong. Their resources are so seriously below those commanded by the average individual or family that they are, in effect, excluded from ordinary living patterns, customs and activities. (Townsend 1979, 31)

The current list of goods and services used to measure material deprivation in the EU is as follows: a household cannot afford to (1) pay its rent or utility bills, (2) keep its home adequately warm, (3) face unexpected expenses, (4) eat meat, fish or a protein equivalent every second day, (5) enjoy a week's holiday away from home once a year, (6) have a car, (7) have a washing machine, (8) have a color TV, (9) have a telephone. A person is counted as being materially deprived if she lives in a household that, for financial reasons, cannot afford at least three of these nine items; a person who cannot afford four or more of the items is considered severely materially deprived.

Two things are important in order to understand the concept of material deprivation: the items on the list are determined by asking the population whether they are, indeed, perceived as really necessary possessions (and using some statistics to validate them). The background idea is that every item should (a) reflect the lack of an ordinary or minimal living pattern common to a majority or large part of the population in the EU and most of its member states; (b) allow international comparisons (i.e., convey the same information value in the various countries and not relate specifically to a "national" context); (c) allow comparisons over time; and (d) be responsive to changes in the living standard of people (Fusco, Guio and Marlier 2013). These items are thus also context-sensitive and relative and can and do change over time. Access to the Internet and having a PC are items that can be expected to be on that list soon. One of the proposals for a new material-deprivation measure is to have thirteen items on the list: five 'personal' items (things the person cannot afford but would like to have) and eight 'household' items (things the household cannot afford) (Guio, Gordon and Marlier 2012). Not being able to afford four of these renders one materially deprived. The five personal items are being able to replace worn-out clothes with new (not secondhand) ones; owning two pairs of properly fitting shoes, including a pair of all-weather shoes; being able to spend a small amount of money each week on oneself without having to consult anyone; having regular leisure activities and getting together with friends or family for a drink or meal at least once a month. The eight household items are replacing worn-out furniture; having a meal with meat, chicken, fish or vegetarian equivalent every second day; meeting unexpected expenses; taking a one-week annual holiday away from home; avoiding arrears (mortgage or rent, utility bills, hire purchase / installment plan commitments); having a computer with an Internet connection; keeping the home adequately warm and having a car or van for private use.

The items on this list are not the result of any normative reasoning like, for example, the items on Nussbaum's list, and they do not aim to reflect things people are or should be entitled to as a matter of social rights in the EU or its member states. Hence, this list also does not converge with any right to have items that would trigger any obligation on the side of the state, although it can be used to guide social policies. A second important thing to consider is that this list of items is the same for all member states of the EU and is therefore absolute in contrast to the at-risk-of-poverty lines, which are determined using national standards. So the monetary poverty line and the measure of material deprivation provide researchers and policy makers with different kinds of information. A look at the respective statistics makes that point clear: while in 2011 the monetary poverty rate was between 9.8 percent in the Czech Republic and 22.2 percent in Bulgaria, the rates of material deprivation differ much more. In Bulgaria, the country with the highest rate of materially deprived people in the EU, the rate was 60.1 percent in 2011, while in Sweden, the country with the lowest rate, it was 4.2 percent (for more details, see Table 2.4). It is also possible, as is done, for example, in the national statistics in Austria, to combine both measures and to differentiate four groups: those who are neither at risk of poverty nor materially deprived, those who fit onto either one category or the other and, the last and most disadvantaged group of people, those who live in households that are both at risk of poverty and materially deprived. The official statistics in Austria call the last group of people 'manifest poor'.

In the European Union, official statistics measure child poverty by counting the children in households that are at risk of poverty or materially deprived as well. The at-risk-of-poverty rate is higher for children under eighteen than for the age group between eighteen and sixty-four (see Table 2.5). In 2011, 19.3 percent of the children (6.3 million children) under six years were living in at-risk-of-poverty households compared with 16 percent of persons between 18 and 64 (51 million persons). It is worth noting that the numbers differ significantly between the member states of the EU, and even rich countries have high numbers of child poverty; for example, Germany (15.6% of children under six at risk-of-poverty) and Sweden (15.7% of children under six at risk of poverty).

Table 2.4 Rate of material deprivation and at-risk-of poverty rate in Europe

	2005		2008		2011	
	Material deprivation	At-risk-of-poverty	Material deprivation	At-risk-of-poverty	Material Deprivation	At-risk-of-poverty
EU (27 countries)	20	16.4	17.5	16.5	18.4	16.9
New member states (12)	47.5	18.9	35.4	17.3	34.1	17.5
Euro area (18 countries)	13.8	15.3	13.9	16.1	15.4	16.9
Belgium	13.3	14.8	11.6	14.7	12.9	15.3
Bulgaria	:	14	55	21.4	60.1	22.2
Czech Republic	22.7	10.4	16.2	9	16.1	9.8
Denmark	7.6	11.8	5.4	11.8	6.9	13
Germany	11	12.2	13	15.2	12.4	15.8
Estonia	26.6	18.3	12.4	19.5	21.5	17.5
Ireland	11.2	19.7	13.6	15.5	22.7	15.2
Greece	26.3	19.6	21.8	20.1	28.4	21.4
Spain	11.9	20.1	10.8	20.8	13.2	22.2
France	13.2	13	13.1	12.5	12.4	14
Italy	14.3	18.9	16.1	18.7	22.3	19.6
Cyprus	31.2	16.1	24.9	15.9	29.8	14.8
Latvia	56.8	19.4	35.7	25.9	49	19
Lithuania	51.7	20.5	22.2	20	35.1	19.2
Luxembourg	3.9	13.7	3.5	13.4	4.7	13.6
Hungary	39.7	13.5	37.1	12.4	42.2	13.8
Malta	15.2	14.3	13.7	15.3	17.1	15.6
Netherlands	7.5	10.7	5.2	10.5	6.6	11
Austria	8.3	12.3	13.7	12.4	9.5	12.6
Poland	50.8	20.5	32.3	16.9	26.4	17.7
Portugal	21.2	19.4	23	18.5	20.9	18
Romania	:	:	50.3	23.4	47.7	22.2
Slovenia	14.7	12.2	16.9	12.3	17.2	13.6
Slovakia	42.6	13.3	27.8	10.9	22	13
Finland	10.8	11.7	9.1	13.6	8.4	13.7
Sweden	5.7	9.5	4.6	12.2	4.2	14
United Kingdom	12.5	19	11.3	18.7	13.3	16.2

Source: Eurostat, www.ec.europa.eu/eurostat/

The measure of material deprivation (and severe material deprivation) is also interesting in this regard. In total, more than 3 million children under the age of six were living in severely deprived households in the EU in 2011, as were nearly 9.5 million children under eighteen and more than 28 million persons between the age of eighteen and sixty-four

80 A Philosophical Examination of Social Justice and Child Poverty

Table 2.5 At-risk-of-poverty rate in Europe, by age

Geo/time	under 6	under 18	18–64	under 6	under 18	18–64	under 6	under 18	18–64
	2005			2008			2011		
EU (27 countries)	19.1	20.0	14.7	19.0	20.4	14.7	19.3	20.8	16.0
New member states (12)	25.4	26.4	17.6	20.1	23.1	15.4	20.7	24.0	16.5
Belgium	20.2	18.1	12.0	17.1	17.2	12.2	21.7	18.7	12.9
Bulgaria	:	18	12	26.1	25.5	17.0	27.7	28.4	18.2
Czech Republic	17.6	17.6	9.4	11.3	13.2	8.3	12.5	15.2	9.1
Denmark	13.5	10.4	11.0	9.3	9.1	11.3	8.5	10.2	13.1
Germany	11.1	12.2	11.9	15.1	15.2	15.4	15.6	15.6	16.4
Estonia	23.3	21.3	16.8	13.0	17.1	15.0	14.7	19.5	18.0
Ireland	17.8	23.0	16.0	14.4	18.0	13.4	13.9	17.1	15.1
Greece	18.8	20.4	17.1	21.5	23.0	18.7	21.3	23.7	20.0
Spain	22.1	26.0	16.4	25.1	28.2	17.3	25.1	29.5	20.8
France	14.3	14.4	11.6	15.0	15.6	11.6	18.0	18.8	13.5
Italy	21.7	23.6	16.4	23.0	24.7	16.3	24.5	26.3	18.5
Cyprus	13.5	12.8	11.1	14.1	14.0	10.8	13.0	12.8	11.5
Latvia	19.6	22.0	18.2	21.5	23.6	19.4	20.4	24.7	20.2
Lithuania	24.1	27.2	19.0	19.3	22.8	16.8	18.5	25.2	20.2
Luxembourg	21.5	20.2	12.8	20.3	19.8	12.9	20.8	20.3	13.1
Hungary	19.6	19.9	13.2	19.5	19.7	12.0	21.2	23.0	13.6
Malta	14.5	17.6	11.4	18.3	20.4	12.0	18.6	23.0	13.1
Netherlands	14.4	15.3	10.2	12.7	12.9	9.9	14.7	15.5	10.5
Austria	14.7	14.9	11.1	14.5	14.9	10.9	15.9	15.4	11.0
Poland	27.5	29.3	20.4	19.6	22.4	16.3	19.7	22.0	17.1
Portugal	20.4	23.7	15.9	16.3	22.8	16.3	18.7	22.4	16.2
Romania	:	:	:	26.3	32.9	20.0	28.2	32.9	21.0
Slovenia	11.5	12.1	10.4	10.4	11.6	10.5	14.7	14.7	11.7
Slovakia	15.7	18.9	12.7	17.8	16.7	9.5	21.1	21.2	12.4
Finland	11.9	10.0	10.5	13.3	12.0	11.8	13.3	11.8	12.8
Sweden	9.8	10.2	9.1	13.4	12.9	11.2	15.7	14.5	12.5
United Kingdom	25.3	22.9	16.2	24.0	24.0	14.7	18.1	18.0	14.1

Source: Eurostat, www.ec.europa.eu/eurostat/

(see Table 2.6). While Denmark has very low rates (1.9% of children under six), other countries such as Bulgaria and Romania have rates of severe material deprivation of children as high as 40 percent. It cannot be said, though, that material deprivation of children is nonexistent in many rich countries of the EU: in Germany, more than 700,000 children

Table 2.6 Number of people in severe material deprivation in Europe, by age (in thousands)

Geo/time	under 6	under 18	18-64	under 6	under 18	18-64	under 6	under 18	18-64
	2005			2008			2011		
EU (27 countries)	3,379	11,668	32,500	2,926	9,404	26,341	3,122	9,470	28,113
New member states (12)	1,814	6,800	19,941	1,230	4,348	12,968	1,195	4,025	12,384
Belgium	70	197	419	50	165	377	73	187	382
Bulgaria	:	:	:	159	521	1,823	171	584	1,977
Czech Republic	65	293	744	41	156	447	48	149	405
Denmark	17	46	122	12	30	69	7	39	97
Germany	169	783	2,565	334	955	3,147	249	737	3,066
Estonia	9	35	98	4	13	38	5	22	80
Ireland	33	94	110	28	78	156	36	117	218
Greece	66	195	795	60	200	720	106	322	1,072
Spain	148	439	1,098	168	446	1,040	135	434	1,459
France	256	812	1,972	318	859	2,065	362	929	1,984
Italy	274	779	2,372	328	985	2,712	424	1,299	4,141
Cyprus	6	22	57	5	17	43	7	26	65
Latvia	39	163	529	22	76	231	37	116	410
Lithuania	63	245	661	31	83	244	23	96	346
Luxembourg	1	3	5	0	1	2	0	1	5
Hungary	150	536	1,434	145	417	1,145	157	536	1,501
Malta	2	6	13	1	5	11	2	6	18
Netherlands	48	126	250	25	82	161	27	104	293
Austria	18	58	162	44	118	346	33	86	210
Poland	692	2,709	8,216	341	1,305	4,317	310	934	3,165
Portugal	74	200	539	45	234	607	65	222	511
Romania	:	:	:	446	1,613	4,180	398	1,426	3,944
Slovenia	3	15	65	4	19	90	6	20	82
Slovakia	65	261	768	31	122	399	30	110	389
Finland	11	42	132	11	34	121	10	35	116
Sweden	14	72	125	12	38	83	8	28	74
United Kingdom	367	1,022	1,892	259	831	1,767	390	906	2,099

Source: Eurostat, www.ec.europa.eu/eurostat/

under the age of eighteen are severely deprived; in France, more than 900,000. The numbers and rates for 'normal' material deprivation are even higher.

Besides measuring child poverty with the indicators used for the whole population, the EU has also started to develop child-specific measures, adapting the material-deprivation index, and to define specific goods and services for children (Guio, Gordon and Marlier 2012). A final list of eighteen items was developed, composed of thirteen children's items (also collected on the household level) and five household items. The children's items are (1) some new (not secondhand) clothes; (2) two pairs of properly fitting shoes, including a pair of all-weather shoes; (3) fresh fruits and vegetables daily; (4) one meal with meat, chicken, fish or vegetarian equivalent daily; (5) books at home suitable for the children's age; (6) outdoor leisure equipment; (7) indoor games; (8) a suitable place to do homework; (9) regular leisure activities (sports, youth organizations, etc.); (10) celebrations on special occasions; (11) possibility of inviting friends around to play and eat from time to time; (12) participation in school trips and school events that cost money; (13) one-week annual holiday away from home. The household items are (14) replacement of worn-out furniture; (15) avoidance of arrears (mortgage or rent, utility bills, hire purchase / installment commitments); (16) a computer and an Internet connection (enforced lack; i.e., cannot afford but would like to have); (17) keeping the home adequately warm (enforced lack); (18) a car or van for private use (enforced lack). The EU does not use this list to actually measure child poverty, but it might do so in the future as the pressure to gather knowledge about child poverty rises.

A different approach is used by UNICEF, which also developed measures for children's well-being in rich countries (UNICEF IRC 2013, 2012). UNICEF distinguishes the following six dimensions: material well-being, health and safety, educational well-being, family and peer relationships, risky behaviors and subjective well-being. The indicators for material well-being were very close to the poverty measures used by the EU and reflected both income poverty and material deprivation. Income poverty was captured by the relative child poverty rate (percent of children living in households with equivalent incomes below 50% of national median) and the child poverty gap (distance between national poverty line and median incomes of households below poverty line); material deprivation was captured by using an index of child deprivation (percent of children lacking specific items) and a family affluence scale (percent of children reporting low family affluence). The use of both income poverty and material deprivation is based on the insight that being income poor does not necessarily say much about the actual living conditions of a child because other factors are also relevant. The index of child deprivation used fourteen items, a child being deemed to be deprived if she lacks at least two of them: (1) three meals a day; (2) at least one meal a day with meat, chicken or fish (or vegetarian equivalent); (3) fresh fruit and vegetables every day; (4) books suitable for the child's age and knowledge level (not including schoolbooks); (5) outdoor leisure equipment (bicycle, roller skates, etc.); (6) regular leisure activities (swimming, playing an instrument, participating in youth organizations, etc.); (7) indoor games (at least one per child, including educational baby toys, building blocks, board games, computer games); (8) money to participate in school trips and events; (9) a quiet place with enough room and light to do homework; (10) an Internet connection; (11) some new clothes (i.e., not all secondhand); (12) two pairs of properly fitting shoes; (13) the opportunity, from time to time, to invite friends home to play and eat; (14) the opportunity to celebrate special occasions such as birthdays, name days, religious events, and the like. The second component of material deprivation was the affluent family scale, which was measured by the responses to four questions the children were asked: (1) Does your family own a car, van or truck? (2) During the past twelve months, how many times did you travel away on holiday with your family? (3) How many computers does your family own? (4) Do you have your own bedroom? The results for the children's material well-being dimension reveal that the eastern European countries show the highest rates of both components of material deprivation, while the Scandinavian countries fare much better (for more details, see Table 2.7). The USA, Germany and Canada are found in the middle. Besides calculating the rankings of OECD countries with significant information in each dimension, UNICEF also calculated an overall score for each country that was not an aggregate of indicator scores per se. Rather, the overall score was an average of how each country ranked across all six dimensions. One interesting and maybe surprising result was that the USA was in the fourth last overall place and only Lithuania, Latvia and Romania had a worse overall score. The low ranking of the USA was also due to its having the second highest child poverty rate.

Besides these large-scale surveys, there are uncountable smaller studies that use different approaches, methods and indicators we cannot present here. It is important to note, though, that there is a growing consensus about the fact that child poverty is a multidimensional phenomenon that cannot be adequately captured by a single measure alone or smaller studies, as the EU and UNICEF also acknowledge. This leads to the extended lists that combine monetary thresholds with deprivation indicators. While this is certainly progress, some researchers call for even more multidimensionality and demand the inclusion of health, education and emotional well-being (Minujin et al. 2006). We already mentioned that more differentiation regarding the dimension

Table 2.7 Child well-being in rich countries

		Overall well-being (average rank)	Material well-being	Health and safety	Education	Behaviors and risks	Housing and environment
1	Netherlands	2.4	1	5	1	1	4
2	Norway	4.6	3	7	6	4	3
3	Iceland	5	4	1	10	3	7
4	Finland	5.4	2	3	4	12	6
5	Sweden	6.2	5	2	11	5	8
6	Germany	9	11	12	3	6	13
7	Luxembourg	9.2	6	4	22	9	5
8	Switzerland	9.6	9	11	16	11	1
9	Belgium	11.2	13	13	2	14	14
10	Ireland	11.6	17	15	17	7	2
11	Denmark	11.8	12	23	7	2	15
12	Slovenia	12	8	6	5	21	20
13	France	12.8	10	10	15	13	16
14	Czech Republic	15.2	16	8	12	22	18
15	Portugal	15.6	21	14	18	8	17
16	United Kingdom	15.8	14	16	24	15	10
17	Canada	16.6	15	27	14	16	11
18	Austria	17	7	26	23	17	12
19	Spain	17.6	24	9	26	20	9
20	Hungary	18.4	18	20	8	24	22
21	Poland	18.8	22	18	9	19	26
22	Italy	19.2	23	17	25	10	21
23	Estonia	20.8	19	22	13	26	24
23	Slovakia	20.8	25	21	21	18	19
25	Greece	23.4	20	19	28	25	25
26	USA	25.8	26	25	27	23	23
27	Lithuania	25.2	27	24	19	29	27
28	Latvia	26.4	28	28	20	28	28
29	Romania	28.6	29	29	29	27	29

Source: UNICEF Office of Research (2013). 'Child Well-Being in Rich Countries: A Comparative Overview', Innocenti Report Card 11, UNICEF Office of Research, Florence.

of space is needed. Calculations of relative income poverty will come to different results in different regions; housing costs, for example, are usually higher in urban regions, and even within them, at the neighborhood level vast differences can exist. Another issue is the level of application of deprivation measures like the ones discussed. The knowledge one can extract for the EU is that deprivation is much higher in eastern member states than, say, in Germany and Austria, but what the data we presented does not show is that within these two countries, one can easily find significant differences between regions and neighborhood. It is not a surprise that there are many regions in Germany where material deprivation among children is nearly nonexistent, while in other regions it is a more prevalent issue. Besides space, the dimension of time needs to be acknowledged; how long a person is poor and during which phase in the life course, for example, during childhood, and whether poverty is a returning issue is highly relevant information. The dynamics of poverty are crucial and underexplored, which can also be attributed to the lack of data (Addison, Hulme and Kanbur 2009). Time is also relevant in the sense that it is valuable information to know if certain phases of life are particularly prone to poverty, as is the case for childhood. It is puzzling that members of society regularly deemed as in need and worthy of particular protection and support, called by politicians 'the future of a society', are more often living in poverty.

Before examining the injustice of child poverty, we need to point out two further aspects in relation to the aims and scope of this chapter. Firstly, we will focus on child poverty and studies that examine it in welfare states such as the countries of the European Union, the USA and, in some cases, Canada and Australia. We will, however, exclude the poorer states of the EU, such as Bulgaria and Romania, from our examination. The main reason is that, although such countries are members of the EU and certainly higher developed than many other countries in this world, they are still not on par with the richer states in the EU or the USA. The data we presented before on the breadth and depth of child poverty in these countries shows that sufficiently. Evidence shows that in highly developed countries severe forms of child poverty also exist but fortunately on a smaller scale (Weinreb et al. 2002). Secondly, despite this focus, we are confident that our conclusions are applicable to many more countries and contexts of child poverty. It holds generally that child poverty negatively affects the functionings children can achieve and the capabilities they can develop during childhood and in later life. This is in no way a problem exclusive to rich countries; in fact, evidence convincingly suggests that the problems are even greater and more severe in poorer countries in Europe and, indeed, everywhere else in the world. Still, child poverty in Romania and Bulgaria is less severe and widespread than it is in many African or Asian countries. It should be kept in mind that, using the monetary measure alone, the poor in richer states would be the middle class in others and among the affluent in many more.

2.2 The Ill-Being and Ill-Becoming of child poverty: physical and mental health

We have presented five criteria a functioning needs to fulfill in order to count as one children are entitled to it as a matter of justice: (a) it must reflect a truly important dimension of children's well-being or well-becoming (which means that it is important for the achievement of one or more other important capabilities as an adult); (b) its choice must be based on the best available (empirical) knowledge about children's lives and development; (c) the functioning can be distributed in a meaningful way and can therefore be secured by the institutional design of a society; (d) it must be objectively determinable and not merely subjective; and (e) it must also take into account children's own views.

We have also offered a sixth criterion that allows the selection of functionings of particular importance because they are fertile and have positive effects on the development and achievement of other functionings and capabilities. For most of these criteria, there is only little dispute if they support physical and mental health, which is certainly an important part of children's well-being and well-becoming. The central role that health plays is based on broad scientific knowledge. Furthermore, children themselves value their own health, although this is dependent on a certain level of maturity and competence. Health, at least many aspects of it, is objectively measurable, both physical and mental health. The claim that health, perhaps especially mental health, is something that can be secured for everyone on the basis of the institutional design of a society is, on the other hand, more problematic. Health is surely influenced by other factors as well, such as genes and the natural environment, which are to a lesser extent alterable; likewise, temporary phases of ill health are a normal aspect of life. There will always be ill health, early death and suffering that cannot be prevented; the argument here is not that health is totally controllable, like, say, the distribution of a specific toy, but that it is, to a sufficient extent, socially determined (Marmot and Wilkinson 2003).

Different pathways for this social determination have been discussed, and a recent review stressed the connection between education and health, working conditions and health, neighborhood conditions and health, income and wealth and health, and race and health (Braveman, Egerter and Williams 2011). All of these influence health to a great extent and are the subject of public concern, especially as they are alterable. Evidence now points in the direction that child poverty is one of the social factors that severely influences health. Thus, even if, on the individual level, there are many cases in which society cannot do much to secure health for children or secure that they become healthy adults, the influence of social factors on health is still large enough to claim that they should be changed accordingly and that ill health due to unnecessary factors is unjust. Again, for older children we have to add that they can – at least to some extent – choose not to be healthy or risk their health because they prefer to realize other options, such as smoking or engaging in risky sports. It seems also clear that health counts as valuable for the current well-being during childhood as well as the well-being as an adult. It is therefore not a child-specific function in the sense that adults are not entitled to it as a matter of justice – at least in the form of having the real freedom to be healthy. In any case, concerning younger children, it is clear that they should actually be healthy and that giving them the choice to decide for themselves is not a realistic and morally permissible option here.

Moreover, health is a fertile functioning and ill health, a corrosive disadvantage. Some reasons for this claim are closely connected to the research about the relation between poverty and health, which we will discuss later, but in general it is reasonable to view health as fertile because it influences nearly all other functionings and capabilities children can reach. Sridhar Venkatapuram has offered a view of health from a capability perspective that is best understood as the ability to achieve valuable functionings and capabilities (Venkatapuram 2013, 2011). Health functions here as a kind of supercapability from which all other capabilities and functionings are more or less dependent. Viewed from the perspective of ill health, this claim can be interpreted as follows: in the most severe form of ill health, which leads to death, it is obvious that no other functionings or capabilities can be achieved and that it is corrosive in an absolute sense. However, we do not want or need to defend such a strong claim here; indeed we are fine with the notion of health as an important and fertile functioning that positively influences the achievement of other functionings and capabilities both during childhood and adulthood. For example, studies have shown that health in childhood influences the socioeconomic status in later life (Palloni 2006). WHO, too, endorses such an understanding in its definition of health as a resource for everyday life (Williamson and Carr 2009), and it should be obvious that the health status of a child profoundly influences central aspects of her life, such as going to school and learning and playing and meeting friends. The lack of health per se is not automatically a violation of social justice, but if it is the result of preventable and changeable social causes, this aspect becomes effective. At this point we make the connection between child poverty, health and social justice.

Health is also corrosive in the sense that it affects the family members, especially the close caregivers of the child who is not healthy. We cannot explore this aspect in any detail, but we would like to at least mention that being healthy or being ill goes beyond the individual person in such a condition. Especially forms of chronic ill health as well as disabilities demand much from caregivers, even preventing them from achieving some important functionings and capabilities themselves. The intersection between poverty and health is also clear here: if a family or parents do not have the resources to pay for professional help and care, they are dependent on the state and a health care system to support them. Otherwise, the chronic illness of a child can easily become a corrosive disadvantage for the parents and other family members.

Two more things have to be added here. The first one is related to defining health. We do not have a comprehensive definition, being aware of the difficulties to define health and its counterpart ill health or disease; debates in the literature do not yield, as far as we can see, to one unanimous conclusion (Venkatapuram 2013; Ereshefsky 2009). We are, however, convinced that we do not need such a definition for our argument. We will present studies that show how child poverty affects various indicators of health in terms of diseases and maladies that children are more likely to suffer from if they are poor. We will also show that childhood poverty leads to ill health in later life and a higher morbidity and mortality. These arguments do not need to rest on a definite conception of health but make use of the very plausible assumption that to suffer from certain diseases is a strong indicator of ill health. Furthermore, we want to stress again that the threshold against which we measure the effect of child poverty on the functioning of health as well as the other functionings we analyze are concerned with the inequality between poor and nonpoor children on the population level. It is unjust if children who are poor are more likely to be ill, even though certainly not all poor children are ill because of their poverty and ill health is something that is also common among nonpoor children. The insights we will present point in the direction that child poverty affects the health of many of these children and more so compared with their nonpoor peers, and this comparison shows that being healthy or having ill health is not an individual issue alone but rather a social one. The fact that nonpoor children have in general better health also shows that the state is in fact in a position to do better for those children in poverty.

The second one is that we choose to distinguish between physical and mental health because both are indeed equally important, but the latter is often neglected. In most examinations on why health is an issue of (social or global) justice, particularly in regard to the relation of poverty and health, the clear focus lies on physical health and on such issues as vaccinations and access to health care, sanitation and clean water in order to prevent severe illnesses that still kill millions of people, adults and children alike.

We understand the reason for this focus – physical health is without any doubt a more severe and pressing problem in many places in this world, and it usually leads in a more direct or faster way to death than mental illness. On a global scale, the priority on physical health can therefore be justified in the context of social justice in modern societies, which have already reached a higher level of welfare and health even for many children in poverty and where child mortality from preventable illnesses is fortunately rather rare. One can and should not dismiss mental health but rather acknowledge that children have a right to be physically and mentally healthy. Mental health issues are on the rise and are a significant burden for the individual who suffers from a mental health problem and her family, and on the epidemiological level, it is a great challenge for health care systems, the economy and the state (Prince et al. 2007; Wittchen et al. 2011).

The complex nature of mental health presents a further challenge: it is far less explored than physical health. In some dimensions, there is a clear and close connection between mental health and subjective well-being as well as happiness, which seems to stand in the way of making mental health an issue of justice in the same way as physical health (Cabezas, Graf and Schweiger 2014). We are aware of these issues as well as of the fact that mental health cannot be fully explored without leaving room for subjective evaluations and how children actually feel; we will explore some related issues in more detail when we come to see how children experience poverty. First, however, we will stick to the 'hard' medical and psychological evidence that already reveals important aspects of the relationship between child poverty and mental ill health.

Having these considerations in mind, what can we say about the effect poverty has on children's health – as children and as the adults they will become? The medical evidence is clear: poverty during childhood affects many different aspects of the health of children, and it has long-ranging effects on adult health as well.

Let us elaborate this point by first looking at mental health. Poverty during childhood has been found to precede anxiety disorders, depression, post-traumatic stress disorder and academic underachievement (Nikulina, Widom and Czaja 2010; Santiago, Wadsworth and Stump 2011); it has been shown to be detrimental to cognitive outcomes and to affect brain development, leading to behavioral disorders as well (Kim et al. 2013; Welsh et al. 2010). The reasons for these influences are still disputed, and many mediating mechanisms have been discussed. A recent overview of the evidence regarding the influence of childhood poverty on mental, emotional and behavioral health in the USA has proposed the distinction between individual, relational and institutional factors (Yoshikawa, Aber and Beardslee 2012). Important factors found include the influence of family poverty on parenting stress, depressed parental mood, marital conflict and household violence; all of these correlate with neglect and reduced parent investment in the child. The lack of cognitively stimulating materials and experiences appears to contribute in particular to differences in cognitive development, which also affects the benefit children can obtain from schooling and further education. Neighborhood poverty, again, is related to an insecure environment, the quality of schooling and the availability of youth programs; exposure to these stressors may overwhelm children and influence their neural development. Studies that observed the influence of childhood poverty on adult mental health also found it to be correlated to a range of mental health problems and psychological disorders (Evans and Cassells 2014; Gilman et al. 2002; Najman et al. 2010). This evidence on the ill-being and ill-becoming due to child poverty makes clear that poverty heightens the risk of growing up in an adverse environment but that lack of money alone is not the cause for mental ill health. Rather, we must look at what is often caused by the combination of a low socio-economic status and the lack of a comprehensive welfare system; namely, stress and insecurity, which affect families and children living in these circumstances in such a negative way. Evidence also shows that children in low socioeconomic level families show self-harming behavior such as overdose and self-injury, which, in turn, shows that poverty takes a high toll on the minds of children and adolescents (Ayton, Rasool and Cottrell 2003). While it is true that children in rich families might also develop mental ill health due to all the above-mentioned reasons, living in poverty makes it much more likely. Likewise, it is a problem of justice because poverty can be prevented. The effects of poverty during pregnancy have also been researched – it can act as a chronic stressor, and high levels of prenatal stress are suspected of negatively affecting the brain development of the fetus, which in turn leads to lower general intellectual and language abilities in toddlers (Laplante et al. 2004).

When it comes to physical health, studies have demonstrated many negative influences of child poverty on both children and adults: The low socioeconomic status of the mother is correlated with lower birth weight and preterm birth, both significant health risks for the infant (Dunkel Schetter and Lobel 2011). A recent study found that the effects of childhood poverty are especially predictive of cardiovascular disease and type II diabetes and that they appear in large part to be biologically embedded, such that later improved life circumstances have only a modest ameliorative effect (Raphael 2011). Another study followed 9,760 participants biennially from 1992 through 2006. Its results suggest that early-life socioeconomic experiences directly influence adult chronic disease outcomes for coronary heart disease (CHD), diabetes and stroke (Nandi et al. 2012). Asthma, too, seems to be influenced by the socioeconomic status of the child (Williams, Sternthal and Wright 2009). Due to these health risks, people growing up in poverty have a higher mortality rate and die younger than their nonpoor peers (Galobardes, Lynch and Smith 2004); child mortality itself is linked to socioeconomic position (Pritchard and Williams 2011). The pathways are, again, multifactorial (Melchior et al. 2007): the environment is linked to a range of influencing factors, for example, lack of heating and poor ventilation; these can trigger processes called biological embedding, by which experiences during early childhood alter the neurological and physical development (Hertzman and Boyce 2010; Hertzman et al. 2010). Risky behaviors that become chronic, possibly influencing adult health, are another mediating mechanism. Moreover, children who grow up poor often stay poor as adults, and this adulthood poverty is a major influence on adult health and mortality. In a recent review Dennis Raphael described how childhood poverty has cumulative effects on health and translates into adulthood:

> Cumulative effects are illustrated by findings that the longer children live under conditions of material and social deprivation, the more likely they are to show adverse health and developmental outcomes. These can be cognitive deficits that contribute to lack of school readiness for children (e.g., physical health and well-being, social competence, emotional maturity, language and cognitive development, and communication skills and general knowledge) upon entering the education system. Cumulative adverse experiences during early childhood predispose children towards learned helplessness where children feel unable to act effectively upon their world. Such helplessness is a strong determinant of health in general and a precursor of adopting health threatening behaviours. (Raphael 2011, 25)

It is not always possible to disentangle these influences, which can lead to vicious circles over the life course. Child poverty leads to ill health, and both can contribute to lower educational outcomes; lower educational outcomes, in turn, lead to a lower socioeconomic position in later life, which, again, is related to several factors that can contribute to ill health. This cycle is then passed on to the next generation, to children who are once again born poor and have fewer life chances and a higher risk of staying poor and being less healthy. An example of how child poverty affects physical health, affecting as a consequence other important functionings, is the issue of obesity. It is now well established that childhood poverty increases the probability of being obese, an effect that can already be observed in very young children and babies (Conrad and Capewell 2012). Obesity is therefore not a lifestyle choice of these children but the result of the environment they are born into (Johnson, Pratt and Wardle 2011). Obesity during childhood is connected to a wide range of further health risks, being linked, in particular, to cardiovascular disease and diabetes but also to mental health problems, such as depression (Levine 2011; Pizzi and Vroman 2013). Again, we by no means wish to deny that obesity during childhood also happens in well-off families but rather opt to reinforce the idea that more children in poverty are affected due to their being poor, which is sufficient for our claim that child poverty violates the claims of these children to be healthy. In an older review, Richard Reading presented good reasons why poverty is, in fact, the cause for ill health and health disparities in a society, reasons that still hold: research is consistent; the relation between poverty and child health can be found in every country; there is historical evidence that shows this relation is not new; there is an incremental relation; and the relation between health and poverty has been shown for many different forms of material and social deprivation (Reading 1997).

In conclusion, the evidence we presented here shows that child poverty and physical and mental health are connected; child poverty influences it negatively and has negative effects on adult health as well. It undermines the equality of opportunity to well-being. Epidemiological studies, however, can give an insight as to the extent of the problem. A recent estimation for the USA concluded that approximately 245,000 deaths in the year 2000 were attributable to low levels of education, 176,000 to racial segregation, 162,000 to low social support, 133,000 to individual-level poverty, 119,000 to income inequality and 39,000 to area-level poverty (Galea et al. 2011). Another study suggests that in the European Union, 700,000 deaths and 33 million prevalent cases of ill health were caused by socioeconomic inequality (Huisman et al. 2013). We cannot put a definite number on the injustice of ill health caused by child poverty, but statistics attest that millions of children are living in poverty in modern welfare states. If there is sufficient evidence that many of them are ill simply because they are poor and that being poor puts them at a higher risk of becoming ill than their nonpoor peers, it is enough to criticize this situation as unjust as well as to claim that these societies are failing the demands of justice for children. They let children down on their justified claims to well-being and well-becoming and deprive them of a fertile functioning, which in turn affects the achievement of other important functionings and capabilities.

One might counter our conclusion about the relation between health and poverty by pointing to parents and families, shifting the blame from the institutional design of society to them. They choose to live under such circumstances and bring children into the world, and they do not move to better neighborhoods, give them better food and care or take them to regular medical checkups. Child poverty is, indeed, in most cases also family poverty (important exceptions are orphans in state care and unattended minor refugees) and the parents' living conditions and socioeconomic status do have significant influence on their children. We will address this issue in the next chapter, where we will analyze the role of close caregivers and their responsibilities toward children in some detail and refute the argument that parents and families are the primary agents for securing social justice for children. For now, we would like to point to the fact that parents and families in poverty usually have very limited options to influence the health of their children due to structural deficiencies, a fact that is to be taken into account when conceptualizing their responsibilities. Parents' behaviors are partially determined themselves by socioeconomic position and how one grows up and is socialized, a claim supported by considerable evidence (Pinderhughes et al. 2001; Russell, Harris and Gockel 2008).

2.3 The Ill-Being and Ill-Becoming of child poverty: social inclusion and education

The next two functionings we would like to explore are social inclusion and education. Again, we see good reason that they should pass the test and fulfill the five criteria we laid out above and also the sixth, which puts higher priority on fertile functionings and the prevention of corrosive disadvantages. Both are important for the well-being and well-becoming in the sense that they are both essential for an adult as well. They can be measured objectively with the usual caveats. It also seems not unreasonable to assume that children themselves view social inclusion and education as important, although maybe the latter not in the same way as adults think of it. Both are influenced by the institutional design of a society, and each and every child can achieve both functionings under the right circumstances. Even children with severe cognitive disabilities have a right to be educated in a way appropriate to their capacities. In addition, we claim that both are fertile functionings, and we will introduce some arguments to bolster that assumption in the following.

We will use very broad conceptions of both social inclusion and education, leaving the decision to further define them again to the respective studies we examine. We employ a negative approach, one that is satisfied with showing that child poverty actually negatively affects social inclusion and education and that children in poverty have a less of a chance to achieve those two functionings than their better-off peers. We therefore do not have a threshold for what each and every child is entitled to, a specific kind of education in terms of what they need to learn or how long they should go to school. Other specialists can answer these questions much better; there are probably differences between the respective education systems that must be taken into account. What seems obvious is that for children growing up and living in modern societies, education is not a matter of learning to read and write alone but also of being prepared for what a highly complex and differentiated society and its social, economic, political and cultural institutions demand. This is the aspect of well-becoming that is always relative to the standards in a given context and that is also risky to some extent, given that we cannot foresee the future. It can be the case – there have been many cases in the past – that children are educated and learn things they cannot use because technology changes or the knowledge and skills are no longer useful. The content and also the threshold in education and social inclusion that is necessary in order to fulfill the demands of social justice is therefore highly context sensitive and evolving. Studies on the future of education show this in an impressive manner (Redecker et al. 2011). Furthermore, we are not able to set different thresholds for different ages, although it is something that would be equally necessary to effectively guide policies. Such a more in-depth examination of education and child poverty, one that analyzes different age groups and different contexts (states or regions), is surely a worthy venture, which, however, goes beyond the limited scopes and aims of our treatise.

We will begin with the functioning of social inclusion, using, as we have just stated, a very broad understanding of it. Social inclusion is closely connected to material resources, on the one hand, and to the public infrastructure (in a broad sense), on the other hand. It encompasses being able to do and have things that are viewed as essential or normal in a society and that are necessary to keep up social relations with people outside one's own family. Such an approach to social inclusion (or its counterpart, social exclusion) is now used in many different contexts, but the concept has also been criticized for being too vague and for being unclear about what it wants to capture due to, among other reasons, the existence of so many different definitions available; a recent review names eighteen different definitions (Morgan et al. 2007). Many approaches share striking similarities with deprivation measures as originally proposed by Townsend, but instead of looking at goods (which dominate the lists of both the EU and UNICEF), they also consider such other contexts of participation and inclusion as employment, politics and decision-making and culture and leisure. The benchmark used to define these contexts or activities is the same as with deprivation indicators: what is essential or normal in a specific society. For example, Burchardt, Le Grand and Piachaud defined four dimensions for adults in the United Kingdom, which can probably be viewed to cover all modern welfare states: (a) consumption, (b) production, (c) political engagement and (d) social interaction. They have also set four corresponding indicators: (a) equivalent household net income under half median income, (b) not employed or self-employed, in education or training, looking after family, (c) nonvoter, not a member of community organizations and (d) lack of someone who can offer personal support (Burchardt, Le Grand and Piachaud 2002). Two things become obvious when considering this approach: one activity (consumption) is, again, measured using income, and two of the others go certainly beyond what many would understand as poverty (political engagement and social interaction). Surely people can lack the last two without being (materially) poor for various reasons.

The concept of social inclusion/exclusion has been less often applied to children; we suppose that this reflects the (implicit) assumption that children are less active than adults (or that there are fewer important contexts in which children should be included). On the contrary, we want to make the point that children can be included in or excluded from many different contexts that matter for them, their well-being and their well-becoming: school, political participation, leisure and friends, health care, social services, rights, a safe and clean environment, among others. Such contexts matter highly to children (Ridge 2002). The social inclusion/exclusion paradigm offers valuable insights into understanding child poverty and its effects on the well-being and well-becoming of children. It highlights the relations between the different dimensions of social life; for example, between material goods and income and other forms of participation. It also shows that income alone is often not enough for one to be (fully) included in a society, since other factors like ethnicity, age, education, employment and health are equally important and lead to exclusion processes. This certainly has implications for social policy: benefits alone will not be enough to solve the problem of social exclusion. The fact that social exclusion is a relational concept poses another issue and shows that social relations are of utmost importance. Inclusion and exclusion are processes that unfold through the interactions within certain social environments and contexts and reshape the opportunities persons have. There is a link between the main assumption of the capability approach, namely that capabilities and functionings are dependent on different conversion factors, and this relational dimension of social inclusion/exclusion. Being excluded means to be cut off from important conversion factors other people have access to as well. Social inclusion/exclusion is also more of a process than a static concept (Millar 2007). One is included through activities, doing certain things on a regularly basis and being part of social groups. Social inclusion is therefore not a functioning one can acquire at a certain point in time and keep without putting constant effort into it. Social inclusion has also a spatial dimension; where children live and how their neighborhood and environment look have a great influence on what they can do and have and on what kind of relations they can have to other people (MacDonald and Marsh 2005).

Social inclusion has two sides, an internal and an external one. The external side can be evaluated by looking at what children in poverty are actually doing and having; the internal side, on the other hand, has an emotional aspect and refers to the actual feeling and knowing that one is included and accepted. The concept of respect and the functioning of being respected as a human of equal worth, which we will discuss later in this chapter, also comes into play here. Both the internal and external dimension of social inclusion are fertile: the internal dimension is closely related to self-efficacy and other positive self-relations of self-trust and self-esteem, which in turn are fertile for the development and achievement of other capabilities and functionings – children that have them are more likely to explore their potentials and try to succeed. The external dimension of social inclusion is fertile because having social relations and being accepted and recognized by others and in the social world one lives in gives a child much more valuable options and makes it easier to realize them. Social inclusion is important if a child needs help; for example, if she struggles at school or if she has problems with her parents; it is important in later life because it can provide networks and is a form of social capital that has been shown to be beneficial especially for economic status (Pichler and Wallace 2008).

Hence, social inclusion in capability terms refers to the ability to achieve functionings and capabilities as a child that are viewed as essential in the target society and to be respected as a human of equal worth. Therefore, social inclusion/exclusion is a relational concept that cannot be defined without reference to the target society. This has two implications: at first, social inclusion has intrinsic and instrumental value for children, but it is a neutral concept in relation to its specific content in a specific context.

We are aware that our claim that children have a right to be included as a matter of justice runs the risk of being interpreted as if we supported the existing capitalistic shaping of society and those behaviors and norms that it demands (Bowring 2000). This would be highly problematic, since it would mean that we support a social, political and economic formation that is one of the main causes of child poverty itself. While the claim that children are entitled to be included holds, being something of the utmost importance for their well-being and well-becoming, this does not imply that we are not critical of many social practices that children want to be part of or that they are actually included in. Social inclusion can also imply adhering to racist, sexist or ableist behaviors and attitudes and fitting into a strict social hierarchy. Such social inclusion is still beneficial for children because the costs of not fitting in are very high, but it is also obvious that such exclusionary patterns of inclusion are highly problematic from a moral point of view and affect negatively all of those excluded by these practices. It is disputable whether social inclusion can ever function without certain excluding mechanisms, but there are certainly forms and modes of inclusion that are less problematic than others. Likewise, children are in a very weak position to stand up against the societal norms they are confronted with, and demanding that they be critical and strong enough to withdraw from consumerist behaviors would overburden them.

Furthermore, social inclusion happens on different levels and can take many different forms. To be included in a specific group may come at the cost of exclusion from other groups. For example, children and adolescents can be included in a street gang and experience many of the positive functions of inclusion through this, but by doing so, they more or less willingly choose not to be included in the larger society in all aspects. Deviant and criminal behavior is simultaneously the ticket into one group and out of the societal mainstream. On the other hand, there are differences between states and cultures within states. Being socially included in Germany might imply having and doing different things than being included in the United States of America, even if there are certain similarities between all highly developed societies. What we claim is that child poverty distorts opportunities for these children to be socially included in the society they live in; this holds for all modern societies. One of the main reasons is that inclusion and money are closely related, and as general features of all modern societies, inclusion reflects this capitalistic consumerist culture.

For now, we want to focus on the external side of social inclusion, which has been largely researched since poverty research itself moved from one-dimensional measures of income poverty to the concept of social exclusion and material deprivation. Social exclusion may be due to a number of different reasons, and lack of money is, although very significant, just one of them (Tisdall et al. 2006). Money buys membership in societies in which inclusion has high costs: cell phones, toys, clothes, leisure activities, sport clubs, trips, going out, eating at the mall and inviting friends. However, money is not the single factor for social inclusion; living conditions, social status, appearance, race and ethnicity, gender, health, education and disability also count. Not all of these are influenced by child poverty (or are a defining part of it), but most are. Children living in poverty have less access to transportation to come and go and meet friends, and their neighborhoods are less secure and provide less space for them to play safely and in a clean and welcoming environment. Children are also less often included due to the stigmatizing by others and prejudices against them, as when they are accused of being lazy, unclean or deviant. The shame that children in poverty feel can also lead to processes of self-chosen exclusion and to isolation and loneliness. Children with health problems or disabilities need more resources to be able to take part in many activities, resources that are often missing from families in poverty. Poor neighborhoods, poor health and poor inclusion go together (Cattell 2001). The social inclusion of children in poverty is more difficult for all these reasons, and many of them are not able to realize this important functioning in an adequately qualitative way. When we described ways to measure poverty, we presented data demonstrating how children in low-income families were more likely to face problems when trying to be socially included; the data were measured by the access to child-related social goods and activities that (partly) constitute what it means to fit in and belong to a society. If they are missed, children feel left out – and with good reason: they are actually not included in a comprehensive understanding. Similar findings have been reported using different methodologies and measures for particular countries in Europe as well as the USA, Canada and Australia (Kahn and Kamerman 2002; Phillips et al. 2013).

There is an abundance of literature on education from a capability perspective (Hart, Babic and Biggeri 2014; Walker and Unterhalter 2010).

Most of the available empirical evidence on the relation of child poverty and education focuses either on cognitive skills or on schooling and academic achievement. Education is, however, more than that; the value of education is poorly reflected if one looks only at schooling and subsequently at the relation between formal education and other socioeconomic characteristics, a relation that is important and, in particular, relevant for the intergenerational transmission and reproduction of poverty.

Education here means any kind of learning and acquiring of skills and knowledge, and in this broad sense it is the condition and grounding of many other functionings and capabilities. The good command of one's mother language is necessary for inclusion in the society and the interaction with other people; it is necessary to acquire further knowledge and skills and to achieve further capabilities and functionings. If one knows how to read, one can acquire all kinds of information available in that language. If one knows how to ride a bike or how to swim, one has obviously more choices of leisure activities and of getting from one place to another at one's disposal. Acquiring manners and social skills, so-called soft skills, becoming acquainted with the customs and habits of one's culture and society, make it a lot easier for one to appear in public, to interact with other people, to feel 'at home'. Soft skills have become ever more necessary in the fast-changing economy of modern societies, in which formal education is just one aspect of qualification. Not only do children learn throughout childhood – yes, childhood can be characterized as life's main learning phase – but the societal framing of childhood is that it should be a protected phase for learning and acquiring skills necessary for the child's well-being as an adult. Education points, in particular, toward an understanding of childhood as a preparatory stage. Besides this orientation toward adulthood, education has certainly an intrinsic and instrumental value for children themselves as well, one that is also empowering and gives them more options and freedom as they mature, learn and become able to do more things. Still concerning education, we would like to argue that children are entitled to realize it as a functioning and that it would be wrong and unreasonable to advocate for it in the form of a capability. Children have an entitlement to actually learn and acquire necessary and fruitful skills and knowledge they need for their further flourishing. A child does not need the capability to choose whether she wants to learn a language and to write and how basic mathematics works for her well-being and well-becoming but actually needs to acquire them on a sufficient level.

It is interesting to note here that our advocacy for the actual realization of education during childhood will almost certainly lead to the result that in adulthood, too, people have it as a functioning, not only as a capability. Other important functionings or capabilities can be altered in later life, perhaps even denied. One can hurt herself or choose to destroy one's health, one can choose to live a life in isolation or one can choose not to engage in politics, but it is very unlikely that one can choose to unlearn. If a child is educated and learns to read, write and acquire other knowledge and skills, it will be the case that at least some of them, maybe the most basic and important ones, will stick. A person might forget what she learned in biology and physics, but to count and make basic calculations or speak in one's first language are hard to unlearn or willingly forget. Therefore – and we consider this a positive – education is a functioning that, if properly acquired in childhood, stays with one for the whole life course, unless severe mental illness or dementia destroys it. This points to another beneficial function of education; namely, that others are not able to destroy it so easily either and that it can aid in overcoming adverse situations, whether it be a personal crisis, life event or the rise of an oppressing regime.

Research about the relation of education and poverty is striking. Children in poverty fall behind in academic achievement very early, and their cognitive skills are less well developed. Recent studies confirm that this inequality becomes stronger during childhood and that children who grow up in poverty acquire a lower formal education than their nonpoor peers (Engle and Black 2008). Poverty influences school readiness, drop-out and attendance habits (Zhang 2003; Welsh et al. 2010). School is, for poor children, a less comfortable experience than it is for their nonpoor peers, and they struggle more often to get along (Horgan 2009). Sufficient evidence suggests that teachers treat children from poor families worse and that the grades of children are influenced by that (Ladd 2012; Auwarter and Aruguete 2008). Without any doubt, these effects on education during childhood also affect the later life of these children. It is much more difficult to catch up and acquire educational attainment as an adult, simply because there is much less support to invest the time needed, because the education systems are still designed in a way that supports linear biographies and because adults generally are slower in acquiring skills and knowledge. Some doors to education are more or less closed forever due to early developments and failings in achievements. The reasons for these low results of children in poverty are, again, manifold, and research has not established a single best explanation (Ferguson, Bovaird and Mueller 2007). We have already mentioned that the home environment and whether it is stimulating or not plays a crucial role in the development of cognitive and emotional skills. Parenting style and parents' expectations of what they think their children can achieve are another factor associated with education outcomes. Such negative influences of parents on the educational achievements and development of their children is not the result of less interest in their children and in most cases also not the result of willing neglect, but the result of the parents' own limitation due to their poverty and own knowledge. Sometimes it also reflects their own experiences during childhood with teachers and in school. Other equally relevant factors are the health of the child and whether she has to be absent from school often due to health problems, as well as whether the parents have enough time and resources to support their child (Fiscella and Kitzman 2009).

Both teachers' perceptions and expectations and the school itself play an important role as well. Children from poor families are more likely to go to schools that are worse equipped, have more children with social and behavioral problems and a less stimulating learning environment. These factors reinforce each other, and children in poverty grow up with fewer conversion factors that would help them realize their potential. According to the research of Chris Power and Clyde Hertzman, the corrosive disadvantage of child poverty in relation to education can be characterized as follows (Hertzman and Power 2003): Circumstances in the early years of life influence the cognitive, social and behavioral skills needed for readiness for school. Children who are not ready for school are more likely to experience low expectations of teachers, lose confidence, have difficulties making friends and face repeated academic failure. Readiness for school also influences school attendance and educational performance; these are important for educational achievement. Both home characteristics (material circumstances, parental involvement with and aspirations for their children) and school characteristics are important. Feeling disengaged with and unsupported by school plays a role in developing health-damaging behaviors, such as cigarette smoking, and in developing sources of identity based around peer relationships and youth culture.

While psychologically important, these identities can result in behaviors such as nonattendance and law breaking, which further damage educational prospects. Early parenthood, too, can be an important source of identity but one that makes it harder to stay on at school and gain qualifications. Leaving school and not going on to education, training or employment leaves young people vulnerable to unemployment, with paid work restricted to unskilled and semiskilled jobs. These jobs are characterized by low payment and job insecurity, which may bring further health costs in terms of higher rates of absence due to sickness, disability and coronary heart disease. The environment of home and neighborhood can place further strains on physical and mental health. In consequence, poor adult circumstances take an additional toll on health, in part because they are implicated in the maintenance of health behaviors linked to chronic diseases such as coronary heart disease and cancer that underlie inequalities in health in adult life.

We now want to turn our attention to one important aspect of the well-becoming of children and their inclusion as adults. An essential part of the social inclusion of adults, different from that of children, is that they are able to provide for themselves and their families through paid work and labor. Modern societies are also working societies in the sense that work and labor are highly valued, a major source for self-esteem, self-respect and self-worth and the main source of income and wealth, which in turn translate into a variety of resources and goods. Work and labor are, so to speak, the main source to access important conversion factors for the majority of the population, being intrinsically valuable for many. These positive functionings of work and labor explain why their absence has such harsh consequences for many and why unemployment is one of the main sources for ill-being. One of the theories that tries to capture this relationship is Marie Jahoda's (Jahoda 1981; Jahoda 1982) who distinguished manifest (income) and latent (time structure, social inclusion, goals, identity and status, activity) positive functions of employment. From them, she derived why unemployment is such a harsh experience, one that takes high tolls on the physical and mental health, social inclusion and private life of the unemployed. The usefulness of Jahoda's model has been empirically tested over the years, and recent studies confirm that unemployment has such a detrimental effect on mental and physical health and social inclusion because it leads to a deprivation of the manifest and latent functions (Paul and Batinic 2009). Only a few people are adequately equipped to effectively cope with involuntary unemployment, especially over a longer period of time. Unemployment also affects the lives of children whose parents are unemployed and who are confronted with the stress that their parents experience and the stigma of unemployment they have to battle, which seems to directly affect the child's health.

We do not have a definite answer as to whether having paid employment is of such importance that it should be considered a capability that each and every one is entitled to as a matter of justice or whether the important thing is not having a paid job but rather having the opportunity to take care of oneself and those one cares about. We do not want to explore this issue here, although we still hold that the effects of child poverty on the material and economic well-being in later life and the ability to participate in the labor market is of importance. We acknowledge that children are born with different talents and different natural internal capacities that will also influence what they can become in later life, but such natural differences cannot be held responsible for the differences in employment outcomes we can find in many modern societies. Findings suggest rather that employment opportunities – and with them also opportunities to gain a certain social status and income and wealth – are heavily influenced by the socioeconomic position of the parents. Again, we find here that the equality of opportunity to well-being defined as important functionings and capabilities is not realized for all children, but those who are poor have it much harder and are significantly disadvantaged. The main causes for unemployment on the side of the individual are low-level formal education, health issues and, as we are able to witness today, age: right now, millions of young people across Europe are jobless as a consequence of the economic crisis. Both education and health are related to childhood poverty, as we have shown, and it is therefore not surprising that it is more likely for children from poor families to experience labor difficulties when they are older. Recent statistics convincingly underpin this claim: in the USA, the unemployment rate of persons with an academic degree (bachelor's, master's, professional or doctoral) ranges between 4 and 2.2 percent; for persons with less than a high school diploma it reaches 11 percent. Earnings are also highly correlated to formal education (see Table 2.8). The same results can be found in the European Union, where 17.9 percent of the persons whose highest finished level of education is

Table 2.8 Education, unemployment and earning in the USA

Education attained	Unemployment rate in 2013 (%)	Median weekly earnings ($)
Doctoral degree	2.2	1.623
Professional degree	2.3	1.714
Master's degree	3.4	1.329
Bachelor's degree	4	1.108
Associate's degree	5.4	777
Some college, no degree	7	727
High school diploma	7.5	651
Less than a high school diploma	11	472

Note: Data are for persons 25 and over. Earnings are for full-time wage and salary workers.
Source: Current Population Survey, US Department of Labor, US Bureau of Labor Statistics http://www.bls.gov/emp/ep_table_001.htm

less than primary, primary or low secondary education are unemployed, compared with 8.6 percent of those with high secondary and postsecondary (nontertiary) education and 5.6 percent of those with a finished tertiary education. Employment status, material resources, education, health and social inclusion are closely entangled and influence each other (Gallie, Paugam and Jacobs 2003). They show that modern societies are not well equipped to realize equality of opportunity for well-being for all its members and that it is especially hard for those who come from disadvantaged backgrounds.

In summary, what the empirical research shows is that child poverty is corrosive in regard to education and social inclusion of children, and both also affect the opportunities of inclusion in later life. They have also a wider effect on what can be called the capability to be a citizen with an equal standing. Elizabeth Anderson has argued that the capability set that people are entitled to as a matter of justice can be defined by looking at what they need to act as equals in a democratic society (Anderson 2010). This line of thought is similar to that of David Miller, who, not coming from a capability perspective, argues that there are two different types of equality: the first type of equality means equality in the distribution of certain goods (or functionings and capabilities), which should be equalized, and the second type refers to equality of social standing and the ideal of a society in which all meet on the same level (Miller 1999). While both are vague concepts, they bring forward the important idea of respect and being respected, which is closely connected to other important functionings and capabilities like self-esteem and self-worth. It is a simple fact that in modern working societies, social status, education, employment and income and wealth go hand in hand and that disadvantages during childhood that translate into inequalities as an adult in these areas work against the ideal of equality proposed by Anderson and Miller. We should look not only at the outcomes of child poverty but also at the well-becoming, which is an equally important part of justice for children, and under the conditions of a working society, children should be equipped with all necessary functionings that let them become productive, equally respected and included citizens.

2.4 The subjective experience of child poverty

So far, we have discussed how child poverty leads to ill-being and ill-becoming, especially in relation to health, social inclusion and education. We now want to turn to the subjective experience of child poverty, how children themselves view their situation and articulate it and how they feel about it. We have already mentioned that child poverty influences mental health, for example, depression. We have built our case so far on objective knowledge that is more or less free of subjective assessments and ignores how children feel about poverty and if their subjective well-being or happiness is altered by it. The reason why we now want to give a voice to children that are actually living in poverty is threefold. First, we believe that children living in poverty have a right to be heard. We will explore here the difference between a consultative and an authoritative view as presented by Harry Brighouse (2003) and further expanded by David Archard and Marit Skivenes (2009). This will also shed some more light on our claim in Chapter 1 that children's views should be taken seriously in drafting a list of important functionings and capabilities that matter for children`s well-being and to which they are entitled as a matter of justice. Second, we will argue that listening to children and taking notice of their subjective experiences deepens our understanding of the injustices they live with. Third, we will show that the way a child experiences poverty is – to a large extent – not arbitrary and that it therefore carries normative weight. In this context, the concept of humiliation will be of central importance.

Brighouse has argued that children should be listened to in matters affecting them but that they should not be granted an authoritative view over their own circumstances. In the end, adults have the right (and the duty) to act in the child's best interest, which sometimes might go against the child's will. This view is an advancement over how children were treated for a long time, but it still leaves them at adults' disposal. The term 'consultative view' already implies that the child's perspective has a certain value for those who have to act in the child's interests but that this value is limited. Adults, in contrast, should be seen, as Brighouse argues, as authoritative in respect to choices that affect them, except for a few cases in which it is clear they are not competent enough to decide for themselves; for instance, when they have severe cognitive disabilities or mental disorders that temporarily render them incompetent.

Archard and Skivenes came to a very similar result after analyzing in detail several cases in which children's views were heard and weighed in the context of legal decision-making in the domains of health in the United Kingdom and custody and child protection in Norway. They add, however, that children also have a right to be heard independently from the instrumental value that comes by listening to them (as they provide useful information) and that children's views are therefore more than consultative. The issue we discuss in this chapter is different from the context in which the distinction of consultative and authoritative was developed. Brighouse, Archard and Skivenes are concerned with the participation of children in decision-making processes that affect their lives such as custody, medical treatment and probably also wider public matters, such as compulsory schooling. They also make use of the concept of best interest, which is commonly used in the children's rights approach, and seek to balance the right of a child to be heard and to decide with the right of the child having her interests and well-being protected. It is not, they all agree, in the best interest of children to give them full command over their lives.

We are, however, concerned with a criticism of child poverty as unjust, and in most treatises criticizing certain injustices, views of the victims of these injustices are not decisive. The reasons to do so are very similar to those that resulted in opting for an objective account of justice as we developed it in the previous chapter. The foundational work has to be done more or less unrelated to how people actually feel or what preferences they have. As Sen, among others, has noted on several occasions, there is a need for objective measures because impoverished circumstances can make the victims of poverty allies of those who oppress them (Sen 1999; Khader 2011). Adaptive preferences demand an objective account of justice that has enough bite and argument on its side to allow for the critique of injustices, even if they are supported by those who suffer from them.

But why, then, is it important to listen to children living in poverty? We think that the distinctions between an authoritative view and a consultative view complemented by a right to be heard, introduced above, is particularly important here. Victims of injustices have a right to be heard by those who talk and write about those injustices. They have a right to be included in the analysis, even if that does not change how one designs a theory of justice and even if that does not alter substantially the outcome of the philosophical work. People living in poverty are often treated as if they lack competence and knowledge; they are treated as passive objects of help, welfare and charity. They are rarely viewed as if they have much to contribute to overcoming their poverty and designing poverty-alleviation measures (Deveaux 2013). This view, however, has been criticized by participatory poverty research and poor-led initiatives for a long time now (Chambers 1997; Brock 1999). In fact, poor adults are often treated like children, in the sense that their choices and views are not seen as authoritative.

In summary, there are issues of inequalities in power and also in epistemic power, as in the power to decide who is poor and what matters for being accounted poor. Children in poverty are particularly powerless, and their agency is often neglected. We believe that it is important to acknowledge that children in poverty have something to say about their situation and that this is of value for a normative theory about their lives. These children have a right to be included in the evaluation of their situation even if we can include them only indirectly and through the reception of participatory and qualitative studies of child poverty. This right is independent of our claim that this will enlarge and deepen our knowledge base and that taking into account subjective views on poverty, therefore, also has also an instrumental value. This right to be heard is a form of respect that each and every child is entitled to and is thus rooted in a fundamental aspect of our theory of justice for children. We add as well that the process of participatory work with children in poverty is itself valuable for these children, as it can have empowering effects (Pascal and Bertram 2009). It can show these children that there are people who care about how they live; it can offer them the experience of being heard and an awareness that their views actually matter to someone, if just to a researcher or research team.

The instrumental value of subjective views on poverty is that it can bring to attention issues that remain otherwise undetected and overlooked. Children in poverty can point toward what matters most to them; this alone is reason enough to at least reflect carefully about their status in a theory of justice. Surely this is also dependent on the competence and maturity of the child, and many children might downplay important injustices that happen in their lives because they are not aware of them or because they cannot know how corrosive a specific deprivation will be over the long run. It can be expected that children also have more to say about their actual well-being or ill-being than about their well-becoming or ill-becoming. The subjective experience of harm is focused on what is actually happening and not on what will or can happen in a few years from now. Their views are consultative in the best understanding of it: they give us more information, they help us make better decisions about what matters in a criticism of poverty and make better evaluations of their lives, and they give us an impression about what poverty does to children on the subjective level – how they feel it. Still, an injustice is an injustice even if these children do not experience poverty as harmful and even if they find ways to be happy and to adapt to their situations. This kind of information is also valuable, though. Another important instrumental value of first-person knowledge about poverty is that it can help design better poverty-alleviation measures or better implement them in practice.

There are different approaches to listening to children in poverty and to giving them a place in our theory. We want to make a distinction between 'thinking small' and 'thinking big' to explore them, a distinction first suggested by David Hulme in an article on the situation of a poor family in Bangladesh, which he researched for more than twenty years (Hulme 2004). Hulme starts with the observation that most poverty research 'thinks big', in the sense that the researchers care mostly about statistics; that is, about how many people are poor and how many things they are missing and so on. He claims that while this thinking big is of course valuable, it is also in danger of overlooking what poverty is on the individual or family level, how it is actually experienced and lived and what it does to a person and his or her family. This is something that cannot adequately be reflected in statistics that show how many millions of people are poor and how much income they have. Hulme claims especially that social embedding and the many different dimensions of poverty are best understood by 'thinking small'; that is, by doing small-scale research that focuses on the story of one person or one household or one small community – this alone allows us to capture the breadth and depth of what it actually means to live in poverty. This thinking small is akin to the concept of 'thick descriptions' of poverty, in the sense that detailed accounts of a single story reflect the many different aspects and dimensions of poverty.

Thick descriptions provide a window into the reality of poverty. They do not and cannot aim to cover varieties of poverty or give an understanding of different socioeconomic positions or how poverty looks in different regions or states. A single story of an individual or a family is not more than that, but it is 'thick', as is every individual life, and it also makes the injustices connected to poverty more visible and tangible. Thinking big as the counterpart of this kind of thinking small means having 'thin descriptions', abstract knowledge about many persons stripped of their individuality. That knowledge comes in statistics that can show us how many people live under the poverty line, how well they are educated and how many people live in a specific household. Data like this are valuable, no doubt, and are necessary to guide and monitor policies as they can tell us how many people moved in or out of poverty. The individual stories behind these numbers, however, are gone – why a specific individual struggles to come out of poverty, what problems lie in her past and what aspirations she has for herself and her children. Hulme is right with respect to the fact that there is no 'either or' between thinking small and thinking big, but we need both if we want to understand poverty. There is also a need for thinking small and using thick descriptions in normative criticism of poverty and theories about its injustice.

We would like to take a third route, which we see as being somewhat in the middle and can perhaps be described as 'thinking intermediate'. In this section, we will not discuss a thick description of child poverty, although we would welcome such an approach – it could certainly enrich the philosophical thinking about it. We will rather present knowledge gathered by qualitative and participatory studies that let children express and articulate their views on their own poverty and on poverty in general. Such studies give insight into important aspects of the subjective experience of poverty by providing many voices, not simply a single one or a few, as does a 'thick description'. We will acknowledge what children have to say and that they have a right to be heard by us, but we are also able to do that on a level that allows the representing of many experiences from different children living in different environments and under different conditions.

Child poverty is a harmful experience for most children; they are aware of their situation and cope with it in many different ways. Some children are better equipped to cope than others, and some prove very resilient. It is therefore not surprising that the experiences of children living in poverty vary to a great degree. Qualitative studies on child poverty were recently summarized by Tess Ridge; we present here some of her key findings (Ridge 2011; Ridge 2009). The studies she surveyed cover children from five to seventeen. The first important insight is that children are aware of a wide range of impacts poverty has on their lives. Ridge presents children's views on such issues as school, family and peer relations, the working situation of the parents, their neighborhood and public infrastructure, their economic situation and material deprivation and their emotions and feelings. Children also report how they try to cope with their situation, ignore it or retreat from social relations or try to support their parents and siblings. The second finding is that, in the view of children, child poverty has three central dimensions of disadvantage: material and economic deprivation, social exclusion and disruption or distortion of social relations, and emotional costs. Children worry about the family's income; they are aware that they have fewer resources and goods. They value friendships but have problems making and keeping friends. They are the victims of bullying and of the discriminating behavior of adults as well. They feel stigmatized, excluded and of little worth. Many children are frustrated and angry, as they have less than others and are afraid of how the future will turn out.

Health, too, is an issue; children report that they are often sick, that they are cold in the winter and that heating and ventilation are often broken and seldom repaired. Health is also an issue because parents or caregivers are sick or disabled, and children are burdened with the care themselves. This attests, once again, to the multidimensionality of child poverty and how different disadvantages intersect and foster each other. Child poverty does not simply attack one functioning but more than one at a time, making it even more complicated to cope with. Other reviews of qualitative literature come to the same conclusions (Attree 2006; Attree 2004); we would like to quote one case study here to illustrate how deprived living conditions, social stigmatization and health intersect:

> Eight-year-old Ben lives with his mother and two brothers in an overcrowded ground floor flat. Shortly after the family moved in, a severe damp and mold problem developed. An environmental health inspector has declared the property unfit for human habitation on two separate occasions. "It's the smell that's almost the worst thing. It's so bad when you come into the flat" describes Ben's mother, Sandra. The damp and mold is having a severe impact on the children's health, which is affecting their education because they are missing school so often due to illness. "My oldest little boy [Ben] is having difficulties at school. And he's had so much time off, so when you have lots of time off it makes things much worse." The children's mental health is also being affected. Ben is being teased at school because his clothes smell of damp, which is affecting his self-confidence. "It's not right...to be told that you smell. Kids are so cruel. [Ben] was teased for it. He's seeing the child psychologist now because he has low self-esteem." The condition of the house makes it difficult for him to have friends round to play, which is impacting on his social development. "When my friend comes round he says [my home] stinks and when I go to school this boy says my clothes stink...but Mummy washes them" (Ben aged eight). (Ridge 2009, 33)

The third insight is that different agents in the lives of these children, especially peers, shape the experience of child poverty. Children in poverty do not merely lack specific functionings (or resources) they experience this lack as harmful, especially in interaction with other people, children and adults alike; within different institutions, the harm of poverty becomes pressing. These experiences add insult to injury; on the one hand, they are embedded in a societal climate in which poverty is framed to a large extent as personal failure and in which the blame for child poverty is put on parents and families; it is often accompanied by sexism, which targets lone mothers as bad mothers, unable to keep a husband that could care for them and their children; the same framing is also prevalent in the discourse about poverty and obese children (Maher, Fraser and Wright 2010). Such an atmosphere is equally present in the experience of children, who are well aware of how they and their families are perceived in the public and by others. While the political discourse claims to view children as innocent victims of poverty who deserve our help, the experience of many children in poverty is a different one. On the other hand, the experience of child poverty is framed in a consumerist society that entangles self-realization and identity with brands: having certain goods, wearing certain clothes, doing certain leisure activities (Elliott and Leonard 2004). A child being bullied for not having something is the collateral damage of such a culture. The role of peers poses several ethical challenges, as they themselves are not fully competent and hence also not fully responsible for their actions, often just reproducing cultural norms and values.

We now introduce the concept of 'humiliation' to capture the subjective experience of poverty by children. We do not want to include all aspects of poverty articulated by children as important, but, in our judgment, a central one. Humiliation is the counterpart to respect and the functioning of being respected. There is also some overlap between being respected and mental health in the sense that being mentally healthy also means achieving positive self-awareness in the form of self-trust, self-esteem and self-respect. Humiliation has two distinct dimensions: on the one hand, it can describe a certain kind of emotion and feeling; one feels humiliated. On the other, it can describe certain kinds of actions perceived as humiliating. In many cases they go hand in hand: a humiliating action leads to the feeling of being humiliated on the side of the victim. This connection is not necessary, though, and some actions judged by many or most as humiliating might not trigger the emotion of being humiliated, and in some cases, people may feel humiliated even if there is no sound reason.

Child poverty is humiliating in both senses: it is typically perceived by children as humiliating and it is an act of humiliation itself. Child poverty is a condition with which acts of humiliation by other people are connected, and being poor is in itself humiliating even if there are no such acts of humiliation by other persons. At least two questions must then be clarified: first, how can humiliation be defined, and second, in what sense can a certain living condition be humiliating in itself without another person committing acts of humiliation?

We borrow our definition of humiliation from Evelin Lindner, who writes that the core of humiliation is an enforced lowering of another person, which attacks the dignity and self-worth of that person (Lindner 2007). We view this in connection with respect and the functioning of being respected, which we have explored in the previous chapter. Children are respected when they are treated in a way that corresponds with their worth as humans. Other theorists, most prominently Martha Nussbaum, use the concept of human dignity to capture this (Nussbaum 2011). Humiliation is an umbrella term that catches the many forms of actions that violate the entitlement to be treated as a person of equal worth while describing the subjective experience of a person who feels she is not treated as an equal by others. It is also possible, we will argue, that children experience this feeling and emotion of being less worthy than others due to their poverty, even if there are no particular acts of humiliation against them. This understanding is much wider than that of Avishai Margalit, for example, who connects humiliation with respect in the sense of being a part of the community of humans (Margalit 1996). Margalit considers humiliation an act that gives other persons good reason to feel expelled from the community of humans, and he reserves the term 'insult' for acts that attack the self-esteem of a person. We prefer a wider understanding of humiliation that also encompasses all such acts of insult. Children in poverty are lowered by others and given the feeling that they are of less worth, which does not necessarily imply a more drastic sense, such as no longer being viewed as human. The insights from qualitative studies discussed before point in this direction and can be captured with our understanding of humiliation. We have here actions of humiliation from peers and adults that hurt children, and we find the whole range of emotional responses and feelings of being humiliated that are known to have potentially severe consequences.

Growing up and living in poverty is in itself humiliating even if children do not encounter humiliating acts by others: it can never be detached from the experience of having less than others without a good reason. This claim is supported in the literature and what children tell us about how they view themselves and their lives. Having less than others is obvious for a child in poverty; even when no one makes fun of her because of it, the child knows, sees and experiences that she has less, that she cannot have the same clothes and toys, make the same trips and live in the same good buildings as others. The persistent inequality in all poverty makes it humiliating. This line of argument adapts the thoughts of Christian Neuhäuser and Julia Müller, who have argued that relative poverty (of adults) is humiliating because the poor know about their poverty and that they have less than what is the normal standard in the society they live in (Neuhäuser and Müller 2011). The argument is not that having few goods or resources is in itself necessarily humiliating but that in a society in which it is normal to have certain goods, those who involuntarily have far fewer can experience humiliation because, as outsiders, they have good reason to feel less worth and less respect. The contingent significance of certain goods, resources or activities is relevant to determining whether not having them is humiliating. We have briefly discussed the concept of material deprivation of Peter Townsend above, which defines poverty using goods and services viewed as essential in a given society, and such a relative approach to poverty is what brings to light why poverty is humiliating even if those who are poor are treated in a friendly manner. In the case of children, we would add, it is furthermore impossible to argue that their having less and being able to do less is a result of choices and bad decisions they made in the past. We would like to refute such a line of argument for adult poverty as well, but we shall leave that point aside here and refer to Neuhäuser and Müller, who have sufficiently argued against it (Neuhäuser and Müller 2011). When it comes to children, it is clear that it is even worse if they rationalize in such a way that they begin to blame themselves for being poor or blame their parents and families.

The concept of humiliation is certainly not only a descriptive one. It has normative weight, and many theories of justice acknowledge it. The absence of (systematic) humiliation is an important aspect of any just society. This applies to both acts and living conditions that can be described as humiliating and to feelings and emotions of humiliation. Put in positive terms, a just society is one in which persons are treated with respect and assured of their equal worth as human beings regardless of what they do, how they live or how old or competent they are. The ability to be in public without being ashamed has long been recognized by capability theorists and also in empirical poverty research (Zavaleta Reyles 2007). While acts of humiliation that target this entitlement are more easily banned, feelings of humiliation are not controllable in that sense. Including them here in our criticism of poverty, thus, somehow opens up the door we shut on subjective assessments as benchmarks for justice. We claim that all the functionings children are entitled to as a matter of justice should be objective and that only they matter when uncovering and criticizing the injustice of child poverty. But using the concept of humiliation points to the direction that there is more than just the instrumental value to listen to the subjective experiences of children in poverty that we have appreciated before. We want to make a proposal on how humiliation, in the subjective sense of a feeling, and the claim for objectivity can work together.

Firstly, it must be noted that feelings of humiliation are to a large extent not arbitrary. There are good reasons to assume that in the overwhelming majority of cases in which children feel humiliated, there are actually acts of humiliation, or these feelings are connected to the experience of the humiliating condition of being poor. The qualitative evidence we have discussed and on which we build our case examines exactly these links between poverty and various experiences of humiliation, and it cannot be said that the feelings and emotions of these children are unjustified or distorted. Today we have sufficient evidence that shame and humiliation are, in general, features of poverty, whether it be in rich or poor societies, and that children and adults alike feel ashamed and humiliated for being poor (Walker et al. 2013). There are certainly cases of children in poverty feeling humiliated without such good reasons, and in some cases, the direct connection to poverty has to be questioned, but if one leaves the individual level and looks at all the evidence brought by different studies, one must acknowledge the consistency of the results.

Secondly, another important aspect is that the expressions of feelings of humiliation are a very important indicator that something is going wrong. The goal of justice for children is not that they will never feel humiliated by others or that they are always to be happy, something that cannot be controlled without employing unethical measures, but that the feelings of humiliation are not systematically attached to a certain social position, especially not to one that is unjust in itself. Under the condition that child poverty is unjust – we hope we have made a good case for that – the fact that these children are systematically humiliated and have to experience feelings and emotions of being humiliated adds another dimension of injustice. Justice still needs objective benchmarks – one of which is that acts and conditions of humiliation can be evaluated without reference to the feelings and emotions they trigger on the side of the victims – but it adds more depth to our criticism, especially a dimension that children care about strongly. This is the third point we wish to make: children do not want to feel left out, excluded, ashamed, humiliated and denigrated. Rather, they want to be respected in spite of their lack of competence or knowledge to articulate it adequately. If we do care about justice for children and their well-being and well-becoming, we also have to care about how they actually feel and the harm they experience. In some cases, as we have stated, we cannot do much about the harm – some experience of harm is part of every human life – and in other cases we will come to the conclusion that the feelings and emotions of a child are misguided and do not violate her claims of justice; these cases, however, do not undermine the general entitlement to be respected and to not feel humiliated by others or by one's social position. We must adapt society in a way that such a picture is possible. Feelings of being humiliated, especially chronic humiliation through repeated experiences of humiliation, are also harmful in undermining self-worth, self-esteem, self-respect and the ability to have trust in the world (Leask 2013). All these can be described, objectively, as highly important functionings for the well-being and well-becoming of a child.

2.5 Conclusions

Children in poverty suffer from deprivation of important functionings and capabilities, which they experience as harmful – especially humiliation, which violates their entitlement to respect and self-respect is important here. Justice for children must also be aware of the particular vulnerability of children and their powerlessness in regard to many of the threats and dangers they face. Child poverty is one of these threats. Children have no real power to evade their poverty and its negative consequences. We believe this to be one of the aspects that make child poverty special and a more severe injustice than adult poverty. Adults in poverty also suffer from ill health, are excluded and have less access to education; they share many feelings and experiences articulated by children, but children are much less able to do anything about their poverty as they are more dependent. Yes, adults in poverty are, too, often powerless themselves and have only limited options and no voice and no political weight, but, for children, the situation is still different; it is a categorical feature of being a child to be vulnerable, and poverty takes advantage of that and leads to severe consequences.

Child poverty affects particularly vulnerable and powerless human beings who are largely dependent on others and need, at least in some important aspects, special and more comprehensive protection than adults. That is a normal feature of being a child and per se not a form of illegitimate oppression, although some features of modern societies do oppress children and exploit their vulnerability and powerlessness. Evidence about the influences and negative effects of child poverty on many different functionings of children – on capabilities and functionings in later life, too – shows that these children are inefficiently protected. They are disadvantaged for the arbitrary reason that they were born poor.

In this conclusion, we wish to mention a few limitations of our examination and issues that need further attention. We have not explored the extent to which the limitation of family income is in itself unjust; rather, we were concerned with it as a corrosive disadvantage and with how it spreads and affects other important dimensions of life. This corrosiveness goes well beyond the functionings we explored; for example, a recent study on poverty and material deprivation in the USA concluded that income poverty harms all different kinds of dimensions of well-being of children.

> Strikingly, children in low-income families are more likely to experience each of the remaining 16 deprivations (excluding low income) compared to children as a whole. In many cases, the deprivation incidence for these children is twice as high or higher. The incidences of parental unemployment and financial stress are remarkably high at 48% and 56%, respectively. Low-income children are also much more likely to suffer from a poor physical environment and live in sub-standard housing conditions and in unsafe or polluted neighborhoods. Of great concern, too, are much higher parental incidences of low education and poor health, with negative consequences in the labor market. Finally, more than one-third of children living in low-income families experience low social/emotional well-being, compared to the already-high incidence of one-quarter among all children. (Ciula and Skinner 2014, 14)

Our focus on 'ordinary' poverty also led us to exclude the most disadvantaged children from our examination, those who live on the street and are homeless, unattended minor refugees and asylum seekers, illegal immigrants and victims of prostitution and trafficking. These children are not part of large-scale national surveys and counting of the poor; there are only estimates of how many children in modern welfare states have to live under these conditions. The body of research concerned with the health, education and social inclusion of such disadvantaged and even more particular vulnerable groups of children shows that the effects are serious (for the case of immigrants and refugees, see: Ruiz-Casares et al. 2010; Fazel et al. 2012; Hodes 2000; for the case of homeless children, see Bassuk 2010; Fantuzzo et al. 2012). The official survey in the USA counted more than 600,000 people living on the street on a given night in January 2013, of whom 23 percent, or

138,149, were children under the age of eighteen; 6,197 of these children were unaccompanied (Meghan, Cortes and Morris 2013). Another report by the National Center on Family Homelessness found that about 1.6 million (1 in 45 children) experienced homelessness over the course of 2010, an increase compared with previous years as a result of the economic downturn (National Center on Family Homelessness 2011). A report from 2007, which collected insights from various European countries, suggested that the problem is also a significant issue, but we were unable to locate any accurate estimation (European Observatory on Homelessness 2007). Street children in eastern European countries, like Romania, are of particular concern, as they face many threats to their well-being (UNICEF 2007). The lack of knowledge about children's lives under such adverse circumstances is problematic in itself, and we fear that this 'invisibility' also delays efforts to help them and make justice for them a reality. We were also not able to do justice to the many issues discussed under the concept of intersectionality, which refers to the intersection of different forms of disadvantage, oppression and discrimination (Norris, Zajicek and Murphy-Erby 2010). Again, we find here very disturbing evidence of how modern welfare states fail children on multiple levels. Race, ethnicity, disability and gender all influence the likelihood of being poor, and they are also independent factors in regard to many functionings of well-being and well-becoming. From our social justice perspective, this can be evaluated as the intersection of the violation of different claims of justice of these children. Justice for children as we conceptualize it means that children and adolescents must not be discriminated against but equally respected for being humans of equal worth, whatever their race, ethnicity, gender or sexual orientation. The fact that poverty is more common among such children is, as a result, a very severe form of discrimination and injustice and must be condemned as such.

Except where otherwise noted, this work is licensed under a Creative Commons Attribution 3.0 Unported License. To view a copy of this license, visit http://creativecommons.org/licenses/by/3.0/

OPEN

3
Responsibilities for Children in Poverty

Children in poverty are the victims of severe injustices. They suffer from deprivations in important functionings and live, thus, in a state of avoidable ill-being and of an increased likelihood of ill-becoming. In this chapter, we will now turn our attention to the question of who is responsible for securing justice for children in poverty and why. We want to examine this question in more detail than just stating that the state and its institutions are responsible or that taking care of children is primarily a task for the family. We would like to go beyond such simplified answers and show what kind of responsibilities persons, collectively and individually, and institutions, the state and other ones, have and for what reasons. The capability approach in general has not dealt often with these questions, being first and foremost a theory about the information that should be used in comparative quality-of-life assessments. It has in particular not engaged with questions of personal responsibility to achieve functionings and capabilities or for closing the door on some of them because of bad choices. Ingrid Robeyns has made the same observation and traced it back to the focus of the capability approach on global and severe poverty.

> There is a remarkable absence of discussion on issues of responsibility in the capability literature, in sharp contrast to political philosophy and welfare economics, where this is one of the most important lines of debate, certainly since the publication of Dworkin's work on justice and equality. Nevertheless, whether or not one chooses to discuss it explicitly, any concrete capability policy proposal can be analyzed in terms of the division between personal and collective responsibility – but this terminology remains largely absent from the capability literature altogether. This may in part be explained by the

fact that much of the work on capabilities deals with global poverty, where issues of responsibility seem to be less relevant since it would seem rather grim to suggest that the world's most destitute people are individually responsible for the respective situations they are in. Philosophical puzzles, such as the issue of expensive tastes (for expensive wine, caviar, fast cars, etc.), are simply beyond the radar screen of the child labourer or the poor peasant. (Robeyns 2009, 114)

Martha Nussbaum, who has expanded the capability approach to a minimal (partial) theory of justice, has not as well addressed in much depth the question of responsibilities, as a result of the fact that she understands the approach as providing guidelines for states to secure a minimal dignity of life for its citizens. Related questions of responsibilities beneath or above the state level are not so much her concern, and it is unclear how responsibilities between states and beyond state borders should be divided to make sure that every human on this planet is put above the threshold in the central capabilities she selected in her list (Gasper 2006). She has outspokenly rejected the idea of establishing a world state but also argued that there is a need for principles of global governance, which she understands as thin and decentralized (Nussbaum 2006). But Nussbaum also agrees – the same applies to Sen and many other capability theorists – that it is important to answer questions of responsibility. We see two main reasons for that: on the one hand, every concept about justice for children should be interested in the means to realize it, especially for children who have been shown to fall short of what they are entitled to. Our interest in justice is fueled by the hope that the clarification of these philosophical issues can also be translated into political change and the design of better policies, although we know that empirical knowledge that goes far beyond the scope of our book is needed to actually do that. On the other hand, every examination of the responsibilities of different agents of justice will also shed some light on the issue that child poverty is a socially produced and sustained condition. Child poverty is not natural, not something that cannot be changed and overcome, and the examination of responsibilities underpins this claim. It is simply not enough to show that child poverty is unjust if this does not lead to coordinated actions; the failure to attribute responsibilities to specific people, individually or collectively, or institutions (like the state) may also lead to diffusion, leading in the end to no one feeling actually responsible. In addition, we want to criticize the common discourse which often blames close caregivers, particularly mothers, for the poverty of their children.

It is therefore necessary to try to name and enumerate particular "agents of justice" and to discuss on what grounds responsibilities can be attributed to them (O'Neill 2001; Deveaux 2013). One core question always concerns the relation between these agents of justice and the victims of the injustices in question. Why are some people, whether individually or as group, or some institutions responsible for changing and enhancing the living condition of others? In which way do they need to be connected to each other? For example, by living together in a country (as particularists would claim), or is it enough that they are simply other humans sharing one world (the cosmopolitans' position; Brock and Moellendorf 2005)? Our account is not explicitly particularist or cosmopolitan – there are, moreover, so many versions of these two out there that it is hard to define them neatly – since we will attribute some responsibilities to the state and some, although far less so, to international institutions. In the case of child poverty in modern welfare states, the debate between particularism and cosmopolitanism is not so important for us: First, most controversies are concerned with how much responsibility can be laid upon richer states (and the people living within them) to support poorer states (and the people living within them) because the latter are overburdened or in a much poorer position to alleviate poverty themselves. In the case of welfare states, it is obvious that they are powerful, at least much more so than poorer states; it would not be fair to ask poorer states to contribute and support richer states in order to alleviate child poverty within them. The issue of child poverty is always an issue of redistribution within rich countries and only to a very limited extent between rich countries, although the economic crisis of the last years in Europe poses some questions in that regard (e.g., the support of Greece and Spain by richer countries in the EU), but we will leave these questions aside. The second important point in the discussion between particularists and cosmopolitans refers to the nature of the relations between richer and poorer countries. Some scholars, most prominently Thomas Pogge, claim that the first harm the second via one-sided trade agreements (Pogge 2007). Virtually no one would claim that the opposite is the case and that poorer states have any substantial responsibilities towards richer states because they would unjustly gain an advantage over them. Thirdly, many particularists claim that the social relations within a state are of particular importance to justify justice and responsibilities attached to it. They conclude that, due to the social basis of justice, cosmopolitanism is not well justified. Whether or not one supports this view, child poverty in welfare states is without a doubt an issue that has to be tackled by that very state, the state and its citizens having some responsibilities. The fourth issue concerns rights and institutions: there exist no social policy institutions on the global level and no functioning legal framework that would guarantee social protection from poverty. This is a major obstacle, and while most cosmopolitans argue that such global institutions are needed, most particularists contend that they will not succeed for various reasons. In the case of child poverty in welfare states, the situation looks different. Here we have states which all have at least some kind of social policy in place; social protection and poverty alleviation is embedded in certain social rights directly granted to families in poverty or children in poverty. It is therefore much less necessary to debate whether global institutions are feasible and if so, in which form. Although we support the view that child poverty in welfare states is best tackled by changing the international and global institutions, most of the work needs to be done in welfare states themselves in terms of designing and implementing more inclusive social policies and allotting enough funds to support poor children and their caregivers. It seems likely that cosmopolitans and particularists will come to very similar conclusions in regard to child poverty in welfare states, both probably agreeing to some extent that its alleviation is first an issue of social justice within a rich state (or a community of them, like the EU) and that global justice is not primarily concerned with it. The reduction of child poverty in richer countries is part of an ideal of global justice but not its primary problem.

Our own account will analyze the relation different agents have to children in poverty, and we will then try to attribute responsibilities based on a set of morally relevant criteria; in this sense, we will defend what the literature calls an agent-centered approach (Deveaux 2013; O'Neill 2001). Instead of focusing on one or two important agents, like the state and the family, we wish to distinguish more of them, including those with limited responsibilities. Furthermore, we wish to emphasize that there are some very important agents who often get neglected in theories of responsibilities; in this context, we point to peers and enterprises, for instance, which raise particularly challenging questions for the concept of responsibilities towards children affected by poverty. All this leads to the conclusion that child poverty is not only a social policy issue but touches many policy areas: the labor market, public infrastructure, health care, education.

Before we outline our own theory, let us briefly comment on one of the few philosophical debates that has emerged on the topic of responsibilities towards children and why we connect our argument only loosely to it and build it mainly on other approaches to responsibilities which have not so far addressed the specific case of children. The debate we have in mind addresses whether there is a responsibility among all adult members of a society (parents and nonparents alike) to share the costs arising from having children and parenting (George 1987; Vallentyne 2002; Casal and Williams 2004; Olsaretti 2013). This issue is a matter of controversy in the literature, but there seems to be a good argument in favor of the pro-sharing argument in terms of the contributions children make, on average and in the long run, to the welfare of a society. Most children will become taxpayers, support the older generations and therefore create a general benefit for the society in question. This again makes it reasonable that those benefiting from the fact that there are enough children in their society (independent from other relationships they have to them) have duties to secure adequate conditions for their upbringing (Olsaretti 2013). But for the purposes of this chapter, where responsibilities towards children in poverty are the focus, we see only limited use for this line of reasoning, first and foremost for two reasons. First, the responsibilities debate typically takes place in the realm of ideal theories of justice, assuming that having and bringing up children happens against fair background conditions. Such strong assumptions help to get to a high degree of philosophical clarity; however, it is often difficult to say what the arguments imply for nonideal circumstances (Sen 2009). We do not want to suggest that this is an impossible or useless enterprise. We prefer to situate our approach to responsibilities from the beginning in nonideal circumstances; this better fits the general orientation of our theory. The second, related reason is a general worry about the strategy of grounding moral responsibilities for children (struck by poverty or not) onto other agents than their parents primarily on their being "public" or "socialized" goods. Especially in contexts where it is unclear if some groups of children (e.g., those living in poverty or those with disabilities or chronic illnesses) will be able to contribute economically to a society it seems to follow from such a perspective that no one but the parents has a responsibility, which is an indefensible conclusion. As will become clear later on, one ground for attributing responsibilities to an agent is that she benefits from a certain situation. But this is only one aspect of a theory of responsibilities, and there are others which are relevant for the injustice of child poverty and which do not get discussed comprehensively in the philosophical debates just mentioned.

3.1 Attributing responsibilities to agents of justice

There are many different ways of attributing responsibilities to agents of justice. We begin by discussing the approach of Iris Young. In *Responsibilities for Justice*, she distinguishes two models of responsibilities

(Young 2011). First, there is the liability model, which can be roughly described by means of two components. It (a) connects responsibility with directly *causing* harmful outcomes and (b) assigns responsibilities only to agents who perform the action in question voluntarily and with adequate knowledge of the situation. The liability model is the dominant one in legal reasoning, and it can also be considered the standard account of moral responsibility found in ethical theory. In this model, it is clear that responsibilities are assigned to concrete agents; there is, from this point of view, no problem for the agent-centered approach we want to develop. Difficulties arise, however, when we are confronted with structural injustices, where the causal relationships of causing harms are often diffuse. As Young argues, such structural injustices are often the result of numerous uncoordinated individual actions, which, taken one by one, cannot always be deemed morally problematic. Taken together, however, they might lead to consequences that impose significant constraints on many members of society, leading to inequality and poverty.

We can easily imagine the story of a child, Sabrina, living with her single mother in London. The mother, let's call her Anne, is not well educated and has to make a living from insecure low-wage service jobs. She would like to give Sabrina a good education and a life in a calm neighborhood, but she struggles to pay the rent for her small flat in one of the most dangerous areas in London, and Sabrina has to go to a public school with a bad reputation. Anne spends a lot of time working and, due to health problems, is increasingly worried about how long she will be able to keep up the current situation; it is likely that things will get worse in the future, leading to feelings of despair and helplessness. Her daughter is often on her own, neglecting her schoolwork and having trouble developing aspirations for her future. Many more aspects of their situation would surely be relevant for an analysis of poverty, but what is important here is that it might be difficult for Anne and Sabrina to blame particular individuals for their difficult circumstances. Of course, it is possible that they are confronted with greedy and abusive employers and landlords, who try to take advantage of their lack of options, or with biased teachers who are convinced that children of single mothers will never be able to get to respectable academic achievements. But it is also conceivable that they usually find helpful persons who understand their situation and are willing to support them: teachers who put in an extra effort to motivate Sabrina or landlords who don't have a problem if the rent is not always paid on time, for instance. Still, despite these morally praiseworthy actions and attitudes, something surely has gone wrong, something that cannot directly be explained by how individuals behave in direct interactions with them. Anne's and Sabrina's lives are characterized by what Young sees as *structural injustice*.

> Structural injustice [...] exists when social processes put large groups of persons under systematic threat of domination or deprivation of the means to develop and exercise their capacities, at the same time that these processes enable others to dominate or to have a wide range of opportunities for developing and exercising capacities available to them. Structural injustice is a kind of moral wrong distinct from the wrongful action of an individual agent or the repressive policies of a state. Structural injustice occurs as a consequence of many individuals and institutions acting to pursue their particular goals and interests, for the most part within the limits of accepted rules and norms. (Young 2011, 52)

For such contexts in which structural injustices exist, Young introduces a second account of responsibilities: the social connection model. Here, the central idea is that everyone participating in and contributing to structural processes that lead to unjust outcomes shares responsibilities for these injustices, even if they do not intentionally act to create the respective harms. Not being at fault in such a sense is not enough to be exempt from responsibilities. These responsibilities are essentially political, demanding that everyone takes steps towards the transformation of unjust structures. Unlike the liability model, which is first and foremost backward looking and focuses on the identification of those who are actively and directly involved in causing harm, the social connection model focuses on the future and the importance of joint actions. On this account, it is not enough that a citizen follows acceptable norms and rules of moral conduct if she wants to be absolved from responsibilities. As long as the society in which she lives possesses unjust background conditions, she is called upon to go beyond her own interests and work towards a fairer society. There are also good reasons to weight the responsibilities stemming from such a social connection model differently for different agents. In one way or another, almost every member of society contributes with her purchasing decisions, preferences on the job market or education choices to a social order with immense inequalities and asymmetries of power. It is, however, surely necessary to rank weights of responsibilities according to a variety of reasons. It is exactly here where an agent-centered approach fits the social connection model. Young introduces four different grounds, or "parameters of reasoning", as she calls them, which are relevant for balancing and weighing responsibilities: power, privilege, interest and collective ability. They are related to the social position of an agent and can be used to identify the kinds and degrees of responsibilities different agents – individual and collective ones – have to confront structural injustices.

Power is relevant because agents are positioned differently in the social structure and have varying options for actions at their disposal. Leading politicians or CEOs of big companies are much closer to processes producing unjust outcomes and in positions to influence them than the unemployed or people with low-wage jobs at the company's bottom rank. As a consequence, it is sensible to connect an agent's power with her responsibilities. Furthermore, responsibilities should be connected to structural processes an agent effectively can influence. It makes no sense to demand actions and behaviors that are not within the reach of an individual; it would even go against the basic moral principle that "ought implies can".

The category of power can be joined with two other influential ways of reasoning about responsibilities and duties. The first is the ability-to-pay principle, which is highly prominent in particular in the design of tax systems (Gaisbauer, Schweiger and Sedmak 2013) and in recent discussions about climate change (Page 2008). It states that the burden of taxation – or any other burden – should be distributed according to the ability to carry the burden and to contribute to the solution of the problem. The ability-to-pay principle is hence often used to justify progressive taxation, where not only the absolute amount of taxes but also the tax rate itself increases according to income or wealth. Three distinct reasons support this principle: First, the ability-to-pay principle rests on the idea of the decreasing utility of wealth and income and that every taxpayer should make about the same sacrifice. For example, person A earns €1,000 per month and person B earns €5,000 per month; both live in Germany. If both have to pay the same amount in taxes, say €200, it is obvious that the living standard of person A is heavily affected while that of person B is nearly untouched. The case is slightly different if both have to pay the same tax rate; for example, 20 percent. Person A would again have to pay €200 and person B €1,000, but it can be argued that the living standard of person A is still more affected and decreased than that of person B. Many tax systems hence favor a progressive taxation, one that would make person A pay 10 percent of her income, which would be €100, and person B 30 percent, or €1,500. Still, the idea of marginal utility suggests that the €100 in taxes are maybe an even bigger sacrifice for person A than the €1,500 paid by person B, which is a reason in favor of even higher progressive taxes. The system, however, already seems to be fairer than one with a "flat tax".

Second, the ability-to-pay principle assumes that it generates more resources and funds. The total income of the persons A and B is €6,000, and if both paid the same absolute amount of taxes, say €200, the total income for the state would be €400; a tax rate of 20 percent that applied to both would amount to €1,200, and a progressive tax rate based on the ability-to-pay principle would amount to €1,600 without harming either A or B to an unjustifiable extent. We are aware that the ability-to-pay principle has its friends and foes, but we think there are good reasons to use it to assign responsibilities for injustices like child poverty: those who are able to contribute more should contribute more. A third supporting reason for progressive attribution of burdens based on the ability-to-pay principle is that it decreases inequalities. Before taxes, B had five times more income than person A, but after taxes, the inequality decreased to a ratio of about 1 to 4.

Another prominent principle connected to the idea of power was introduced by Onora O'Neill in her important article on agents of justice (O'Neill 2001). There she distinguished between primary and secondary agents of justice: primary agents have the power to assign duties and responsibilities to secondary agents and are in a position to use coercive measures if secondary agents do not comply with their duties. O'Neill had in mind that states are typically powerful primary agents. If they are weak or have failed altogether, however, as often happens in states where absolute poverty is prevalent, she argues that international and global institutions have to take on this role. However, in such cases, which are typical for the global poverty discourse and where conflicting interests exist between states, it is extremely difficult to identify institutions that should be seen as powerful primary agents of justice. Since we focus on child poverty in rich welfare states in this book, the situation is clearer and her argument has more force. In general, these states operate quite well, have command over a lot of funds and resources and the power to enforce most of their laws. Sometimes their powers are restricted, of course, but they definitely fit O'Neill's definition of primary agents of justice. Hence, they have the power to set up institutions and rules that help to achieve justice or that can significantly influence and mobilize other, weaker agents – in many different contexts and particularly regarding structural injustices. Rich states – or in the case of Europe, the European Union – can introduce binding laws and policies and therefore provide standards that come up to the demands of social justice.

There are other agents that hold considerable power over others as well and thus possess at least some features of primary agents of justice. Companies, for example, have the power to hold suppliers responsible for producing under fair conditions or to provide incentives for employees to support the local community and do charity work. The wealthy members of a society often have greater influence on policies than the "normal" voter; it makes therefore a big difference if they lobby exclusively for their own interests or instead support measures empowering the weaker members of society. The media constitute another agent, one which is often forgotten but has some real power in terms of influence and shaping the discourse about and attitudes towards poverty. It supplies people with information they have to trust and influences policies in campaigning for or against it. The media cannot hold anyone responsible for what they do or how they think about poverty, but as they certainly influence public opinion, they are an important agent of justice.

There are also those who benefit and who are able to live comfortable lives due to, for instance, the economic order of a society or the world as such. According to Young, such *privileges* also confer responsibilities: those who benefit from unjust structures are morally obliged to initiate change. Furthermore, privileged agents can usually adapt their lifestyles without jeopardizing their well-being, something that also adds to their responsibilities. Privilege *often* goes hand in hand with positions of power, yet this is not necessarily the case. In industrialized countries, for instance, broad parts of the population benefit from unjust international trade relations; at the same time, their power to directly alter them is limited and difficult to grasp. Nevertheless, their privileged position per se grants them special responsibilities. Of course, a full account of responsibilities must also look at the variety of privileges within industrialized countries, which collectively profit from an unjust global order; there is definitely a hierarchy of privileges, and in varying degrees they are connected to different forms and forces of responsibilities.

This idea of privileges is close to the beneficiary principle (Butt 2014; Page 2012), which can be interpreted in at least four different ways. (1) People or institutions have certain responsibilities to victims of injustices insofar as they voluntarily benefited from injustices as a result of a wrongdoing they were at least part of. In this case, the beneficiary principle is closely connected to Young's liability model: the ones held responsible here benefited from an injustice which they at least partially caused, and the beneficiary principle only adds another argument. (2) People or institutions have certain responsibilities to victims of injustices insofar as they involuntarily benefited from injustices as a result of wrongdoing they were at least part of. In this case, the one held responsible did something wrong but did not intend to benefit from the wrongdoing. For example, a company may cheat a family out of its farm in order to build a factory on that land, only to discover that beneath the land there is oil, a fact they were unaware of. Extracting the oil will be much more profitable than building the plant. (3) People or institutions have certain responsibilities to victims of injustices insofar as they involuntarily benefited from the injustices as a result of a wrongdoing they were not part of. In this case, someone is held responsible even though she did nothing unjust and wrong and did not even intend to benefit from it; it "accidentally" happens to her. For instance, someone buys a house in a cheap area; after some time a rich company comes and pressures most other owners to leave. It develops the area, leading to an increase in the value of all houses there. A person who stayed in her house, unaware of what was going on, certainly did not plan that to happen and did not intend to profit; she simply stayed because it was her home and the general situation allowed her to. Is she in any way responsible for undoing this wrong or providing compensation – for example, by giving money to the families that had to leave? (4) People or institutions have certain responsibilities to victims of injustices insofar as they voluntarily benefited from injustices as a result of wrongdoing they were no part of. For example, a person knows that a company is going to develop a neighborhood and that it will use illegal and immoral means to achieve that; she then buys a house in that area to profit from this wrongdoing.

How should we evaluate these examples from a moral point of view? Does it matter if someone benefited voluntarily or involuntarily or if she played a part in the origination of the injustice from which she benefited? The first case, because of its closeness to the liability model, is not very controversial. Causing voluntarily an injustice one benefits from clearly confers a strong responsibility to the respective agent. The second case is mainly relevant for the extent of the responsibility in question. It seems reasonable that a company is responsible not only for giving back the land but also for paying part of the profit it made exploiting the oil. The beneficiary principle in this case extends the company's obligation. The fourth case seems also easy to accept, since one can argue here that the beneficiary took part in something she knew to be wrong, even if she did not dirty her hands directly. The trickiest case is certainly (3): should someone, without doing anything wrong and without intending to benefit, be held responsible? On what grounds can that be? The cases can be made more complicated if certain background information is added: For instance, the house owner who profits from the wrongdoing of the company planned to do the same and already established a sham firm but was just a few days late. Or the company is owned by the house owner's brother, who wanted to help raise the house's market value without telling him. In these two cases, most would agree that the house owner is in some sort of way responsible for trying to undo the wrong that happened, even though it is highly unclear how he can succeed in doing that. Similar examples, on a smaller scale and involving the loss or benefit of no more than US$1,000, have been discussed by Daniel Butt, who concludes that the beneficiary principle should not be legally enforceable on the individual level but can play an important role on the level of institutions or collectives, helping these types of agents determine responsibilities based on an evaluation of how much they benefited (Butt 2014). The beneficiary principle of case (3) responds to a certain moral intuition to owe something to those from whose suffering one benefits but whose extent is still to be determined. Obviously the house owner is neither obliged to sell his house at the higher market price nor give the funds to his wronged neighbors. He might, however, be responsible for helping them sue the company. Thus, we deal here with a responsibility that should not be legally enforceable but still has moral weight.

We have discussed the beneficiary principle in relation to concrete injustices or wrongs that happen to other persons. But as Young suggests, its moral force also applies to cases of structural injustices, where it is very difficult to disentangle who benefits and who does something wrong. The case of Anne and Sabrina, presented as an illustration of structural injustice, makes this clear. We can think of an employer, for example, who will give Sabrina a job in the future. He pays her a very low salary because of her bad education, and she has to work in precarious conditions. The employer thus profits from an injustice that happened long before he takes advantage of poor Sabrina. He might not even intend to exploit her but is pressured by shareholders interested in high profit. He might sincerely think that giving her a low-wage job is better than no job at all, since she will at least be able to pay her bills and keep her apartment. Still, he benefits from the mere existence of people in vulnerable positions in the labor market, forced to take any job they get. Consumers who buy low-priced products because of the exploitation of Sabrina's labor benefit as well. Assuming that they do not know that she works under harsh conditions, what responsibilities should be given them? This small example illustrates how child poverty is, in fact, beneficial for many people. Some of them know about the relationships and voluntarily take advantage of it, but there are many others who are unaware and would even oppose it if they knew what was happening.

Another relevant ground for distributing different kinds and degrees of responsibilities is captured by Young with the term *interests*. Challenging unjust social structures will have a positive effect on certain groups – first and foremost (but not exclusively) on those who are negatively affected by the current inequalities and imbalances of power. It is in their interest that injustices are remedied and that the society they live in becomes a fairer one. Hence, they should also play an active part in these transformations; indeed, a social connection model sees them as agents of justice who bear responsibility for their own situation. One must, of course, proceed with caution here so as not to overburden the least advantaged members of society, attributing their weak social position to their own failure. But without their involvement, dedication and struggles for recognition, it is unlikely that improvements will occur. Furthermore, their firsthand knowledge and experience of the harms they suffer puts them in an epistemologically privileged position; it, too, generates certain responsibilities. In the case of child poverty, it is clear that there is also a wider interest of society and the state to alleviate it because of the many social and economic problems it creates. A society's interest is in having children grow up to become healthy, productive members; this way, they are able to care for themselves and their own children with little state support, from which a society benefits as a whole. The fight against child poverty should, hence, be driven by a state interest to keep the subsequent costs of benefits, unemployment, medical care and the like low.

Monique Deveaux has argued in a similar vein that most agent-centered approaches, in particular that of Thomas Pogge, focus on powerful agents and on institutions either on the national or international level (in questions of global poverty) and that this focus neglects the contribution of the poor themselves to overcoming their poverty (Deveaux 2013). They are conceptualized mainly as beneficiaries with very limited power or none at all to contribute to poverty alleviation and the realization of justice.

> On this framing, the designated moral agents are specifically persons and entities not suffering from poverty but rather responsible for contributing to that poverty, or thought to be capable of alleviating it (or both). By contrast, the would-be recipients are construed as mere recipients of justice, rather than as potential agents of change. [...]

> In the absence of adequate attention to perspectives and needs of the putative recipients of poverty reduction efforts, a focus on agents' duties and capabilities risks marginalizing the role of poor communities in devising and implementing solutions to chronic poverty and inequality. By failing to see the poor as actual or prospective agents of justice, such approaches risk ignoring the root political causes of, and best remedies for, entrenched poverty. (Deveaux 2013, 23–24)

Deveaux uses the concept of agents of justice for all who can and should have an active role in the process of fighting injustice. This is further supported by insights provided by participatory approaches to poverty and pro-poor initiatives, as well as research on ways to empower the poor by taking them seriously (Drydyk 2013; Chambers 2008). Conceptualizing the poor as agents of justice is empowering; it acknowledges that they still have the capacity to alter their lives and that they are not completely dominated. Furthermore, such a view entails that there is a responsibility on the side of other agents of justice to provide poor people with the means and resources – in capability terms, conversion factors – they need to make choices, acquire capabilities and realize functionings. In the case of child poverty, children themselves have an interest in not being poor and not suffering from severe deprivation in functioning; young children, however, cannot articulate that interest, and older children typically do not understand the breadth and depth of the problems they face and their long-term consequences. Consequently, the main beneficiaries in the battle against child poverty are, in this sense, the weakest agents, who are at least to some extent dependent on others who advocate their interests and claim justice for them. That is, it seems, a central difference between children and adults in poverty. Poor adults are often treated like children, which is humiliating and degrading, while children are actually able to act as agents of justice for themselves only to a limited extent. This does not mean that children should be treated as objects without agency or the ability to express some of their interests; but some kind of paternalism is usually justified and needed in order to protect their interests. Again, it is very difficult to draw a line from what age, on a child's view, should be taken as authoritative; the context is certainly relevant to an adequate answer to that question. Especially for younger children, it is very likely that those who have the strongest interest in realizing justice for them are not the children themselves but their parents, families or other caregivers who have a close bond to them. They should have at least such a strong interest as part of their parental responsibilities.

One additional important issue is connected to the idea of interest as a ground for attributing responsibilities to agents of justice: adaptive preferences. We have already argued that adaptive preferences are normal during childhood and that development during childhood itself is always an adaption to the environment in which one grows up and lives. No child is in a position to choose these things autonomously, naturally coming to terms with her situation. This is one of the reasons why functionings, not capabilities, are to be preferred as units of justice for children: it is simply unreasonable to emphasize freedom of choice when the agent in question has only very limited knowledge and experience of what she is choosing. Hence, the normative core of adaptive preferences is tricky to catch in the case of children, because it seems as if, from an objective (adult) point of view, children often tend to alter preferences based on what is made available to them by adults. Children sometimes neglect injustices happening to them; in extreme cases they still love and bond with abusive parents and view themselves as responsible for the parents' behavior. Adaptive preferences can also affect the parents and other caregivers who directly interact with the child daily. Parents can have adaptive preferences in the sense that they do not want their children to be educated or that they neglect their health issues. Here, the issue of parental autonomy, parental rights and duties and the responsibility of other agents of justice to interfere becomes crucial; we will come back to this later, when we discuss the responsibilities of parents and caregivers. For now, we highlight that the idea to put responsibilities on the poor as agents of justice always faces the difficulty that those who should have the most interest in overcoming an injustice often support its existence. In such cases, it might be justified to neglect the choices of the poor and to enforce certain changes, even if it goes against their will. Expert-driven poverty alleviation is sometimes necessary, and in the case of children, even justified. They certainly cannot be expected to always make the right choices and know what is best for them in order to reach justice.

Finally, Young argues that *collective abilities* are relevant. Fighting structural injustices is usually a matter of joint actions. Individuals have to work in a coordinated way in order to effect change. There are typically networks and groups concerned with questions of social justice – NGOs, trade unions, several faith-based organizations – but universities and other educational institutions also unite many individuals. Consequently, their structures can be used to initiate or maintain movements aimed at undermining structural injustices. Their collective abilities provide a very helpful starting point, and it is reasonable to suggest that this particular characteristic puts them in a position where special obligations arise.

In summary, it is crucial for both the liability model and the social connection model of responsibilities to identify *specific agents of justice*. The liability model puts the focus on the intended causation of harm (or the knowing omission of an act causing harm); it is predominantly backward looking and suitable to circumstances where the causal relationships are clear and where agents who deliberately and knowingly bring about and keep up morally untenable outcomes can be located. The social connection model, in contrast, starts from the assumption that many injustices cannot be grasped in this way, because causal relationships are blurry and those contributing to and upholding unjust social structures have no bad intentions. It suggests, however, that there are different grounds for attributing different agents with different kinds and degrees of responsibilities, depending on their social positions. According to Young, primarily the categories of power, privilege, interests and collective abilities can be used to decide who actually has which responsibilities to act.

We think Young's model provides a very helpful way of looking at responsibilities for justice. However, making it fit the special issues we are concerned with in this book requires some additional considerations. The model has to be extended and refined in some parts for our purpose of identifying grounds relevant to assigning responsibilities for acting against child poverty. Let us start by adding another ground, one Young touches on only superficially, one rooted in every child's dependency on love, care and respectively close relationships. We separate the interest of someone that child poverty should be alleviated and overcome from the relation to the child and the particular responsibility that stems from being a parent or close caregiver, having the duty and right of parenting. Young seems less concerned with close relations and how they influence the kind of responsibilities we have. We have argued that her grounds can and should also guide attribution of responsibilities in contexts where the connection between an agent of justice and those who benefit is less blurred. Child poverty, as we have often said, is almost always family poverty, and parents have a major influence on their children. Parents, however, do not only have such an influence, their poverty does not only cause their children to be poor as well; they have different kinds of relations, which are constituted by being a family. Parents have some rights but certainly also responsibilities towards their children; some of them can be caught by using the grounds discussed before. This does not, however, apply to all of them.

The fact of being close to the child, the fact that the child is attached to her parents, which is essential to the child's development, constitutes another strong ground for responsibility. Children depend on having caregivers and being parented – whether by their biological parents or a different person – and it has been shown that continuity of care matters heavily. Parents and caregivers have thus a responsibility solely based on the relation they have to these children, a relation that cannot be broken without causing serious harm. So to our existing list of four grounds on which an agent can be held responsible, we add a new one: the relation of a child being attached to this agent and depending on her to continue to care and take on some responsibility.

The different grounds for attributing responsibility have produced different variations of understanding responsibility. In the liability model it is closely tied to causing an injustice; the social connection model attributes responsibility on other grounds, but it is unclear what this means exactly. Does responsibility of an agent of justice imply that she is to blame? Does it imply that she has the duty to act, a duty that can be enforced by others (primary agents of justice)? How is responsibility tied to autonomy and choice, hence the ability to do something different, and how is it related to knowledge and the ability to know about the result of one's actions, participating in a web of social relations that are structurally unjust? And what do we want to do with these five grounds? Can they help us rank agents of justice and their responsibilities, for instance? Answering these questions is our aim in what follows.

An agent of justice is, so we suggest, responsible if any of the five criteria discussed above can be applied, with two refinements. On the one hand we need to consider knowledge; that is, what an agent of justice has known or could have known with reasonable effort about the results of her actions or the structural injustices she helps to create. The grounds presented by Young, which we also endorse, suggest that not knowing does not mean no responsibilities exist, though it can reduce the responsibility one has. On the other hand we need to put more weight on choice and if an agent might have acted differently or did act differently in the future. The ability to act differently in the past, that is, in creation of an injustice, is important. Nevertheless, the possibility on the part of the agent to alter her actions now and in the future, undoing the injustice or at least helping something change for the better, counts as well. It seems that agents are completely free of responsibilities only if two things can be shown: First, if they did not participate in any actions that led to an injustice or helped create or sustain a structurally unjust context; and second, if they did not benefit in any way from the existence of an injustice and were in no position to alter their actions in a way that would create more justice. Applied to child poverty in welfare states, this means that basically everyone – except for people with severe disabilities or dementia or in coma or for (young) children – has some sort of responsibility and should therefore act to counter child poverty.

Young uses the grounds she specifies under the social connection model to specifically address injustices which are structural. In these circumstances, it is very unclear who is directly or causally responsible for the existence of a harm, making it virtually impossible to attribute responsibilities on the basis of the liability model. Child poverty is certainly such an issue; it is to a large extent a structural injustice rooted in the cultural, social, political and economic order of a society. It is upheld and reproduced by the way capitalistic societies work and how they are supported by nearly all people living within them, directly or indirectly, voluntarily or involuntarily. There is nearly no way to escape these social connections besides moving to a detached island and cutting off all contact to the outside; but doing many little things differently can make a difference: voting for another party, supporting the state and its institutions, not avoiding taxes, buying clean clothes, doing some community work and supporting those who are let down by the state via charity, paying fair prices and – if one is an employer – fair wages. Such actions and behaviors have an effect on poverty and on how it affects children. These effects are often indirect, but it is still important to anchor moral responsibilities in these "small" domains. If many people come up to these demands, important changes will be seen.

We want to use these grounds to assign responsibilities to agents of justice where the causal relation of causing an injustice is simply unclear. These are the cases Young developed her model for, and we follow her in this respect. At the same time, we wish to suggest that they also apply to cases where agents of justice have a more direct relation to the victims of injustices than just via taking part in a context of structural injustice. As Young presents the liability model, only those who willingly and knowingly cause an injustice should be held responsible; we believe this to be too narrow. Those who cause an injustice directly but unwillingly and/ or unknowingly should be held responsible, though to a lesser extent. As we saw in discussing the beneficiary principle, doing something involuntarily and/or unknowingly does not let one off the hook. Moreover, there are many cases in which agents of justice are not far away from the victims of injustice. In the case of global justice, where relations between people living in rich states and poor states are discussed, arguing with closeness is usually beside the point. Thousands of kilometers separate them, and often no emotional bonds are present at all. In the case of child poverty in welfare states, however, many possible agents of justice interact directly with the child and influence her well-being and well-becoming, both directly and indirectly, through contributing to structural injustices within which child poverty is embedded. We therefore argue that these four grounds – power (we will later show that this includes the ability to take collective action), interest, privilege and closeness – together with the main ground of the liability model, causation, are all relevant in attributing responsibilities.

In a nutshell, there are many different ways in which agents of justice can be directly or indirectly connected to the existence and sustenance of child poverty and what it does to children. People can have many different relationships to children in poverty, and we suggest that this position in the child's "environment" matters for the attribution of responsibilities. This category of closeness, the specific nature of the relation to the victims of injustice, can be implicitly found in all other grounds. An agent's power to help can increase if she is closer to victims of injustice and is able to provide direct help (e.g., providing shelter for a homeless child). Likewise, the benefits gained through an unjust situation can also depend on the closeness (e.g., an employer who exploits a single mother benefits more from doing so than the middle-class man who buys the cheap clothes produced by the company to save money). It is also reasonable to think that state institutions such as social welfare departments and their employees have particular responsibilities due to their professional relation to families in poverty and the power they have to influence their lives; the responsibility to treat everyone in a fair way and with due respect certainly falls into this category. A neighbor not detecting that a child is maltreated or undernourished can be excusable, but if a social worker fails to do so, something is certainly wrong (either because the social worker is just not good at her job or because the state failed to provide the working conditions and resources she needed to do it).

Such a broad concept of responsibility as we endorse here makes clear that everyone has some share of responsibility; we cannot just lie back and say that it is not our problem, that others have to solve it. But there is danger involved, too; if everyone is responsible, this easily leads to the conclusion that, in the end, no one is, shifting the responsibility back to the "usual suspects": the state and the families these poor children grow up in. We are well aware of this problem; using the grounds we laid out to clarify and help identify concrete agents of justice and determine their responsibility is what is needed. In the best case, it would even be possible to determine what has to be done. We will not be able to go into these details here, but we will propose a first model of how these five grounds should be ranked and weighed against each other.

Our proposal is vague to some extent, in that we cannot attach exact numbers to each ground and then calculate a given agent's responsibility based on that. Notwithstanding, we will be more specific than most other models are, going far beyond just saying that each and every ground has the same normative force and leaving it wide open which agents should be held responsible.

The strongest reason for being responsible as an agent of justice is if an injustice is caused and upheld willingly and knowingly, even if this happened due to negligence. It seems uncontroversial that such a causal role carries strong responsibility for the agent in question; in fact, this reasoning motivates the liability model. By holding someone responsible we mean that she is the first one to whom the victims of injustice can go and claim that the injustice should be undone or compensated. The respective responsibilities are therefore not only backward looking, as Young's interpretation of the liability model suggests. They have a forward-looking component as well and demand that actions be taken to improve the situation in the future.

Second to that is power, especially the power to be a primary agent and to create institutions and hold other agents responsible. If an agent can help undo an injustice (with reasonable effort, be it noted), she should do so even if she did not cause it. Third on the list is the relation a certain agent has to the child, in particular if it is a caring relation, which is essential for the child. We put this high on the list simply because of the particular needs and vulnerabilities of children. Fourth in our ranking is gaining privileges and benefiting from the existence of an injustice. The fifth and weakest reason to be held responsible is to have an interest in overcoming the injustice, in particular if the interest stems from being a victim of this injustice oneself. Let us support this ranking with an example. Consider a family with three children that is pushed into and held in poverty because of the action of an agent, A. The father was the only one working in the family, but A employed him in precarious and exploitative conditions. He had to work more than he could bear and eventually quit his job due to health reasons, leaving the whole family without an income. It is reasonable that agent A is the first one to be held responsible. We also have agent B, who has nothing to do with what happened but has a lot of power and is well equipped to step in and support the family. In a rich society, the state typically meets these criteria. If agents A and B cannot do anything to help, then it is up to the mother to try to find a job, leaving her children alone during the day. But if she cannot find anything or finds only jobs she cannot accept for good reasons, she will be in a situation in which she no longer is able to provide a decent living for her children. In these circumstances, another agent comes into play: a person in her neighborhood, who works closely with the father's employer and who has benefited from the fact that A exploits his workers and his profits are high. The neighbor did not intend to do anything wrong and was not aware of the schemes of his business partner, but he surely benefited; if there is no one else to turn to, his responsibilities are strong. The children themselves have the weakest obligation in respect to their own poverty. The two younger ones, aged one and three, obviously cannot do anything. The older one, aged ten, could work for the neighbors and support her mother and siblings, but from a moral point of view, this fact can confer only very weak responsibilities.

Three important things should be noted here. Firstly, in many cases more than one reason to be responsible can be applied. The state, for example, is powerful and has some interest in keeping children out of poverty. Then there might be an uncle that is well off and close to the children; he certainly ought to step in and support the mother if the state fails to do so. It is possible that the state might fail but the society has other powerful institutions like charities. Secondly, responsibility rises if more than one reason can be applied. Take a company that has the means to pay fair wages and provide good working conditions but, due to its focus on maximizing profits, exploits women and hence harms both them and their children. This company is more to blame and needs to shoulder more responsibility than an equally powerful company that makes only moderate profit because it pays fair wages but could do more in respect of better work-life-balance programs for its workers. It is again important to keep in mind that the responsibilities individuals have are attached to their positions within an institution. A politician has the responsibility to make the state and its institutions work in such a way that injustices do not occur or are alleviated; this may happen by trying to increase the working conditions and introduce a minimum wage. As a private person, her responsibilities are different and have more to do with paying a fair wage to her cleaner instead of exploiting her, for instance. Finally, it is possible to construct examples in which arguments speak against our weighting or in which the case is less clear. Such an example would be another very rich neighbor who is powerful but did not profit from the precarious conditions the father was employed in. Is she responsible for stepping in even before the mother tries to work to make ends meet, because power ranks higher than closeness? We would agree that, in such a case, the rich neighbor has a responsibility towards these children and has to step in if the mother could provide for her children only by excessive and harmful means like leaving them alone and moving to another country for work.

3.2 Important agents of justice and their responsibilities

In the previous section, we tried to narrow down grounds on which agents of justice can be held responsible and presented a ranking of the grounds. A still missing but equally important point is to identify agents of justice in the first place. Some clarifications are needed before we can do that. One the one hand, we need to distinguish between agents responsible for doing something about the child being poor and agents responsible for doing something about the negative effects of being poor. These are different issues. We argued that child poverty is unjust because it leads to severe deprivations in important functionings. Hence, it is a state of ill-being and leads to ill-becoming; it is a major obstacle to developing important capabilities adults should have. But these negative effects of child poverty can certainly be alleviated to some extent without changing the poverty condition itself, at least if one uses a monetary definition of poverty. Think of the example of social inclusion from the previous chapter. Children in poverty are more likely to be excluded due to a lack of adequate transportation and because they are often stigmatized by other people, including their peers in school. Both aspects could be different without moving the child out of poverty measured by household income. In such a case, the harsh effects of poverty are alleviated, and the deprivation in this aspect might not even occur. Again, household income is just one measure for poverty in welfare states; measures like deprivation indicators could use access to transportation and being stigmatized as indicators for poverty. In that case, providing transportation and a change in the behavior and attitudes of other persons and children towards their poor peers would translate into a move out of poverty. It is also very likely that some agents who cannot do much about the poverty of the child can do a lot in regard to how poverty translates into disadvantages and deprivations. A more inclusive health care system that provides free and low-threshold health care might be combined with outreach social work. Taken together, these measures can certainly make a difference and help increase the health of many poor children. Some agents may be able to do much about the poverty status of the child while not directly influencing other dimensions of its well-being and well-becoming. The employer of the father or mother, for instance, who decides to pay a higher wage and improve working conditions, aiming at more family-friendly working hours, certainly influences what a child is able to do and be. Eventually such changes can move her and her family out of poverty, but the employer still can influence the health and education of the child only indirectly.

Since the relation between poverty and the deprivations discussed in Chapter 2 suggests that poverty is a very important cause for them, we argue that poverty should be targeted directly if possible. Alleviating the effects of poverty is like fighting the symptoms and not the disease. This in no way implies that one should not care about alleviating the effects of child poverty. Setting up more inclusive health care systems that directly target poor children is definitely a good thing. We know that they are a particularly vulnerable group and in need of support. In situations where it is unlikely that poverty can be directly tackled or in which it is foreseeable that progress on that front is coming very slowly, it is necessary to use all means available to counter what poverty does to children, even if they cannot be moved out of poverty. One must not forget, however, that the fundamental normative problem is that children grow up in poverty and that there is a need for a systematic change to this.

Identifying agents of justice for child poverty is a task that should be informed by empirical evidence. The relations between different agents in the child's environment and the way they actually influence her well-being and well-becoming is complex, and we have already indicated that a focus on state and family is too narrow. A very influential theory that guides our specification is the ecological model proposed by Urie Bronfenbrenner, a psychologist who worked on child development (Bronfenbrenner 1979; Bronfenbrenner and Morris 2007). His bioecological model aims to conceptualize child development based on an understanding that development is the change and continuity of biopsychological characteristics of humans over the life course, a development shaped by direct and indirect interactions between the developing human being and her environments. Bronfenbrenner's model, used in empirical work for more than three decades, is also applied in research that aims to understand the effects of child poverty and in social work (Eamon 2001; Jack 1997). Such ecological approaches are especially fruitful in concepts of child well-being and well-becoming, which follow a multidimensional approach and want to understand the embedding of children in different environments and how they are influenced by them (Aldgate 2010; Graf and Schweiger 2015). Bronfenbrenner distinguishes five so-called systems: the microsystem, the mesosystem, the exosystem, the macrosystem and the chronosystem. Bronfenbrenner's model is not a philosophical one; it is also not primarily interested in child poverty and not conceptualized to identify agents of justice in the sense explored before. It simply tells us what different kinds of environments are important in children's lives, as well as something about how child poverty can affect the child through these different systems by affecting the microsystem and the direct interaction between parents and child and other environments in which the child is present, like the school, the neighborhood and social service. Furthermore, this model can provide relevant information for a general concept of justice for children by showing what necessary conversion factors children need to develop – hence for developing functionings and, once they have reached a certain level of freedom, capabilities. In a nutshell, such a bioecological model shows that children's development, the very acquiring of any functioning on which later functionings and capabilities can grow, is a process in which many different agents are present and where they have direct and indirect influence.

This ecological approach gives further weight to Young's approach, according to which one must look not just at those who directly and knowingly cause harm and injustice but at the broader context in which children grow up to see whether this context is suitable and supporting or harming and disadvantageous for some children. In political philosophy and most theories of justice, there is a focus on the state and its institutions (basic infrastructure, as one might say) or on powerful international and global institutions that shape the lives of hundreds of millions of people by their policies and actions. We have already argued with Monique Deveaux that weaker individuals can also be seen as agents of justice, in the sense that they can do something important to overcome an injustice. In general, we think it is very plausible to view both persons and institutions as possible agents of justice. Since all institutions are made up of persons acting within them, the attributed responsibilities are transferred to them as far as they are in institutional roles. For example, if a certain company is called upon to change its behavior, the call is directed more at that company and less at the managers leading it. This becomes clear if a change in management does not lead to a change in the attribution of responsibility on that company. The people running the company are the ones responsible for its actions but only insofar as they have roles within the institution. The managers of the company may have many other responsibilities in their other roles: being members of a particular society, living in a certain community, having children, profiting from structural injustices or injustices they cause directly through their jobs and the like. The same can be said of politicians who are in charge of designing their society's institutions and also those of the world in general through an international agency in which they act and which they support or help design. If one understands agents of justice in this sense, the categories of power and collective ability seem to collapse into each other and become one. An institution is often powerful because it can coordinate the actions of many people through their being members of that institution.

Partially following this ecological approach, we distinguish eight agents according to their relation to the child. The agents are listed such that they grow ever more distant from the child in poverty in terms of direct interaction. This says nothing about other parameters, like influence on the child via indirect interaction or structural injustices or in terms of causing the child's poverty and connected harm and deprivations. We use "agent" in a loose sense and in some cases prefer to name environments and institutions, not particular individuals. In accord with what we said before, however, we always address the relevant individuals within these environments and institutions, since in the end they must start acting against child poverty.

(1) The child herself. The child herself is an active agent interacting with her environments and also influencing and shaping them to some extent. Children in poverty are not mere passive objects. From an early stage on, they position themselves within their living conditions and must try to cope with them in some way, whether successfully or not. Participatory research has revealed many different ways that children try to do so (Ridge 2009). Poverty makes living harder for children; if it is very severe, it can kill them. It would, however, be wrong to deny them any agency when it comes to evaluating their condition or determining how it should be changed. We have argued that any justifiable theory of childhood nowadays incorporates a strong agency aspect that actively involves children in their own development. At the same time, one has to be clear that the exact moral status of their perspective has to be weighed by their age and maturity.

(2) The family and close caregivers. The family is obviously crucial to alleviating child poverty and securing justice for children. Child

poverty most often happens in the family children grow up and live in, and the condition of the family is a major source of the child's ill-being and well-being alike. Furthermore, it largely shapes the future of the child and influences what capabilities and functionings can be developed and achieved. Early development especially is based on interactions between the child and close caregivers, which can hardly be replaced adequately. Attachment and love and care are needed for the healthy development and well-being of a child. Poverty can, as we have already shown, disrupt families and even destroy them (Barnett 2008; Goodman et al. 2009). As the exact meaning of "family" is still in dispute, the mentioned relationships of love and care can – within certain limits – take on different forms depending on the social and cultural context. However, the importance of some form of family relationship for a child's well-being and well-becoming is recognized across different cultures and times.

(3) Friendship, leisure and neighborhood. This category describes all the different agents with which, besides the core family, children in poverty interact in a nonprofessional way. This group is obviously very heterogeneous and encompasses close friends as well as neighbors, school peers and relatives. Although their influence on the poverty condition of the child is typically limited and they are not in a position to alleviate material hardship, they still exercise some influence. For instance, they are crucial for the way a child experiences her situation in terms of social exclusion and feelings of disrespect and humiliation. Children are often excluded, stigmatized and denigrated for being poor by their environment, which is highly stressful. Such experiences are likely to lead to isolation, shame and low self-worth, factors that make reaching important functionings and capabilities difficult.

(4) The social and political institutions on the local and state level (e.g., public infrastructure, health care, education). This group of institutions and persons acting within them is crucial for children's development and well-being. Children in poverty are to a great degree dependent on the existence of public health care, education and social services in order to achieve capabilities and functionings. Without them, they are in danger of ill-being and ill-becoming in various ways, and poor families have no resources to take the place of a failing public infrastructure. Therefore, they are the ones hardest hit by austerity measures that cut the welfare system. It is important to note that these institutions have to be inclusive and set up in a way that they can also be afforded, reached and used by those who need them.

(5) The economy and the labor market. Besides the public infrastructure and the welfare system, the economy and the labor market are probably the most influential institutions when it comes to child poverty, although children are kept out of both to a large extent in many countries. It is a widely shared conviction in many countries, especially in the highly developed world, that children should not work to provide for themselves, and up to a certain age it is certain they cannot do so anyway. The economic position of the family, however, determines the life chances of the children who live in them in many ways. Work, income and wealth, education, health, social status and power are interdependent throughout the life course, even before birth and early childhood. It is therefore no surprise that welfare and workfare are very close and that work and improvements to the family's economic position are seen as primary child poverty alleviation measures in many countries. They enable families to provide for children without aid from the state or other national and international institutions and NGOs.

(6) The community of citizens in a society. Every child is a member of a wider community; in most cases, children are citizens of the states they live and grow up in. Citizenship is important for access to services and institutions and determines which rights children have on the national or local level. The citizenship of their parents or caregivers is equally important. On the one hand, if children and their families are illegal immigrants or have refugee status, they usually have significantly lower opportunities in the country they live in; they may be denied political and social rights. On the other hand, being member of a bigger community provides certain opportunities. In many states, the welfare system is supported by the majority of citizens who finance it, and there is a certain degree of solidarity between them. Whether or not one agrees that justice is dependent on such a mutual sense of community, it is certainly the case that citizens influence each other's well-being even if they never interact directly. Prominent examples are tax systems, to which everyone contributes and which are crucial to financing the welfare system from which the worst-off profit the most. Other examples are political institutions: on the one hand, they might be designed in an inclusive way, supporting poverty alleviation and creating a sense of solidarity; on the other hand, they might opt for gated communities, private schools, cuts in the welfare system and the criminalization of begging, thereby marginalizing poor families and their children.

(7) The economic and political institutions on the international and global level. The local and national economy and labor market, as well as local and national public institutions, are not insular and detached from the international and global level. The global economic and political architecture and the power of transnational companies to avoid taxes, to put pressure on states and to lobby their interests highly influence child poverty and pose challenges for the supporting welfare systems. Especially in poorer countries, poverty alleviation is directly financed and designed by international institutions and NGOs; international treaties and agreements shape such countries' economic and social development and their ability to design and control policies in areas from health care to the labor market (Craig and Porter 2006). Hence, particularly in poor countries dominated by such international rules, child poverty is shaped to a large extent by forces external to their own political and social institutions.

(8) The global community of humans. Humans share one earth, and through the various forms of globalization, the connections between them have intensified. The global chains of production and trade, which certainly produce winners and losers, mass tourism across the whole world and a globalized aid system in which resources from rich countries are transferred to poorer ones in the name of charity are just three examples of how people living in very distant places can effectively influence each other's lives. These connections are typically manifold and interlaced, making it difficult to isolate and specify an individual's exact position in the overall "network". Nevertheless, these relations exist, and their normative dimensions must also be considered in an account of responsibilities.

We now have eight different groups of agents that are obviously involved in the well-being and well-becoming of a child in poverty and her being poor in the first place. Each of these groups and the agents within them, such as companies, deserve a close examination so as to scrutinize their responsibilities based on the grounds we distinguished before. Unfortunately, this would go far beyond the scope of this book, and so we present only a first systematization and ranking. After that, we will focus on two agents, the family and the state, since they are crucial to the alleviation of child poverty.

(a) High level of responsibilities. The group with the highest level of responsibilities encompasses social and political institutions on the local and state level (public infrastructure; health care, school, social care) and close caregivers. Based on our criteria for attributing responsibility, it is clear why these two are so important. Within the family, parents especially are closely related to their children, influencing them heavily and having direct power to alter their lives. They have (or should have) a strong interest in overcoming the child's poverty (this often implies that they themselves escape poverty). At the same time, the family is often weakly positioned to change the poverty condition because it is most likely poor and marginalized, a state that can be reinforced by health issues or related problems. Thus, its power has to be seen in the relevant context, acknowledging that it is often severely limited. The state, on the other hand, is the most powerful agent, especially if it is a modern welfare state. It can hold other agents and parents responsible and define what they owe children. Moreover, the state can be said to be a major source for the existence of child poverty in the first place, because it failed to set up an inclusive labor market and a well-working economy in which everyone finds a decently paid and secure job. The state has a strong interest in alleviating child poverty as well, because it is founded around such ideas as equality of opportunity and justice for adults, to which child poverty is a major obstacle. The state can furthermore be interested in avoiding many of the functional deprivations connected to poverty, since they amount to high costs over the life course (e.g., in the health care system or the social welfare systems that have to pay long-term unemployment benefits to adults who did not get a decent education when they were young). Social and political institutions on the local and state level are in the best position to help – if they are financed and equipped properly, as we assume here for argument's sake – and they can do so without any sacrifice on their own. They can successfully support children and their families and can provide them with such crucial conversion factors as health care, education and public infrastructure. We believe this analysis still widely holds true for the states we focus on. However, we acknowledge that the state's actions are limited insofar as it is embedded in wider international and global relations and institutions. In fact, there is an observable tendency that many states give up some of their power to transnational companies, which are more and more in a position to blackmail rich states and avoid taxes and lobby to weaken labor laws. These are trends that must be observed closely, since they clearly have the potential to alter the account of responsibilities we are developing here.

(b) Midlevel of responsibilities. This group of institutions includes the community of citizens within a society, friendship, leisure and neighborhood, the economy and the labor market, as well as political institutions on the international and global level. The community of citizens has only midlevel responsibilities that include the obligation to financially and politically support institutions and policies necessary for alleviating child poverty. They should do so to the extent they can without their own claims of justice being infringed. Citizens can have more comprehensive responsibilities to help if institutions fail or are not sufficient, as in cases of natural disasters. Persons interacting directly with poor children, like their peers, friends, neighbors and other persons they meet in public, have only midlevel responsibility, too. Naturally, this group has the same types of responsibilities as the community of citizens, since it is a subgroup of it, but there are some additional factors. As these agents are closer to the child, their direct influence is greater, as is their ability to intervene; therefore, their responsibilities have more weight. One very important obligation in this domain is treating the child respectfully and refraining from humiliating and excluding behaviors. Another is to keep the neighborhood safe and child-friendly, not make it a dangerous and insecure place. Surely, friends and peers who are themselves children have fewer responsibilities than adults; they usually belong to the last group we will discuss. But again, the line is difficult to draw; with teenagers, there might be cases where responsibility is relatively high. The economy and the labor market are in this midlevel because of their important influence on the child's poverty by providing families with decent jobs or goods and services at fair and affordable prices. The economy and labor market – together with failed policies to regulate them properly – are among the main initiators of child poverty. Political and economic institutions on the international and global level are often overlooked, and child poverty is conceptualized as a local or national problem – but it is not in any exclusive sense. Every state is embedded in the global economic and political regime, and effective poverty alleviation will have to include significant changes on this level as well.

(c) Low level of responsibilities. The group with the lowest level of responsibilities is composed of the global human community and the child herself. The child is clearly in the weakest position to change her situation, at least until a certain age. We would argue that older children, who have achieved a certain level of competency and are therefore also allowed a certain degree of autonomy and choice for themselves, have a certain degree of responsibility for their choices and actions. They do not have an obligation towards themselves in the strict sense, but if they make deliberately bad choices that lower their well-being and well-becoming – like criminal acts and dropping out of school – they should also face the consequences. Still, the degree to which adolescents should be held responsible is debatable. The global community of humans – we exclude here those in high positions of power – has only weak responsibilities towards children in poverty living in other countries. The possibility of influencing their condition is limited, especially compared to the local and national public institutions available in all developed countries, about which we next speak. This does not mean that they have no responsibilities at all, such as to support change on the global level.

3.3 The family and the state

Having presented a first systematization and ranking of agents of justice, we wish to comment further on the family and the state. The first issue that needs to be addressed is causality and responsibility for the child's being poor. The second is causality for the negative effects of child poverty and whether the parents are largely to blame for it because their behavior is an important mediating factor. The reason for discussing these issues is that if the parents are held responsible but obviously fail to fulfill their responsibility, strong intervention could be justified. We will then explore what the state and society in general owe parents as support for them in taking care of their children.

If the parents of poor children are responsible for their children's poverty and/or for severe but preventable deprivations due to their poverty, the state has basically four options: to support the parents and help them become better parents and escape poverty; to take the children away and put them in state care; to take the children away and give them to other parents; and as a preventive option, to make it less likely that poor parents have children in the first place. All the options are based on the assumption that the parents of poor children are not in a position to prevent and overcome their own poverty and that of their children, at least not without being helped by others. This assumption is very important, because in most literature regarding responsibilities towards children it is argued that the parents have to take care and that it might even be unjust to put the costs of care on other agents, including the state. In the case of poverty such a conclusion is not of much help, because poor parents cannot do what might be reasonably demanded of nonpoor parents under the circumstances of a just society. As soon as a child comes to exist, she has a claim to justice; if her parents fail to provide for her, someone else must. Anything else would be unjust and cruel, since children cannot be held responsible for being born to parents who are ill adapted to meet their needs and claims of well-being and well-becoming. In this sense we take here a child-centered line of argument and are not closely concerned with the question of whether fulfilling claims of justice of poor children puts unjustifiable burdens on other agents. We think that it does not and that each and every citizen has a responsibility to support its state to realize justice for all children, whether or not the citizen is a parent. In the nonideal circumstances in which we live now, this is even less controversial than it might be in an ideally just society, where everyone has a fair share and would be expected to give something from it. Today we are far from that situation.

We begin by discussing briefly the relationship between parents and their children and the rights parents have. It is now widely acknowledged that children have certain rights and parents also have rights and that parents can make and need to make important decisions for their children. Compulsory education is a case in which the state itself exercises a right to determine large parts of children's lives. The tension between parental and children's rights and the right of the state to intervene in the family is obvious. We take here a child-centered approach that argues that in this triangle children are the primary right bearers and parents have rights that flow from them. In terms of justice this means that children have claims of justice towards their parents and that it is the parents' responsibility to fulfill these claims up to a just minimum. Hence, we do not think that a property view of parental rights, which views children as the property of their parents, is appropriate. Under the premise of the capability approach, no person is the property of another, because this would violate the demand of equal respect. This is similar to an argument developed by Harry Brighouse and Adam Swift that argues convincingly that parental rights should be based on the children's rights to be cared for in their interest – though maybe not their best interests, because these are hard to define and unlikely to be accomplished perfectly. There is no society-wide feasible alternative to the family as a place for children to be raised, although in thought experiments such options can be imagined. In theory, it is thinkable that a well-run orphanage might do a better job than any parent could do and that such a society would be more just in terms of equality of opportunity, but this comes at very high costs

(Munoz-Darde 1999; Schoeman 1980). It is very unlikely that parents would be willing to give up their children. They would sooner consider leaving the country or trying other ways to keep and raise their children themselves. The same applies to such ideas as redistributing babies to better (i.e., richer) parents as a generally used mean to secure justice for children. To deprive poor parents of their children simply because they are poor would be fighting one injustice with another. Some practical issues stand against such an idea as well, such as the problem that there might not be enough rich families who would want to raise another person's children. There is also some evidence that suggests that the risk of being abused and mistreated is higher for children raised by those to whom they are not biologically related (Daly and Wilson 1999). Taking away the child is, thus, a last resort. Moreover, attachment theory suggests that taking away a child always mean harming the child; staying with close caregivers the child is attached to is very important for the child. Still, in cases of abuse and severe neglect, taking away the child is justified. This means that parents, even poor parents, have a right to act as parents only as long as they provide their children with a minimally decent life. A similar argument was made by David Archard in his defense of parental rights.

> We have said both that parents' rights are limited and that they are conditional on parents' protecting certain of the children's interests. Failure to protect those interests amounts to a forfeiture of the right, in the same way that failure to obey just laws implies forfeiting one's right to freedom of association. All accounts of parental rights, in order to be plausible, have to make them conditional on parents' meeting certain of their children's interests adequately (Brighouse and Swift 2006, 103).
>
> In sum, the rights individuals have as parents within a liberal society are the rights to bring up their children as they choose so long as they discharge the morally prior duty of ensuring that their children enjoy a minimally decent life. They do not have the rights of property owners to dispose of their offspring as they would their estate. However they are not required, as liberal principles might seem to demand, to bring up their children to enjoy maximally open futures; nor must they do so in such a way as would satisfy a liberal principle of legitimacy. (Archard 2010, 50)

The tricky question in regard to poverty is if being poor falls below the threshold and if parents who can be said to be poor through their own fault should lose their rights as parents. In this case, it would be justified to take away their children, because the harm of being taken away would be less severe than the harm of staying in the family. Poverty would then fall into the same category as abuse and severe neglect, which also count as legitimate reasons for state intervention today. In fact, empirical research shows that children from poor families are more often taken away, and it has also been suggested that social workers are more likely to intervene in poor families than in richer ones, even if the level of neglect or abuse is similar.

We now want to discuss why parents are not fully responsible for being poor and why this leads to the conclusion that even if poverty should constitute falling under the threshold necessary to uphold parental rights, parents should be supported instead of having their children taken away. Most people in poverty are not poor by choice, in the sense that they wish to be poor. The question is whether poor parents can be seen as being poor because they made bad and wrong choices, which lead them to become poor against their will and desire. This would be evaluated as a kind of deserving poverty. The first argument that speaks against such a conclusion is that poverty is very often grounded in childhood, and the intergenerational transmission of poverty suggests that people move through the life course on a trajectory that is very hard to change. It is certainly not impossible to escape poverty, but it is hard to because of the many disadvantages we discussed, like deprivations in health and education. The second argument in favor of our conclusion is the structural nature of poverty. The economic crisis of the last years pushed millions of people into poverty and made it much harder to escape it, showing impressively that the individual is dependent on the economic and social chances she finds. If there are simply not enough jobs available, someone will be unemployed, and if the economy changes in a way that transfers jobs from one country to another, the individual worker with a family and a mortgage to repay simply cannot move along (in fact, in most cases this would not help much, since it would still be too expensive).

The counterargument, that uneducated persons are much more vulnerable to poverty, captures only one dimension and so must be rejected at least partly. Educational choices are in many countries made very early and depend on such things as available schools in the neighborhood or the support from parents. Children cannot control them, and when they reach an age at which they can be held partially responsible for their educational achievements and choices, it is often too late. We do not wish to dismiss adolescents completely, but they are at least partially the victims of their circumstances and the environments in which they grew up, which makes it more likely that they will leave school early, become teenage parents or start to work early in insecure low-wage jobs. Furthermore, education is important, but so are other factors – for example, health and disability. The fact that single parents are much more often poor speaks not so much against these mothers and fathers as it reflects gender inequalities in the labor market (England 2005), the undervaluing of jobs done mainly by women and the lack of economic recognition of care work, as well as the difficulties of supporting young children with a part-time job in an environment which does not have enough affordable child care facilities. Many poor adults have certainly made bad choices and are partially to be blamed for them, especially if they are responsible for children, in which case their bad choices' consequences fall upon others who are particular vulnerable. But all the knowledge and evidence about poverty in welfare states suggests that most people are victims more of their circumstances than of their bad choices.

This conclusion is closely connected to the second point concerned with the behavior of poor parents and how they influence their children's well-being and well-becoming. We saw in the last chapter that parents mediate how poverty affects their children. Two examples from research illustrate this point. An older study on the effects of severe economic hardship on children during the Depression found that parenting behavior plays a crucial role (Elder, Nguyen and Caspi 1985). The most interesting result, however, was that the rejecting behavior of the fathers had a significant negative impact on the psychosocial well-being of their daughters, a behavior related to the physical attractiveness of the daughters. Put simply, fathers treated their daughters better if they were more attractive, which led to higher psychosocial well-being in these girls. This means that the child's development and her well-being and well-becoming were influenced by the economic downturn, and this had influenced a major agent in their lives and the interactions taking place between the child and this agent. More importantly, this interaction was also shaped by a characteristic of the girls themselves, although they had no control over it. In a 2002 study, Mary Eamon investigated the relation between poverty and antisocial behavior of children from twelve to fourteen (Eamon 2002). She found that physical punishment, lower levels of parental emotional support, deviant peer pressure and neighborhood problems all predict antisocial behavior and that children living in poverty are more likely to experience these. The effect of poverty on antisocial behavior is therefore influenced by both the interactions within the family (parenting behavior) and the interactions with peers and with the wider social environment (neighborhood).

Both these examples show how important parents' behavior is in the translation of poverty into negative outcomes in other areas of well-being and well-becoming. How much blame for the outcomes can be attributed to the parents, then, and can it lead to a justification of state intervention? Again, we argue that it is enough to show that parents are not fully responsible for many of their choices that affect their children and that this suggests that the state has a responsibility to support rather than punish them. Parents living in poverty in most cases have limited opportunities – and capabilities and functionings – when it comes to improving their own living conditions and those of their children. Lack of resources translates into a lack of freedoms in this respect, which becomes evident for such things as paying for heating, a better flat, moving to a different neighborhood or paying for repairs and special treatments not covered by general insurance (in some modern and highly developed societies, millions of children and families are not covered by any medical insurance). Trickier from a moral point of view are "choices" such as taking drugs or drinking during pregnancy, child neglect due to addictions or simple bad parenting (as in the two earlier cases). We make a much weaker claim here: namely, that behaviors are themselves partially determined by socioeconomic position and how one grows up and is socialized; this claim seems to be supported by some evidence now (Pinderhughes et al. 2001; Russell, Harris and Gockel 2008). The claim that at least some important aspects of the choices we make are socially determined is, we believe, uncontroversial. The case of fathers treating their attractive daughters better shows that. Under better circumstances, such behavior probably carries little weight or does not happen at all. It is hence something that is not under full control of these fathers, and so we argue that the responsibility should be at least partially shifted from the fathers to the economic downturn and the state, which was unable to compensate adequately. We cannot specify how many of the choices poor people and parents make can be attributed to factors they cannot control themselves, but we would claim the portion is large enough to support our interpretation that the behavioral influence on their children's life is not in their full responsibility and that as they have often limited possibilities to alter their behavior, they cannot be held fully responsible for it. William J. Wilson has come to the same conclusion in his influential study on urban poverty in the USA:

> This is not to argue that individuals and groups lack freedom to make their own choices, engage in certain conduct and develop certain styles and orientations, but it is to say that these decisions and actions

occur within a context of constraints and opportunities that are drastically different from those present in middle-class society. (Wilson 1997, 55)

This does not indicate that they are not responsible at all and that poverty is an excuse for everything. It is certainly not. Let us consider another example: a study has shown that the economic downturn of the last years increased significantly the cases of children suffering from abusive head trauma (shaken baby syndrome; Berger et al. 2011). It seems as if stress caused by unemployment and financial strain leads more parents to behave in this abusive and severely harmful way. In such a case we believe two lessons can be learned: On the one hand, poverty does not excuse such behavior. Parents' responsibility is to support their children, not hurt them. On the other hand, if poverty helps us understand why parents act in such a way, it certainly implies that other agents of justice for children, mainly the state and its institutions, should either alleviate poverty and unemployment in the first place or act preventively to support families and parents so that they do not display this kind of destructive behavior.

Where does this leave us now? Parents are an important mediator, they are not fully responsible for being poor or for all of their (moderately) bad parenting, and there is no really feasible alternative to them, since placing children either in state care or with other, richer parents incurs many other problems. Would it be best if poor parents did not have children in the first place? The state then would not have to intervene, and there would be no issues of responsibility for poverty or bad parenting to begin with. There is actually some support for this claim to be found in the literature, not only with a focus on children that would not be born and then could not be harmed. We leave aside the nonidentity problem and do not discuss whether it would be good if no one had children, considering it to be always harmful. We start with the assumptions that being born is good and that children born into poverty are more likely to have a bad life, in the sense of an unjust life, hampered by deprivations in important functionings and capabilities. We assume furthermore that the state has the ability to intervene and that it could alleviate poverty for these children by supporting their parents or that it could at least alleviate most negative effects of child poverty, limiting them to an extent that is within reasonable range of the risks every other child has to live with. Hence, if the state changes, it can secure justice for children having been born poor, which certainly comes at some costs the state could use otherwise if these children were not born at all. Under these circumstances – and we think they more or less accurately reflect what is possible in all modern welfare states – the state is allowed to enable and responsible for enabling all people, adolescents in particular, with a real choice if and when they want to become parents. It is thus responsible for providing knowledge about reproductive health and helping them plan their parenthood. Again, we are confronted here with a very sensitive issue about which many different opinions exist (e.g., religious groups that argue that family planning is always wrong and the state should never provide mandatory sexual education). Adaptive preferences, or to put it more moderately, unreflecting choices of younger adults and adolescents are an issue here. The reasons why young women get pregnant are multifold and can include gender roles, carelessness, lack of knowledge and the hope of stabilizing a relationship with a baby. Considering this, there is a fine line between education, helping people make good choices for themselves – this is the ideal of the capability approach – and manipulating or pushing them to make a choice that is good for the state. Under the circumstances described above, all adults and, to a lesser extent, adolescents are entitled to become parents if they wish, and the state has the responsibility to support them in making that decision freely and with respect to their own life plans. The state has the further responsibility to support the parents on their way to parenthood, providing prenatal health care and social services in cases where there is an indication that problems exist, as for parents-to-be in poverty. Furthermore, the state certainly has the responsibility to support the parents after birth and in their efforts to be good parents; it is not allowed to compel poor persons to not become parents in the first place for the sake of merely sparing some funds. Reproduction and the capability of becoming a parent and acting as a parent – on the condition that one provides for that child sufficiently, with the help of the state, if needed – are part of what constitutes justice for adults.

Our arguments so far have been concerned with the claim that the state is not allowed to take children away from poor parents solely because they are poor or to hinder them from becoming parents. We have said little about the responsibilities the state has subsequently in regard to children born into poor families or living in families that become poor while the children are young; we also have not explored the responsibilities poor parents have in respect to their children, besides having to care for them sufficiently – for which Brighouse and Adams used the term "interests" and Archard used "a minimal decent living". We wish to use here an argument developed by Anne Alstott, who argues that parents have an obligation to stay and no right to exit their parenthood; based on that responsibility, the state has the responsibility to support them in doing that. She derives the obligation to stay from an analysis of the importance of continuity of care. Put otherwise, children's well-being and well-becoming are dependent, not totally but largely, on continuity of care, on having caregivers who stay and do not leave them.

> No Exit is the flip side of continuity of care. We have seen that society expects parents to provide continuity, and it depends on them to do so. But when parents commit to continuity of care for their children, they limit their own capacity to exit, in two senses. Most obviously, parents undertake to stay with their children for the long term and not to leave them. But in addition, continuity of care requires parents to reshuffle their priorities: parents must strive to meet their children's material and emotional needs, and they must, if need be, limit their own aspirations and forgo opportunities to do so. (Alstott 2004, 51)

Alstott is interested in what continuity of care, hence the no exit obligation, implies for parents – namely, that they are limited in their autonomy, both in local autonomy to make choices (like going on a spontaneous romantic trip) and global autonomy, which concerns long-term choices. Such a parent-centered approach coincides with a child-centered approach that asks not what the state owes to parents but what the state owes to children; from this the parents benefit only because they are the mediators and conversion factors of state resources that cannot be directly given to children due to their limited capacities, vulnerability and powerlessness. Such a child-centered line of argument can even conclude that poverty-alleviating measures targeted at children benefit parents only as a side effect, since they are the necessary mediators. In some policy areas, such an argument is more likely to receive support than a parent-centered approach that claims parents have certain entitlements or rights regardless of the benefits for the children. The parent-centered argument, according to which parents fulfill a necessary responsibility towards children that demands certain sacrifices and in which they deserve to be supported, and the child-centered argument – according to which children are entitled to certain functionings and parents being the best mediators to help realize them, parents need to be supported because of that – come to very similar conclusions.

Parents have basically eight different types of responsibilities towards their children; they show a great overlap in regard to what we demand of justice for children in terms of functionings they are entitled to. The first, as Alstott convincingly shows, is the responsibility to stay parents and not to leave, unless staying is either unbearable for them or would harm the child more. Parents should stay because children need them to. This implies that whenever parents make a decision that could affect their children, they are to take them into account and give them due weight. The second responsibility is to provide for them materially and give them decent living conditions. This encompasses a wide range of functionings: having adequate shelter, clothes, toys, time for play and the like. It is not possible to draft a final list detached from a particular context, but deprivation indicators that select necessary goods in a particular society can be used here. The third responsibility is to meet the health needs of their children and provide them with access to health care when they need it, seeing that they are healthy, develop healthy lifestyles and acquire knowledge about their bodies and minds. The fourth responsibility is to provide for them emotionally and let them experience deep attachments and security. Others have discussed whether a child has a right to be loved (Liao 2006); we see good grounds to deny that (Cowden 2012). An emotion can never be enforced by others – this is the only meaningful interpretation of having a certain right. But parents or other caregivers can be required to let the child experience attachments necessary for her healthy development. The fifth responsibility is to take care of children's well-becoming and see that they acquire functionings that will help them develop important capabilities in the future. This includes being responsible that children get some good options in their life so that they can participate in their own development. Joel Feinberg has prominently argued that children should have a right to an open future (Feinberg 1980). This claim, however, should not be interpreted in terms of maximization (Mills 2003): No one can ever provide a child with a fully open future, because growing up and developing functionings and capabilities always closes the door to other options. The life course is in many ways structured, not only by parents but by the whole environment and the state (Kohli 2007), and nothing more can be demanded from parents than to help their children develop into autonomous beings who have a broad range of options, selected on the available knowledge at that time. Parents are, thus, not to be blamed if they support a child in becoming a journalist and she later becomes unemployed because the news branch is hit hard by new technological developments; at the time, becoming a journalist might have seemed a very good option and life plan. The sixth responsibility of parents is to aim for inclusion in social activities and groups.

They should help their children make friends and be in the public. The seventh responsibility is to give their children room for making decisions themselves according to maturity and competencies. To guide their children, parents are allowed to prevent them from doing things, but children should be heard, be given voice and be able to decide (small) things for themselves from a certain stage on. Parents are responsible for letting children take on some responsibility for their actions. The eighth and last responsibility is to protect children from harm and dangers. This responsibility to protect, based in the vulnerability of children, is never fully comprehensive. Growing up and exploring the world always implies some dangers and the risk of accidents, injuries or other bad experiences. Parents cannot and are not responsible for fully protecting their children; this would be possible only by applying very restrictive measures that would rob the children of other valuable experiences. Parents should therefore protect their children, but exposure to potential risks is always necessary and justified within reasonable limits.

The parents' responsibilities that focus on their own child also imply that they have good reasons to favor the best result for their child, even at the expense of other children. This partiality is unavoidable in parenting not only because of the special relationship between children and parents but also because parents have only little influence on the choices of other parents; it is reasonable for them to expect that other parents will increase the functionings and capabilities of their children even if this has negative side effects on other children. The state, on the other hand, can set up and run education and health care systems which provide every child with a fair chance and produce healthier and better-educated children regardless of their socioeconomic background. As the state has to look after all its children and citizens, it also has the responsibility to interfere with parents' decisions and actions that either harm their own or other children. This leads us to propose a first systematization of responsibilities of the state towards children in poverty based on our examination of justice for children.

At first, the state has to come up with a list of important functionings and capabilities and discuss whether or not these are all of equal value. We argued in Chapter 1 that fertile functionings should be treated with priority because of their positive influence on other functionings and capabilities (e.g., for their instrumental value). We further argued that this means that corrosive disadvantages should be tackled with a higher priority because they undermine many important functionings and capabilities. We discussed lists and methods to select dimension; this is an ongoing effort, particularly in regard to formulation of concrete policies. We are confident that the functionings and capabilities discussed – health, education and inclusion – will be on any such list and also will come out with a high priority.

Secondly, this means that child poverty is a corrosive disadvantage; to put it in positive terms, the functioning of being not poor is a fertile area and so should receive close attention. This implies two different tasks: the first is to alleviate poverty itself, to provide for the material well-being of child and family; as this can be done in many different ways, further scrutiny is needed to see which way shows the best results. The second task is to alleviate the corrosiveness of child poverty, hence its negative influence on other functionings and capabilities. Health, education and inclusion, for example, can be enhanced for children in poverty without alleviating their poverty directly. For example, if it is known that stress due to poverty during pregnancy affects the birth outcome, it could be a good measure to include a mandatory stress screening in prenatal care and to reach out to at-risk women and provide them the opportunity for counseling or other forms of stress management. In some countries such programs have already been set up and show positive results (Loureiro et al. 2009).

Thirdly, in regard to these functionings and capabilities, the state needs to further specify them and set adequate thresholds; it should aim to set them in a way that shows equal concern for each and every child, that minimizes inequalities in them based on such arbitrary and undeserved traits as being poor and that secures an equal opportunity for well-being in later life. It does that adequately only if it invests as many resources in children's well-being and well-becoming compatible with its other responsibilities of justice to all its citizens. Here, again, the idea of a priority view is important: the state should prioritize children in poverty and help them overcome the group-based injustices they suffer from. The limits to this priority view are drawn by the justified claims of other children and adults, which should not be put below the threshold, and also by the supply-side sufficiency view, which claims that the state should not overburden itself.

Fourth, the state is responsible for supporting parents or other caregivers in their responsibilities, which we laid out earlier. It has to give them the means to be good parents to the extent that is possible, but it is also responsible for dimensions of justice that cannot be covered by the parents, such as equality of opportunity for all children. Parents can support their children in being educated and can also make some crucial choices regarding their education, but whether the education system itself produces equal outcomes is far beyond their control. If parents or other caregivers cannot fulfill their responsibilities, the state is obliged to step in. The particular vulnerability of children and their limited capacity to take care of themselves adequately imply necessarily that the state – or if the state fails then a different agent of justice – has to substitute and provide for these children, whether it does so by seeking new guardians for them or by putting them in protectory.

We have derived responsibilities of the state towards children from the perspective of what is owed to these children in order to provide them with well-being and well-becoming. Because poor children most often live in poor families, the costs attached to these state responsibilities cannot be shouldered by them. We have said much about the family and the state, which could lead one to the conclusion that justice for poor children is an issue concerned just with these two agents. This is, however, certainly not what we argue. The responsibilities of family and state derive from their relation to the child, from their power and interest in overcoming child poverty to support these children. Other agents have other reasons to be responsible; the state, as one important primary agent, can influence them much more than the family, which is faced with such problems as how the economy works, how gender roles are attributed and how to deal with the stigma of being poor.

3.4 Conclusions

In this chapter we have explored the issue of responsibilities towards children in poverty, focusing on the relevant agents of justice who can be held responsible for doing something about it. Our model is still vague, but this vagueness reflects both the complexity of the issue and the limits of philosophical inquiry. Based on the criteria presented, to attribute concrete responsibilities to the groups of agents we named would require a much deeper empirical knowledge. To some extent it would not be possible to disentangle relations and interferences. We argued that families in poverty are limited in their power and that parenting behavior is shaped and influenced by how these parents grew up and lived in poverty. It is not possible to disaggregate exactly how much of their harmful behavior can be attributed to circumstances for which they are not responsible themselves and how much responsibility they have to shoulder. Being poor comes with a restriction of freedom, one that is, however, not total. It would be unjust to neglect poor parents completely as agents of justice; this would either degrade them to children, which they are not, or to persons with severe mental disabilities who are not able to make choice for themselves. Likewise, it is not possible to calculate the responsibility of any given company, one that just does what nearly all others do: try to take advantage of their workers, make a profit, avoid taxes and so on. But even without exact calculations, we believe that our extension of Young's model of responsibilities to the issue of child poverty is a step in the right direction. The identification of different reasons for attributing responsibilities and agents of justice can offer initial guidance to coordinated actions necessary to achieve real improvements.

Except where otherwise noted, this work is licensed under a Creative Commons Attribution 3.0 Unported License. To view a copy of this license, visit http://creativecommons.org/licenses/by/3.0/

OPEN

4
Advancing Our Approach to Global Justice for Children

So far, we have outlined a concept of social justice for children in welfare states and criticized child poverty within them as unjust. We have argued that different agents are responsible for securing justice for these children and that the respective extent of their responsibility can be determined, at least approximately, using different criteria relating to the capacities of these actors and their role in the causation of child poverty, as well as their relation to the child and her living condition. The state and its institutions – education system, health care, social protection services and so on – are obviously the most important agents in this respect: as they possess metaresponsibility, they should enforce, if necessary, the responsibility of other agents. We have already discussed the international and global level briefly, acknowledging that it is of importance. We have argued, however, that we view the state and its institutions as the primary agent in the case of child poverty in modern welfare states – they are still strong enough and have plenty of opportunities to shape their own institutions and societies. Still, child poverty in welfare states is more likely to be alleviated and eradicated if the international and global structures within which these states have to act and by which their opportunities and institutions are influenced also change. Nevertheless, welfare states can do much about child poverty even under the present unjust global structure. The situation is different for 'weaker' and developing countries, where child poverty is more widespread and severe. These countries have fewer opportunities, and it is very unlikely that child poverty in these regions can ever be eradicated without thinking about global justice; their problems are simply too closely intertwined with imbalances in the current global order.

It is clear that in poorer countries child poverty is a much more severe and widespread problem than in welfare states, where most poor children reach a level of well-being and well-becoming that is higher than that of most children worldwide. Yet one should never use these differences in the severity of absolute poverty, so to speak, to underestimate or downplay the severity of relative poverty; this is certainly not our intention in this chapter. Child poverty in welfare states is an injustice that weighs heavily and demands coordinated action. An examination of child poverty on the global scale, however, shows how it deprives even the most fundamental functionings and capabilities, leading to starvation, homelessness and death. These forms of deprivation constitute such blatant injustices that one can only wonder why it is still allowed to exist in a world that has reached such a high technological level.

UNICEF (2005) reported that in 2005 every second child in the world (1 billion) lived in poverty, that one in three children (640 million) in developing countries lived without adequate shelter, that one in five children (400 million) had no access to safe water and that one in seven children (270 million) had no access to health services. In 2011, close to 6.9 million children died before their fifth birthday, most of them due to a lack of access to nutrition and basic medical care (UNICEF 2012). These figures alone give a glimpse of how child poverty in poorer countries affects many dimensions of the physical, emotional, social and economic well-being and well-becoming of children and of how our world fails to deliver to these children what they are entitled to as a matter of justice. Hence, in this last chapter we wish to at least outline how we think our approach extends to these issues. We touch upon two aspects of particular importance: first, the task of identifying functionings and of setting thresholds that work as a benchmark for criticizing global child poverty; and second, the need to prioritize the attribution of responsibilities on a global scale.

In Chapter 1 we proposed criteria to help identify functionings children are entitled to as a matter of justice; we do not see why they should not be applicable to any context and to all children in this world. Built into these criteria, however, is the claim that the functionings and respective thresholds have to be interpreted according to the context in which a child lives and that the level of welfare in that country is of particular relevance. As we furthermore argued, thresholds of functionings as well as capabilities are best interpreted in terms of more specified functionings and capabilities. To come back to the earlier example, the adequate threshold for the general functioning of being educated can be the functioning of going to school for nine years or achieving an education that enables one to succeed in the labor market in that society. Thresholds are thus specifications of functionings, and it is possible to understand them in terms of a combination of different such specified functionings. The threshold of the functioning of being healthy can, for instance, be specified using three functionings: (a) living as many healthy life years as the average in that society, (b) receiving all vaccines medical evidence identifies as beneficial and (c) not being affected by more illnesses than others due to arbitrary features that cannot be traced back to voluntary choices as an adult or to innate features that cannot be altered by medical care without subjecting other persons to other injustices.

These three functionings refer to important aspects of being healthy, but whereas the first and the third directly address the status of being healthy, the second one is related to a preventive measure. This points to another important issue; namely, that the thresholds of functionings are often to be translated into functionings that affect the achievement of the respective functioning. The chosen threshold is, then, only an indirect specification. We have largely ignored such problems in the selection of concrete functionings and their thresholds; instead, we used a 'negative' approach to criticize the injustice of poverty by looking at what it does to the poor children compared with their nonpoor peers who live in the same country. We have not judged the effects of child poverty on education by using a particular threshold, but we examined how well children in poverty fare in the education system and what educational achievements they have compared with those of nonpoor school children. It can be criticized that this strategy to disclose injustices gives an inaccurate evaluation because it is possible that all children in a certain society are below the threshold for the functioning of education and that looking at the inequalities produced by child poverty does not give a clear picture of the problem. We are aware of that; unfortunately, we could not come up with a better answer than to say that for the context we are interested in – namely, modern welfare states – we assume that the majority of children are above the threshold and that looking at the inequality and disadvantage produced by poverty is what counts under such advanced circumstances. If one uses the threshold of going to school for six or nine years, nearly all children in modern welfare states reach this threshold, but as we made clear, there still exist injustices in education – a deprivation in the functioning to be educated – that are related to the socioeconomic position of the child. Furthermore, we did not tackle the question of whether comparative weighting of different functionings is reasonable and feasible, even necessary in some circumstances, but assumed that at least the four functionings examined in more detail are highly important – but are they equally important?

For an expansion of our approach to cover global child poverty, these issues become even more problematic, since a sufficient answer for welfare states – to look at relative poverty and the disadvantages it produces – is surely not enough for developing countries. It could be argued that there is a much more urgent need to prioritize certain functionings in poorer countries – for example, health and nutrition – and to give them more weight than, say, education. Such a prioritization should not be understood as devaluing education. Poverty alleviation relies on improving education and also empowering poor people to become agents of justice; the role of education is crucial. Furthermore, as was argued in some detail, education can be seen as a fertile functioning, influencing many other aspects of a person's life and the lives of whole communities. Still, without having one's nutrition and basic health secured, education's value is usually marginal; thus there is good reason to secure first what is essential for survival and only then secure other functionings and capabilities. This reasoning has strong parallels to Henry Shue's arguments for a basic right to subsistence:

> No one can fully, if at all, enjoy any right that is supposedly protected by society if he or she lacks the essentials for a reasonably healthy and active life. Deficiencies in the means of subsistence can be just as fatal, incapacitating, or painful as violations of physical security. The resulting damage or death can at least as decisively prevent the enjoyment of any right as can the effects of security violations. (Shue 1996, 24)

On the global level, using such absolute thresholds and specifying functionings that define them is necessary. This is a very tricky task, and poverty research is limited in what functionings it can use as well, since some are easier to measure and to survey than others. In some cases, the functionings used to measure poverty are the result of the data available. Sabina Alkire, a pioneer in the application of the capability approach in global poverty measurement, used the following six indicators to measure child poverty in Bangladesh (Alkire and Roche 2012):

(1) Nutrition. Children who are more than two standard deviations below the international reference population for stunting (height for age) or wasting (weight for height) or are underweight (weight for age). The standardization follows the algorithms provided by WHO's Child Growth Reference Study.

(2) Water. Children who use water from an unapproved source, such as open wells or springs, or use surface water (time to reach the water source is not included because this information was not available for the Bangladesh Demographic and Health Survey 1997).
(3) Sanitation. Children who use an unapproved sanitation facility, such as a pit latrine without slab, open pit latrine, bucket toilet or a hanging toilet.
(4) Health. Children who have not been immunized by age two. Children are deprived if they do not receive at least eight of the nine vaccinations – bcg, dpt1, dpt2, dpt3, polio0, polio1, polio2, polio3, measles – or do not receive treatment for an illness involving an acute respiratory infection or diarrhea.
(5) Shelter. Children who live in a house with no flooring (i.e., a mud or dung floor) or inadequate roofing (overcrowding was not taken into account because the Bangladesh Demographic and Health Survey 1997 does not register the number of rooms used for sleeping).
(6) Information. Children with no access to a radio or television (i.e., broadcast media). This indicator applies only to children above age three.

Alkire herself is well aware that this selection reflects just a few dimensions of child poverty and that other important information is missing, but these pragmatic choices can be justified in empirical research – having some knowledge of a few functionings is always better than having none. For a concept of global justice, this is certainly not enough. Unfortunately, philosophers have seldom engaged with this task in such a way that they came up with functionings or capabilities that can really be measured. Nussbaum and others do write about the problem but do not provide us with many answers; it is unclear what the exact thresholds for capabilities on Nussbaum's list are, for being healthy, for example, or being able to use one's senses. Not long ago, Ingrid Robeyns called the capability approach radically underspecified (Robeyns 2006), a critique that is still valid. For children, developing beings that change significantly over a rather short period of time, these problems are even more compelling, and issues of poverty dynamics and evolving functionings and capabilities are more relevant. We do not aim to come up with a definite list of functionings and respective thresholds for these functionings in terms of specified measurable functionings either. What is important, though, is to tackle the problem of differences between contexts. The functionings described above and used by Alkire in the context of Bangladesh show that over 90 percent of children live in a house with no flooring or inadequate roofing, and the deprivation rates for nutrition, sanitation and information (access to broadcast media) are nearly 60 percent. These numbers speak for themselves and make the injustice of child poverty in Bangladesh and other developing countries clearly visible. But in regard to the nature and effects of child poverty in modern welfare states, these functionings provide us with barely any information at all. Still, there is poverty, and in the course of this book we have presented some of its moral implications. The fact that it cannot be measured using the functionings employed by Alkire in Bangladesh must not lead to the conclusion that the living conditions of the respective children are free from any problems.

Against this background, where should the thresholds be set? In which functionings should they be specified? There is a real danger in setting them either too low or too high. We see two different basic strategies for handling the questions, though with important variances. The first is to differentiate between countries and allow them to set their own thresholds, at least within reasonable limits. This approach is favored by Nussbaum and also by Sen, who has a far more pragmatic approach and leaves the selection of the relevant functionings and capabilities up to the respective nations or societies. Nussbaum has made her approach clear on numerous occasions:

> Setting the threshold precisely is a matter for each nation, and, within certain limits, it is reasonable for nations to do this differently, in keeping with their history and traditions. (Nussbaum 2011, 41)
>
> Indeed, part of the idea of the list is its *multiple realizability*: its members can be more concretely specified in accordance with local beliefs and circumstances. It is thus designed to leave room for a reasonable pluralism in specification. The threshold level of each of the central capabilities will need more precise determination, as citizens work toward a consensus for political purposes. This can be envisaged as taking place within each constitutional tradition, as it evolves through interpretation and deliberation. (Nussbaum 2000, 77)

There are at least two problems with this solution, of which Nussbaum and others are well aware; still, no one has come up with a sufficient answer so far. On the one hand, this differentiating approach produces results that seem to contradict the aim of a concept of justice; namely, to provide all children with sufficient functionings that they need for their well-being and well-becoming. Again, we use the example of education. Mario Biggeri and his colleagues researched child poverty in Afghanistan and used the percentage of primary-school-age children who are not enrolled in school to measure educational functioning (Biggeri, Trani and Mauro 2010). Interpreting this in normative terms in a concept of justice, we say that every child of primary school age is entitled to go to school. For a child in a welfare state like Germany or the United Kingdom, the threshold would be different due to the fact that nearly all children of that age are enrolled, making it much more reasonable to take completion of secondary education as a minimum standard. In the language of justice, each and every child in Germany is entitled, as a matter of justice, to finish secondary education because this is the basic threshold for the functioning of education. If one uses these two different thresholds, a puzzling and disturbing result is that a child who does not finish secondary education in Germany is evaluated as being wronged, while a child in Afghanistan in the same circumstances is not. This seems questionable, as these two children are different in no feature save the arbitrary one of birthplace. It would be unjust in itself, so it appears, to tolerate exactly the same deprivation for one child and criticize it for the other. Is the child living in Afghanistan not entitled to the same level of functioning in education as the child in Germany? Is she of unequal worth? Does she not have the same entitlement to well-being and well-becoming?

On the other hand, Nussbaum and others claim that for some functionings or capabilities, the threshold should be universal and in some even strictly egalitarian in the sense that every human is entitled to the same. An example for adults would be voting rights, which should be, according to Nussbaum, distributed equally; it would be unjust if a society decides to let only men vote or to let them vote for their household. An example for children would probably be the functioning to live free of exploitation (which is on the list of Biggeri); it seems reasonable and necessary to claim that each and every child, no matter in which society, is entitled to being equally free of exploitation, with all the relevant protections in place. The question then arises: what functionings and capabilities (of children) should be universal, and what thresholds should be used? Furthermore, it is not obvious who should be able give answers to these questions, and, again, the issue of power arises forcefully.

We believe that these difficulties give us enough reasons to dismiss this strategy and be in favor of the second one, which sets universal thresholds for all children wherever they live. This implies that the threshold children are entitled to reach in a specific functioning is the same in Austria, the USA, Bangladesh, India and South Africa. As we said in regard to some functionings, this is also claimed by proponents of the first strategy. We gave as examples voting rights and freedom from exploitations, where any differentiations between different members of society are clearly always wrong. But we go a step further and demand this feature for each and every functioning that matters for justice.

The crucial question, then, is how to set such universal thresholds, which should neither be too high, so that they cannot be reached by most countries, nor too low, so that many forms of injustices cannot be detected and criticized. We agree that solving this problem cannot be done by relying on philosophical reasoning alone and that empirical knowledge that goes beyond the scope of what we are able to provide here is needed. Nonetheless, we believe that a concept of global justice still has to come up with some answer that goes beyond simply handing over the problem to the social sciences or politicians.

Our solution is to claim that the threshold for each functioning (or capability, if it comes to older children) should be set at a level as high as it is already for the majority of children in welfare states. Let us explain this solution in more detail: the first assumption is that today's world is highly unjust and that children across the globe are hindered from developing and sustaining high levels in all important functionings. They die too young, they suffer from preventable diseases and they lack sufficient education as well as inclusion and political participation. We assume that this world could do a much better job and that its political, cultural, social and economic institutions could be designed and implemented in a much better way, reducing or even setting aside the inequalities between children – and between the countries they live in. We assume that all children in this world could reach the level of functioning reached by a majority of children in modern welfare states if the world just looked different. This is one main reason that we propose a universal threshold – it gives a clear picture of a world in which it is not enough that children in poorer countries are a little bit healthier than they are today, get a little more education and are a little less likely to be deprived of shelter, food and clean water. Doubtless, such a world would already constitute an improvement, but it is not one we should aspire to. The goal must be to improve the well-being and well-becoming of all children to a level that some children worldwide – and a majority of children in welfare states – enjoy today, simply because we can do it. We know that this account is connected to a very high level of sufficiency, one that is not even realized for all children in modern welfare states, but everything else seems too low. We do not strive for perfection with these thresholds either, and it should be clear enough that the level of well-being and well-becoming that the majority of children in welfare states enjoy (the best indication for a just threshold, in our view) are still far away from a maximum. In the first chapter, we have already dismissed a maximizing view in well-being and well-becoming for two reasons: first, it is too demanding on the side of those who are responsible for securing it for children, and second, it is highly unclear how such a maximum could be defined in the first place. Our threshold, instead, takes up a more realistic stance concerning what should be achieved; that it is already achieved for many children in many countries also counters the objection that such high thresholds are not feasible. If a few countries can do it, why should the whole world not be able to set up a much more inclusive welfare system, with social protection, education, health care and so on? Still, our approach leaves a lot of room for differentiation and different ways to realize justice for children. Here it is important not to mix thresholds of functionings with the conversion factors to achieve them. A threshold can, according to our account, take the form of enabling each and every child a comprehensive education that prepares them with the necessary skills and competencies to become active members of society, to make informed decisions and to be aware of the equal worth of all humans. This threshold has to be set in accordance with the levels of well-being and well-becoming currently achieved in modern welfare states and is, in this sense, not relative. It is oriented toward what is reasonably achievable and goes beyond typical capability theorists' rather relativist approaches. It is important to note, however, that we are dealing here with a threshold in terms of specified functionings – and so we argue for a universalist account (one adaptable through time and in general circumstances on a global level, though).

But the conversion factors to achieve this threshold can be very different. They can refer, for example, to a public school system that limits the role of private schools or to an active role by organizations and the early inclusion of children and adolescents in regional decision-making processes. Modern welfare states today show a wide range of such conversion factors, and it is often not clear which yields better results; it seems that there are always trade-offs to be considered and that a conversion factor that is highly beneficial to achieve one functioning has a slightly negative effect on a different functioning or that two conversion factors can come into conflict with each other. There is plenty of room for each society and state to design its own institutions. Such a universal threshold is also in line with what we did over the course of this book in regard to child poverty in welfare states and highly developed societies. Even within them, children in poverty fall short in comparison with their nonpoor peers and are contingently disadvantaged in many dimensions. These societies would be much more just if they enabled all children living within them to reach what is reached for the majority of children who are not poor.

The second question that seems crucial for a concept of global justice for children concerns attributing responsibilities. We have proposed a first systematization for children in welfare states, and the main difference to this in respect to global child poverty is probably the responsibility we can lay upon poor states and their institutions. Poorer countries, where child poverty is most severe and widespread, are much weaker than in the USA and European welfare states. These states have far less power and fewer opportunities to counteract child poverty in their countries, to secure justice for these children and allow them to achieve a sufficient level in each important functioning (Babb 2009; Williamson 2011). Most theorists of global justice acknowledge this inequality between states, especially the international political and economic order's role in producing and reproducing these inequalities, keeping poorer countries from developing and from building stronger social protection systems and achieving a higher level of welfare for their citizens.

> Poor countries need trade for development. They do not get fair trading opportunities under the WTO regime; but one that failed to sign up would find its trading opportunities even more severely curtailed. Any poor country is forced to decide about whether to sign up to the WTO rules against the background of other rules that it cannot escape and that make it extremely costly not to sign up. One such rule is, for instance, that the people and firms of poor countries may not freely offer their products and services to people in rich countries. This rule enables the rich countries to exact a price for whatever limited access to their markets they are prepared to grant. Part of this price is that the intellectual property rights of rich-country corporations must be respected and enforced. Poor-country governments must help collect rents for those corporations, thereby driving up the cost of pharmaceuticals and foodstuffs for their own populations. Paying this price makes sense perhaps for poor countries, given their calamitous circumstances. But this calamity is due to a rule that the rich countries impose unilaterally, without any consent by the poor. (Pogge 2007, 43)

This leads us to conclude that the responsibilities of the agents of justice in regard to global child poverty should be weighted differently and that the agents on the international and global level have a much higher responsibility, while the states high up on the list when it comes to child poverty in welfare states move down. They are to a substantial extent the victims of injustices themselves and have only limited options to move their citizens, adults as well as children, out of poverty. Still, these states share some responsibility and are obliged to do what is in their power to secure justice for children living in their societies and to adapt their cultural, social, political and economic institutions in such a way that they provide the necessary conversion factors to let all children achieve a just threshold in each important functioning. Poor states are partially responsible for their own situation, and justice demands that they try to alter and enhance their capacities to change. This also applies to the people living in these states. We see here an analogy between poor states and poor parents: even if they have responsibilities of justice, as David Miller (2007) argues, for example, as soon as they are not able to fulfill them adequately, a different agent of justice, in this case richer and more powerful states, has to substitute. It would be unjust to hold poor states responsible for the costs of children's suffering, because they cannot be said to be responsible.

Furthermore, in the global context, some of our endorsed considerations on the sufficiency principle gain additional force (see Chapter 1). We urged an interpretation of the sufficiency principle combining a demand-side view with a supply-side view, claiming that those in privileged positions must give sufficient attention to inequalities in the distribution of functionings and capabilities. The meaning of 'sufficient attention' however, depends in large part on how urgent the needs of the 'demand side' are; that is, the people who are suffering. In addition, we presented a priority view consisting of three elements for tackling functionings. It asks how important a functioning is, how severe and widespread its deprivation, and what is needed to overcome the deprivation in this dimension. From these considerations it follows that alleviation of global child poverty is even more urgent than alleviation of child poverty in welfare states. Again, this diagnosis must not lead to the conclusion that relative child poverty is nothing to worry about. It is evident that global poverty (a) jeopardizes even children's most basic functionings (in fact it often leads to death), (b) exists to an extremely high degree and (c) can be alleviated considerably by relatively small changes to the global order. It therefore triggers strong claims of responsibilities on the supply side.

This brings us to a further group of agents that are assumed to have different kinds of responsibilities for global child poverty in respect to child poverty in welfare states: other persons in the global community of humans. We gave these agents of justice a rather low ranking in regard to child poverty in welfare states because most members have only limited capacities to change something and have only limited responsibility for the existence of child poverty. We took into account that the majority of agents in this global community are themselves poor or have a low status of well-being because they live in poorer countries. This is still true in the case of global child poverty, but nonetheless, many agents in the global community, people who live in welfare states, who are therefore much richer and have much more resources, can make a real difference. If a middle-class adult in a welfare state adopts a poor child from another welfare state, this child's situation will probably improve; this improvement, however, has to be weighed against possible harms; for example, when a child is removed from her biological parents and has to move to another country or the burden that is put upon the parent-to-be. In the case of global child poverty, our skepticism regarding a responsibility that can be translated into a duty to adopt poor children without sufficient means seems less reasonable. Daniel Friedrich has recently defended such a duty to adopt (Friedrich 2013); as applied to the case of child poverty, it is true that moving a child likely to die or suffer severely over her whole life in her home country – perhaps even against her will and the will of her parents – to a middle-class parent or family in a welfare state would certainly improve her condition to such an extent that our counterarguments become less valid. This implies that there might indeed be such a duty to adopt, maybe with some caveats; for example, that this duty apply only to those who wish to have children in the first place or only as long as child poverty is as severe as it is now.

We note again that a concept of global justice for children should also make use of an ecological approach, such as the one proposed, and differentiate between different agents and their responsibilities. This implies giving the poor themselves and poor children, as they reach a certain level of competencies and maturity, a role in the alleviation of poverty and in the design and implementation of measures of justice (Deveaux 2013). Reasons for doing so are not limited to the fact that the poor have a right to be heard and included in decisions affecting them; there are also pragmatic reasons built on the knowledge that measures that take the poor seriously and are developed on the basis of real knowledge about them and their situation work better. Besides, taking the agency of the poor seriously is empowering (Drydyk 2013). This aspect of participation and empowerment of poor people is both relevant for global (child) poverty as it is for (child) poverty as it typically occurs in welfare states. In both contexts the poverty knowledge of poor people and their interest in overcoming their poverty and their children's give them, as we argued in Chapter 3, certain responsibilities, albeit limited ones, for action against child poverty. However, there is a relevant difference to be noted, too. The severe poverty of the global poor and their typically very limited scope of action leads to the conclusion that they have almost no responsibility toward poor children living in welfare states. On the contrary, it makes sense to assert that poor people in welfare states have certain responsibilities toward poor children in developing countries or failed states. They profit, albeit to a smaller degree than many of their fellow countrymen, from an unjust global order and often they contribute with their consumption, at least to some degree, to the upholding of structural injustices on a global level. It therefore makes sense to think about their relationship to poor children on a global level in terms of responsibilities and to call upon them to rethink their actions and behaviors in some aspects, as is generally done for members of affluent states. Naturally, the kinds and weights of responsibilities of agents within these societies differ; application of the grounds for attributing responsibilities that we identified in Chapter 3 will lead to the conclusion that generally the responsibilities of poor people in affluent societies toward the global poor are low compared with those of their rich and powerful fellow countrymen. However, they should not be completely ignored.

4.1 Conclusions

In this section, we have given some ideas how our critical theory of child poverty, which we developed first and foremost for modern welfare states in affluent societies, can be extended to the global level. We have defended the view that it is important to aim for relatively high thresholds in the most important functionings (and capabilities, if applicable) for children, independent from where they happen to be born. The basic commitment of the capability approach to show equal concern and respect for every human being points, in our interpretation, clearly toward this goal. It does not seem fair to apply different standards for well-being and well-becoming based on completely arbitrary features, and a reasonable point of reference seems to be provided by what has been already achieved for most children in welfare states. We are aware that this goal is, in practice, hard to achieve and often changes and that improvements have to be implemented pragmatically and in small steps. Still, a normative concept of justice should also open up horizons that are worth aspiring to. For this, it is not necessary to develop a transcendental theory of justice that tries to fully specify the concept in all details (Sen 2009). It is enough to work with the realistic and rather simple conception of justice we have developed in this book.

We acknowledge that what we have discussed here about a global concept of justice for children is just preliminary and is insufficient in many aspects. Capability theorists need to do more work to specify the functionings and capabilities children are entitled to and how the thresholds for each of them should be set. Our solution needs to be scrutinized in more detail to be proven a viable alternative to the most common strategy of using different thresholds in different nations, which we dismissed. Our examination of the attribution of responsibilities to different agents of justice is also just a first dip into a much wider issue. Nonetheless, we have argued that such an expansion of justice from the domestic to the global level is needed and that this demands aiming high and not being satisfied with making the lives of children in poverty just a little less harmful and deprived but making real progress. The fact that hundreds of millions of children are born into circumstances where even the most basic goods are missing and where it is just not possible for them to have a minimally decent life is surely not their fault and can never justify claiming less for them than what we claim for children who had the luck to be born in a welfare state. As a matter of justice, each and every child matters the same and has the same entitlements.

Except where otherwise noted, this work is licensed under a Creative Commons Attribution 3.0 Unported License. To view a copy of this license, visit http://creativecommons.org/licenses/by/3.0/

References

Adams, Harry William. 2008. *Justice for Children: Autonomy Development and the State*. 1st ed. Albany: State University of New York Press.
Addison, Tony, David Hulme, and Ravi Kanbur, eds. 2009. *Poverty Dynamics: Interdisciplinary Perspectives*. 1st ed. Oxford/New York: Oxford University Press.
Alanen, Leena, and Berry Mayall. 2001. *Conceptualizing Child-Adult Relations*. London/New York: Routledge/Falmer.
Alcock, Pete. 2006. *Understanding Poverty*. 3rd ed. Basingstoke: Palgrave Macmillan.
Alkire, Sabina. 2002. *Valuing Freedoms: Sen's Capability Approach and Poverty Reduction*. 1st ed. Oxford/New York: Oxford University Press.
Alkire, Sabina, and José Manuel Roche. 2012. "Beyond Headcount: Measures That Reflect the Breadth and Components of Child Poverty." In *Global Child Poverty and Well-Being*, edited by Alberto Minujin and Shailen Nandy, 1st ed., 103–133. Bristol: Policy Press.
Alstott, Anne. 2004. *No Exit: What Parents Owe Their Children and What Society Owes Parents*. 1st ed. Oxford/New York: Oxford University Press.
Amerijckx, Gaëlle, and Perrine Claire Humblet. 2014. "Child Well-Being: What Does It Mean?" *Children and Society* 28 (5): 404–415. doi:10.1111/chso.12003.
Anderson, Elizabeth. 1999. "What Is the Point of Equality?" *Ethics* 102 (2): 287–337.
———. 2010. "Justifying the Capability Approach to Justice." In *Measuring Justice: Primary Goods and Capabilities*, edited by Harry Brighouse and Ingrid Robeyns, 1st ed., 81–100. Cambridge/New York: Cambridge University Press.
Anderson, Joel, and Rutger Claassen. 2012. "Sailing Alone: Teenage Autonomy and Regimes of Childhood." *Law and Philosophy* 31 (5): 495–522. doi:10.1007/s10982-012-9130-9.
Archard, David. 2003. *Children, Family, and the State*. 1st ed. Live Questions in Ethics and Moral Philosophy. Aldershot/Burlington: Ashgate.
———. 2004. *Children: Rights and Childhood*. 2nd ed. London/New York: Routledge.
———. 2010. *The Family: A Liberal Defence*. Basingstoke/New York: Palgrave Macmillan.
Archard, David, and Colin M. Macleod, eds. 2002. *The Moral and Political Status of Children*. 1st ed. Oxford/New York: Oxford University Press.
Archard, David, and Marit Skivenes. 2009. "Balancing a Child's Best Interests and a Child's Views." *International Journal of Children's Rights* 17 (1): 1–21. doi:10.1163/157181808X358276.
Arndt, Christian, and Jürgen Volkert. 2006. "Amartya Sens Capability-Approach – ein neues Konzept der deutschen Armuts- und Reichtumsberichterstattung." *Vierteljahrshefte zur Wirtschaftsforschung* 75 (1): 7–29. doi:10.3790/vjh.75.1.7.
Arneson, Richard. 2006. "Distributive Justice and Basic Capability Equality: 'Good Enough' Is Not Good Enough." In *Capabilities Equality: Basic Issues and*

Problems, edited by Alexander Kaufman, 17–43. Routledge Innovations in Political Theory 18. London/New York: Routledge.

Arneson, Richard, and Ian Shapiro. 1996. "Democratic Autonomy and Religious Freedom: A Critique of Wisconsin v. Yoder." In *Political Order*, edited by Ian Shapiro and Russell Hardin. Vol. 38. Nomos. New York/London: New York University Press.

Atkinson, Anthony B., and Eric Marlier, eds. 2010. *Income and Living Conditions in Europe*. 1st ed. Eurostat Statistical Books. Luxembourg: Publications Office of the European Union. http://ec.europa.eu/eurostat/en/web/products-statistical-books/-/KS-31-10-555 (last accessed on January 27, 2015).

Attree, Pamela. 2004. "Growing Up in Disadvantage: A Systematic Review of the Qualitative Evidence." *Child: Care, Health and Development* 30 (6): 679–689. doi:10.1111/j.1365-2214.2004.00480.x.

———. 2006. "The Social Costs of Child Poverty: A Systematic Review of the Qualitative Evidence." *Children and Society* 20 (1): 54–66. doi:10.1002/chi.854.

Auwarter, Amy E., and Mara S. Aruguete. 2008. "Effects of Student Gender and Socioeconomic Status on Teacher Perceptions." *Journal of Educational Research* 101 (4): 242–246. doi:10.3200/JOER.101.4.243-246.

Ayton, Agnes, Hufrize Rasool, and David Cottrell. 2003. "Deliberate Self-Harm in Children and Adolescents: Association with Social Deprivation." *European Child and Adolescent Psychiatry* 12 (6): 303–307. doi:10.1007/s00787-003-0344-0.

Babb, Sarah L. 2009. *Behind the Development Banks: Washington Politics, World Poverty, and the Wealth of Nations*. 1st ed. Chicago, IL: University of Chicago Press.

Bagattini, Alexander. 2014. "Child Well-Being: A Philosophical Perspective." In *Handbook of Child Well-Being: Theory, Indicators, Measures and Policies*, edited by Asher Ben-Arieh, Ferran Casas, Ivar Frønes and Jill E. Korbin, 1st ed., 163–186. Dordrecht/New York: Springer.

Ballet, Jérôme, Mario Biggeri, and Flavio Comim. 2011. "Children's Agency and the Capability Approach: A Conceptual Framework." In *Children and the Capability Approach*, edited by Mario Biggeri, Jérôme Ballet, and Flavio Comim, 1st ed., 22–45. Basingstoke/New York: Palgrave Macmillan.

Barnett, Melissa A. 2008. "Economic Disadvantage in Complex Family Systems: Expansion of Family Stress Models." *Clinical Child and Family Psychology Review* 11 (3): 145–161. doi:10.1007/s10567-008-0034-z.

Bassuk, Ellen L. 2010. "Ending Child Homelessness in America." *American Journal of Orthopsychiatry* 80 (4): 496–504. doi:10.1111/j.1939-0025.2010.01052.x.

Ben-Arieh, Asher. 2010. "Developing Indicators for Child Well-Being in a Changing Context." In *Child Well-Being: Understanding Children's Lives*, edited by Wendy Rose and Colette McAuley, 129–142. London/Philadelphia: Jessica Kingsley Publishers.

Beresford, Peter, David Green, Ruth Lister, and Kirsty Woodward. 1999. *Poverty First Hand: Poor People Speak for Themselves*. 1st ed. London: Child Poverty Action Group.

Berger, Rachel P., Janet B. Fromkin, Haley Stutz, Kathi Makoroff, Philip V. Scribano, Kenneth Feldman, Li Chuan Tu, and Anthony Fabio. 2011. "Abusive Head Trauma during a Time of Increased Unemployment: A Multicenter Analysis." *Pediatrics* 128 (4): 637–643. doi:10.1542/peds.2010-2185.

Besharov, Douglas J., and Lisa Laumann. 1997. "Don't Call It Child Abuse If It's Really Poverty." *Journal of Children and Poverty* 3 (1): 5–36, 10.1080/10796129708412203.
Biggeri, Mario. 2003. *Capability Approach and Child Well-Being*. Studi e Discussioni, no. 141. Dipartimento di Scienze Economiche, Università degli Studi di Firenze: Scienze Economiche, Università degli Studi di Firenze.
Biggeri, Mario, Jérôme Ballet, and Flavio Comim, eds. 2011. *Children and the Capability Approach*. 1st ed. Basingstoke/New York: Palgrave Macmillan.
Biggeri, Mario, and Renato Libanora. 2011. "From Valuing to Evaluating: Tools and Procedures to Operationalize the Capability Approach." In *Children and the Capability Approach*, edited by Mario Biggeri, Jérôme Ballet, and Flavio Comim, 79–106. Basingstoke: Palgrave Macmillan.
Biggeri, Mario, and Santosh Mehrotra. 2011. "Child Poverty as Capability Deprivation: How to Choose Domains of Child Well-Being and Poverty." In *Children and the Capability Approach*, edited by Mario Biggeri, Jérôme Ballet, and Flavio Comim, 1st ed., 46–75. Basingstoke/New York: Palgrave Macmillan.
Biggeri, Mario, and Marina Santi. 2012. "The Missing Dimensions of Children's Well-Being and Well-Becoming in Education Systems: Capabilities and Philosophy for Children." *Journal of Human Development and Capabilities* 13 (3): 373–395. doi:10.1080/19452829.2012.694858.
Biggeri, Mario, Jean-François Trani, and Vincenzo Mauro. 2010. *The Multidimensionality of Child Poverty: An Empirical Investigation on Children of Afghanistan*. OPHI Research in Progress. Oxford: Oxford Poverty and Human Development Initiative. www.ophi.org.uk/wp-content/uploads/OPHI-RP19a.pdf (last accessed January 27, 2015).
Bostock, Lisa. 2002. "'God, She's Gonna Report Me': The Ethics of Child Protection in Poverty Research." *Children and Society* 16 (4): 273–283. doi:10.1002/chi.712.
Bowring, Finn. 2000. "Social Exclusion: Limitations of the Debate." *Critical Social Policy* 20 (3): 307–330. doi:10.1177/026101830002000303.
Braveman, Paula, Susan Egerter, and David R. Williams. 2011. "The Social Determinants of Health: Coming of Age." *Annual Review of Public Health* 32 (April): 381–398. doi:10.1146/annurev-publhealth-031210-101218.
Brennan, Samantha, and Robert Noggle. 1997. "The Moral Status of Children: Children's Rights, Parent's Rights, and Family Justice." *Social Theory and Practice* 23 (1): 1–26, 10.5840/soctheorpract19972311.
———, eds. 2007. *Taking Responsibility for Children*. 1st ed. Studies in Childhood and Family in Canada. Waterloo: Wilfrid Laurier University Press.
Brighouse, Harry. 2003. "How Should Children Be Heard?" *Arizona Law Review* 45 (3): 691–711.
Brighouse, Harry, and Adam Swift. 2006. "Parents' Rights and the Value of the Family." *Ethics* 117 (1): 80–108. doi:10.1086/508034.
Brock, Gillian, and Darrel Moellendorf, eds. 2005. *Current Debates in Global Justice*. 1st ed. Studies in Global Justice 2. Dordrecht: Springer.
Brock, Karen. 1999. *It's Not Only Wealth That Matters – It's Peace of Mind Too: A Review of Participatory Work on Poverty and Ill-Being*. Washington, DC: World Bank.
Bronfenbrenner, Urie. 1979. *The Ecology of Human Development: Experiments by Nature and Design*. Cambridge: Harvard University Press.

Bronfenbrenner, Urie, and Pamela A. Morris. 2007. "The Bioecological Model of Human Development." In *Handbook of Child Psychology*. Vol. 1: *Theoretical Models of Human Development*, edited by William Damon and Richard M. Lerner, 6th ed., 793–828. Hoboken: Wiley.
Bugental, Daphne Blunt, and Joan E. Grusex. 2007. "Socialization." In *Handbook of Child Psychology*. Vol. 3: *Social, Emotional, and Personality Development*, edited by William Damon and Richard M. Lerner, 6th ed., 366–428. Hoboken: Wiley.
Burchardt, Tania, Julien Le Grand, and David Piachaud. 2002. "Degrees of Exclusion: Developing a Dynamic, Multidimensional Measure." In *Understanding Social Exclusion*, edited by John Hills, Julian Le Grand, and David Piachaud, 1st ed., 30–43. Oxford: Oxford University Press.
Burchardt, Tania, and Polly Vizard. 2011. "'Operationalizing' the Capability Approach as a Basis for Equality and Human Rights Monitoring in Twenty-First-Century Britain." *Journal of Human Development and Capabilities* 12 (1): 91–119. doi:10.1080/19452829.2011.541790.
Butt, Daniel. 2014. "'A Doctrine Quite New and Altogether Untenable': Defending the Beneficiary Pays Principle." *Journal of Applied Philosophy* 31(4): 336–348. doi:10.1111/japp.12073.
Cabezas, Mar, Gunter Graf, and Gottfried Schweiger. 2014. "Health, Justice, and Happiness during Childhood." *South African Journal of Philosophy* 33(4): 501–511. doi: 10.1080/02580136.2014.967593.
Camfield, Laura, Martin Woodhead, and Natalia Streuli. 2009. "What's the Use of 'Well-Being' in Contexts of Child Poverty? Approaches to Research, Monitoring and Children's Participation." *International Journal of Children's Rights* 17 (1): 65–109. doi:10.1163/157181808X357330.
Casal, Paula. 2007. "Why Sufficiency Is Not Enough." *Ethics* 117 (2): 296–326. doi: 10.1086/510692.
Casal, Paula, and Andrew Williams. 2004. "Equality of Resources and Procreative Justice." In *Dworkin and His Critics*, edited by Justine Burley, 150–169. Malden: Blackwell.
Cattell, Vicky. 2001. "Poor People, Poor Places, and Poor Health: The Mediating Role of Social Networks and Social Capital." *Social Science and Medicine* 52 (10): 1501–1516. doi:10.1016/S0277-9536(00)00259-8.
Chambers, Robert. 1997. *Whose Reality Counts? Putting the First Last*. 1st ed. London: Intermediate Technology.
———. 2007. *Poverty Research: Methodologies, Mindsets and Multidimensionality*. http://www.ids.ac.uk/files/Wp293.pdf (last accessed January 27, 2015).
———. 2008. "Participation, Pluralism and Perceptions of Poverty." In *The Many Dimensions of Poverty*, edited by Nanak Kakwani and Jacques Silber, 1st ed., 140–164. Basingstoke/New York: Palgrave Macmillan.
Ciula, Raffaele, and Curtis Skinner. 2014. "Income and Beyond: Taking the Measure of Child Deprivation in the United States." *Child Indicators Research*, May. doi:10.1007/s12187-014-9246-6.
Comim, Flavio, Mozaffar Qizilbash, and Sabina Alkire, eds. 2008. *The Capability Approach: Concepts, Measures and Applications*. 1st ed. Cambridge/New York: Cambridge University Press.
Conrad, David, and Simon Capewell. 2012. "Associations between Deprivation and Rates of Childhood Overweight and Obesity in England, 2007–2010: An

Ecological Study." *BMJ Open* 2 (2): e000463–e000463. doi:10.1136/bmjopen-2011-000463.
Cowden, Mhairi. 2012. "What's Love Got to Do with It? Why a Child Does Not Have a Right to Be Loved." *Critical Review of International Social and Political Philosophy* 15 (3): 325–345. doi:10.1080/13698230.2011.572426.
Craig, David, and Doug Porter. 2006. *Development beyond Neoliberalism? Governance, Poverty Reduction, and Political Economy*. 1st ed. London/New York: Routledge.
Crocker, David. 2008. *Ethics of Global Development: Agency, Capability, and Deliberative Democracy*. Cambridge/New York: Cambridge University Press.
Currie, J., and C. Spatz Widom. 2010. "Long-Term Consequences of Child Abuse and Neglect on Adult Economic Well-Being." *Child Maltreatment* 15 (2): 111–120. doi:10.1177/1077559509355316.
Daly, Martin, and Margo Wilson. 1999. *The Truth about Cinderella: A Darwinian View of Parental Love*. 1st ed. Darwinism Today. New Haven: Yale University Press.
DeNavas-Walt, Carmen, and Bernadette D. Proctor. 2014. *Income and Poverty in the United States: 2013*. P60-249. Current Population Reports. Washington, DC: United States Census Bureau. www.census.gov/content/dam/Census/library/publications/2014/demo/p60-249.pdf (last accessed January 27, 2015).
Deneulin, Séverine, and Lila Shahani, eds. 2009. *An Introduction to the Human Development and Capability Approach: Freedom and Agency*. 1st ed. London/Sterling/Ottawa: Earthscan/International Development Research Centre.
Deveaux, Monique. 2013. "The Global Poor as Agents of Justice." *Journal of Moral Philosophy*, 1–25. http://booksandjournals.brillonline.com/content/journals/10.1163/17455243-468102
Dixon, Rosalind, and Martha Nussbaum. 2012. "Children's Rights and a Capabilities Approach: The Question of Special Priority." *Chicago Public Law and Legal Theory Working Paper*, no. 384. http://papers.ssrn.com/sol3/papers.cfm?abstract_id=2060614.
Drydyk, Jay. 2013. "Empowerment, Agency, and Power." *Journal of Global Ethics* 9 (3): 249–262. doi:10.1080/17449626.2013.818374.
Dunkel Schetter, Christine, and Marci Lobel. 2011. "Pregnancy and Birth Outcomes: A Multi-level Analysis of Prenatal Maternal Stress and Birth Weight." In *Handbook of Health Psychology, Second Edition*, 1st ed., 431–463. New York: Psychology Press.
Durrant, Joan, and Ron Ensom. 2012. "Physical Punishment of Children: Lessons from 20 Years of Research." *Canadian Medical Association Journal* 184 (12): 1373–1377. doi:10.1503/cmaj.101314.
Dworkin, Ronald. 2000. *Sovereign Virtue: The Theory and Practice of Equality*. Cambridge: Harvard University Press.
———. 2002. "Sovereign Virtue Revisited." *Ethics* 113 (1): 106–143. doi:10.1086/341579.
Eamon, Mary Keegan. 2001. "The Effects of Poverty on Children's Socioemotional Development: An Ecological Systems Analysis." *Social Work* 46 (3): 256–266. doi:10.1093/sw/46.3.256.
———. 2002. "Poverty, Parenting, Peer, and Neighborhood Influences on Young Adolescent Antisocial Behavior." *Journal of Social Service Research* 28 (1): 1–23. doi:10.1300/J079v28n01_01.

Edwards, Janice Berry, Maria Gomes, and Monique A. Major. 2013. "The Charged Economic Environment: Its Role in Parental Psychological Distress and Development of Children, Adolescents, and Young Adults." *Journal of Human Behavior in the Social Environment* 23 (2): 256–266. doi:10.1080/10911359.2013.747350.

Elder, Glen H., Tri Van Nguyen, and Avshalom Caspi. 1985. "Linking Family Hardship to Children's Lives." *Child Development* 56 (2): 361–375.

Elliott, Richard, and Clare Leonard. 2004. "Peer Pressure and Poverty: Exploring Fashion Brands and Consumption Symbolism among Children of the 'British Poor.'" *Journal of Consumer Behaviour* 3 (4): 347–359. doi:10.1002/cb.147.

England, Paula. 2005. "Gender Inequality in Labor Markets: The Role of Motherhood and Segregation." *Social Politics: International Studies in Gender, State and Society* 12 (2): 264–288. doi:10.1093/sp/jxi014.

Engle, Patrice L., and Maureen M. Black. 2008. "The Effect of Poverty on Child Development and Educational Outcomes." *Annals of the New York Academy of Sciences* 1136 (1): 243–256. doi:10.1196/annals.1425.023.

Ereshefsky, Marc. 2009. "Defining 'Health' and 'Disease.'" *Studies in the History and Philosophy of Biology and Biomedical Sciences* 40: 221–227.

European Observatory on Homelessness. 2007. *Child Homelessness in Europe – an Overview of Emerging Trends*. Belgium: European Federation of National Organisations Working with the Homeless. http://feantsa.org/spip.php?rubrique171&lang=en (last accessed January 27, 2015).

Evans, Gary W., and Rochelle C. Cassells. 2014. "Childhood Poverty, Cumulative Risk Exposure, and Mental Health in Emerging Adults." *Clinical Psychological Science* 2 (3): 287–296. doi:10.1177/2167702613501496.

Fantuzzo, John W., Whitney A. LeBoeuf, Chin-Chih Chen, Heather L. Rouse, and Dennis P. Culhane. 2012. "The Unique and Combined Effects of Homelessness and School Mobility on the Educational Outcomes of Young Children." *Educational Researcher* 41 (9): 393–402. doi:10.3102/0013189X12468210.

Fazel, Mina, Ruth V. Reed, Catherine Panter-Brick, and Alan Stein. 2012. "Mental Health of Displaced and Refugee Children Resettled in High-Income Countries: Risk and Protective Factors." *Lancet* 379 (9812): 266–282. doi:10.1016/S0140-6736(11)60051-2.

Feinberg, Joel. 1980. "A Child's Right to an Open Future." In *Whose Child? Parental Rights, Parental Authority and State Power*, edited by Hugh LaFollette and William Aiken, 1st ed., 124–153. Totowa: Littlefield, Adams, and Co.

Ferguson, H., S. Bovaird, and M. Mueller. 2007. "The Impact of Poverty on Educational Outcomes for Children." *Paediatrics and Child Health* 12 (8): 701–706.

Fiscella, K., and H. Kitzman. 2009. "Disparities in Academic Achievement and Health: The Intersection of Child Education and Health Policy." *Pediatrics* 123 (3): 1073–1080. doi:10.1542/peds.2008–0533.

Fisher, Gordon M. 2002. *The Development of the Orshansky Poverty Thresholds and Their Subsequent History as the Official U.S. Poverty Measure*. Washington, DC: United States Census Bureau. https://www.census.gov/hhes/povmeas/publications/orshansky.html (last accessed January 27, 2015).

Franklin-Hall, Andrew. 2013. "On Becoming an Adult: Autonomy and the Moral Relevance of Life's Stages." *Philosophical Quarterly* 63 (251): 223–247. doi:10.1111/1467–9213.12014.

Friedrich, Daniel. 2013. "A Duty to Adopt?" *Journal of Applied Philosophy* 30 (1): 25–39. doi:10.1111/japp.12003.

Fusco, Alessio, Anne-Catherine Guio, and Eric Marlier. 2013. "Building a Material Deprivation Index in a Multinational Context: Lessons from the EU Experience." In *Poverty and Social Exclusion around the Mediterranean Sea*, edited by Valerie Berenger and Florent Bresson, 1st ed., 43–71. Boston: Springer. doi: 10.1007/978-1-4614-5263-8_2.

Gaisbauer, Helmut P., Gottfried Schweiger, and Clemens Sedmak. 2013. "Ethical Obligations of Wealthy People: Progressive Taxation and the Financial Crisis." *Ethics and Social Welfare* 7 (2): 141–154. doi:10.1080/17496535.2013.779003.

Gallie, Duncan, Serge Paugam, and Sheila Jacobs. 2003. "Unemployment, Poverty and Social Exclusion: Is There a Vicious Circle of Social Exclusion?" *European Societies* 5 (1): 1–32. doi:10.1080/1461669032000057668.

Galobardes, Bruna, John W. Lynch, and George Davey Smith. 2004. "Childhood Socioeconomic Circumstances and Cause-Specific Mortality in Adulthood: Systematic Review and Interpretation." *Epidemiologic Reviews* 26 (1): 7–21. doi:10.1093/epirev/mxh008.

Gardner, William. 2015. "The Developmental Capability Model of Child-Well-Being." In *The Well-Being of Children: Philosophical and Social Scientific Approaches*, edited by Gunter Graf and Gottfried Schweiger, 50–66. Berlin: DeGruyter.

Gasper, Des. 2006. "Cosmopolitan Presumptions? On Martha Nussbaum and Her Commentators." *Development and Change* 37 (6): 1227–1246. doi:10.1111/j.1467-7660.2006.00520.x.

George, Rolf. 1987. "Who Should Bear the Cost of Children?" *Public Affairs Quarterly* 1: 1–42.

Gilbert, Ruth, Cathy Spatz Widom, Kevin Browne, David Fergusson, Elspeth Webb, and Staffan Janson. 2009. "Burden and Consequences of Child Maltreatment in High-Income Countries." *Lancet* 373 (January): 68–81. doi:10.1016/S0140-6736(08)61706-7.

Gilman, Stephen E., Ichiro Kawachi, Garrett M. Fitzmaurice, and Stephen L. Buka. 2002. "Socioeconomic Status in Childhood and the Lifetime Risk of Major Depression." *International Journal of Epidemiology* 31 (2): 359–367. doi: 10.1093/ije/31.2.359.

Goodman, Lisa A., Katya Fels Smyth, Angela M. Borges, and Rachel Singer. 2009. "When Crises Collide: How Intimate Partner Violence and Poverty Intersect to Shape Women's Mental Health and Coping?" *Trauma, Violence and Abuse* 10 (4): 306–329. doi:10.1177/1524838009339754.

Graf, Gunter. 2015. "Conceptions of Childhood, Agency, and the Well-Being of Children." In *The Well-Being of Children: Philosophical and Social Scientific Approaches*, edited by Gunter Graf and Gottfried Schweiger, 1st ed, 2–15. Berlin: DeGruyter.

Graf, Gunter, and Gottfried Schweiger, eds. 2015. *The Well-Being of Children: Philosophical and Social Scientific Approaches*. 1st ed. Berlin: DeGruyter.

———. 2014. "Poverty and Freedom." *Human Affairs* 24 (2): 258–268. doi:10.2478/s13374-014-0224-y.

Guio, Anne-Catherine, David Gordon, and Eric Marlier. 2012. *Measuring Material Deprivation in the EU: Indicators for the Whole Population and Child-Specific Indicators*. Eurostat Methodologies and Working Papers. Luxembourg: Office for Official Publications of the European Communities. http://ec.europa.eu/

eurostat/de/web/products-statistical-working-papers/-/KS-RA-12–018 (last accessed January 27, 2015).

Hart, Caroline, Bernhard Babic, and Mario Biggeri, eds. 2014. *Agency and Participation in Childhood and Youth: International Applications of the Capability Approach in Schools and Beyond.* 1st ed. New York: Bloomsbury Academic.

Hertzman, Clyde, and Tom Boyce. 2010. "How Experience Gets under the Skin to Create Gradients in Developmental Health." *Annual Review of Public Health* 31 (1): 329–347. doi:10.1146/annurev.publhealth.012809.103538.

Hertzman, Clyde, and Chris Power. 2003. "Health and Human Development: Understandings from Life-Course Research." *Developmental Neuropsychology* 24 (2–3): 719–744. doi:10.1080/87565641.2003.9651917.

Hertzman, Clyde, Arjumand Siddiqi, Emily Hertzman, Lori G. Irwin, Ziba Vaghri, Tanja A. J. Houweling, Ruth Bell, Alfredo Tinajero, and Michael Marmot. 2010. "Bucking the Inequality Gradient through Early Child Development." *BMJ* 340: c468. doi: 10.1136/bmj.c468.

Hodes, Matthew. 2000. "Psychologically Distressed Refugee Children in the United Kingdom." *Child Psychology and Psychiatry Review* 5 (2): 57–68.

Holzer, Harry J., Diane Whitmore Schanzenbach, Greg J. Duncan, and Jens Ludwig. 2008. "The Economic Costs of Childhood Poverty in the United States." *Journal of Children and Poverty* 14 (1): 41–61. doi:10.1080/10796120701871280.

Horgan, Goretti. 2009. "'That Child Is Smart Because He's Rich': The Impact of Poverty on Young Children's Experiences of School." *International Journal of Inclusive Education* 13 (4): 359–376. doi:10.1080/13603110802707779.

Hulme, David. 2004. "Thinking 'Small' and the Understanding of Poverty: Maymana and Mofizul's Story." *Journal of Human Development* 5 (2): 161–176. doi:10.1080/1464988042000225104.

Jack, Gordon. 1997. "An Ecological Approach to Social Work with Children and Families." *Child and Family Social Work* 2 (2): 109–120. doi:10.1046/j.1365-2206.1997.00045.x.

Jahoda, Marie. 1981. "Work, Employment, and Unemployment: Values, Theories, and Approaches in Social Research." *American Psychologist* 36: 184–191.

———. 1982. *Employment and Unemployment: A Social-Psychological Analysis.* 1st ed. Cambridge/New York: Cambridge University Press.

Johnson, Fiona, Michelle Pratt, and Jane Wardle. 2011. "Socio-Economic Status and Obesity in Childhood." In *Epidemiology of Obesity in Children and Adolescents: Prevalence and Etiology,* edited by Luis A. Moreno, Iris Pigeot, and Wolfgang Ahrens, 1st ed., 377–390. New York: Springer. www.springerlink.com/index/10.1007/978-1-4419-6039-9_21.

Kahn, Alfred J., and Sheila B. Kamerman, eds. 2002. *Beyond Child Poverty: The Social Exclusion of Children.* 1st ed. New York: Institute for Child and Family Policy at Columbia University.

Kay, E., M. Tisdall, John M. Davis, Malcolm Hill and Alan Prout, eds. 2006. *Children, Young People and Social Inclusion: Participation for What?* 1st ed. Bristol: Policy Press.

Kelleher, J. Paul. 2013. "Capabilities versus Resources." *Journal of Moral Philosophy,* http://booksandjournals.brillonline.com/content/journals/10.1163/17455243-4681031.

Khader, Serene J. 2011. *Adaptive Preferences and Women's Empowerment.* 1st ed. Oxford/New York: Oxford University Press.

Kim, Pilyoung, Gary W. Evans, Michael Angstadt, S. Shaun Ho, Chandra S. Sripada, James E. Swain, Israel Liberzon, and K. Luan Phan. 2013. "Effects of Childhood Poverty and Chronic Stress on Emotion Regulatory Brain Function in Adulthood." *Proceedings of the National Academy of Sciences*, October, 1–6. doi:10.1073/pnas.1308240110.

Kingdon, Geeta Gandhi, and John Knight. 2006. "Subjective Well-Being Poverty vs. Income Poverty and Capabilities Poverty?" *Journal of Development Studies* 42 (7): 1199–1224. doi:10.1080/00220380600884167.

Kohli, Martin. 2007. "The Institutionalization of the Life Course: Looking Back to Look Ahead." *Research in Human Development* 4 (3–4): 253–271. doi:10.1080/15427600701663122.

Ladd, Helen F. 2012. "Education and Poverty: Confronting the Evidence." *Journal of Policy Analysis and Management* 31 (2): 203–227. doi:10.1002/pam.21615.

Landrigan, Philip J., and Lynn R. Goldman. 2011. "Children's Vulnerability to Toxic Chemicals: A Challenge and Opportunity to Strengthen Health and Environmental Policy." *Health Affairs* 30 (5): 842–850. doi:10.1377/hlthaff.2011.0151.

Lanius, Ruth A., Eric Vermetten, and Clare Pain, eds. 2010. *The Impact of Early Life Trauma on Health and Disease: The Hidden Epidemic*. Cambridge/New York: Cambridge University Press.

Lansdown, Gerison, and UNICEF Innocenti Research Centre. 2001. *Promoting Children's Participation in Democratic Decision-Making*. Florence: UNICEF International Child Development Centre. http://www.unicef-irc.org/publications/pdf/insight6.pdf (last accessed January 27, 2015)

Laplante, David P., Ronald G. Barr, Alain Brunet, Guillaume Galbaud du Fort, Michael L. Meaney, Jean-François Saucier, Philip R. Zelazo, and Suzanne King. 2004. "Stress during Pregnancy Affects General Intellectual and Language Functioning in Human Toddlers." *Pediatric Research* 56 (3): 400–410. doi:10.1203/01.PDR.0000136281.34035.44.

Lawrence, Catherine R., Elizabeth A. Carlson, and Byron Egeland. 2006. "The Impact of Foster Care on Development." *Development and Psychopathology* 18 (01): 57–76. doi:10.1017/S0954579406060044.

Leask, Phil. 2013. "Losing Trust in the World: Humiliation and Its Consequences." *Psychodynamic Practice* 19 (2): 129–142. doi:10.1080/14753634.2013.778485.

Lee, Nick. 2001. *Childhood and Society: Growing Up in an Age of Uncertainty*. Buckingham, UK/Philadelphia: Open University Press.

Levine, James A. 2011. "Poverty and Obesity in the U.S." *Diabetes* 60 (11): 2667–2668. doi:10.2337/db11-1118.

Liao, S. Matthew. 2006. "The Right of Children to Be Loved." *Journal of Political Philosophy* 14 (4): 420–440. doi:10.1111/j.1467-9760.2006.00262.x.

Lindner, Evelin Gerda. 2007. "In Times of Globalization and Human Rights: Does Humiliation Become the Most Disruptive Force?" *Journal of Human Dignity and Humiliation Studies* 1 (1): 1–30. http://www.humiliationstudies.org/documents/evelin/HumiliationandFearinGlobalizingWorldHumanDHSJournal.pdf (last accessed January 27, 2015)

Lister, Ruth. 2004. *Poverty*. 1st ed. Key Concepts. Cambridge/Malden: Polity.

Loureiro, Maria Isabel, Ana Rita Goes, Gisele Paim da Câmara, Manuel Gonçalves-Pereira, Teresa Maia, and Luís Saboga Nunes. 2009. "Priorities for Mental Health

Promotion during Pregnancy and Infancy in Primary Health Care." *Global Health Promotion* 16 (1): 29–38. doi:10.1177/1757975908100748.

MacDonald, Robert, and Jane Marsh. 2005. *Disconnected Youth? Growing Up in Britain's Poor Neighbourhoods*. 1st ed. Basingstoke/New York: Palgrave Macmillan.

Macleod, Colin M. 2010. "Primary Goods, Capabilities and Children." In *Measuring Justice – Primary Goods and Capabilities*, edited by Harry Brighouse and Ingrid Robeyns, 174–192. Cambridge/New York: Cambridge University Press.

Maher, JaneMaree, Suzanne Fraser, and Jan Wright. 2010. "Framing the Mother: Childhood Obesity, Maternal Responsibility and Care." *Journal of Gender Studies* 19 (3): 233–247. doi:10.1080/09589231003696037.

Margalit, Avishai. 1996. *The Decent Society*. 1st ed. Cambridge/London: Harvard University Press.

Marmot, Michael, and Richard Wilkinson, eds. 2003. *Social Determinants of Health: The Solid Facts*. 2nd ed. Copenhagen: Centre for Urban Health World Health Organization. http://www.euro.who.int/__data/assets/pdf_file/0005/98438/e81384.pdf (last accessed January 27, 2015).

McAuley, Colette, and Wendy Rose, eds. 2010. *Child Well-Being: Understanding Children's Lives*. 1st ed. London/Philadelphia: Jessica Kingsley.

Meghan, Henry, Alvaro Cortes, and Sean Morris. 2013. *The 2013 Annual Homeless Assessment Report to Congress (AHAR)*. Washington, DC: U.S. Department of Housing and Urban Development. https://www.hudexchange.info/resources/documents/ahar-2013-part1.pdf (last accessed January 27, 2015).

Melchior, Maria, Terrie E. Moffitt, Barry J. Milne, Richie Poulton, and Avshalom Caspi. 2007. "Why Do Children from Socioeconomically Disadvantaged Families Suffer from Poor Health When They Reach Adulthood? A Life-Course Study." *American Journal of Epidemiology* 166 (8): 966–974. doi:10.1093/aje/kwm155.

Millar, Jane. 2007. "Social Exclusion and Social Policy Research: Defining Exclusion." In *Multidisciplinary Handbook of Social Exclusion Research*, edited by Dominic Abrams, Julie Christian, and David Gordon, 1st ed., 1–16. Chichester: Wiley.

Miller, David. 1999. *Principles of Social Justice*. 1st ed. Cambridge/London: Harvard University Press.

———. 2007. *National Responsibility and Global Justice*. 1st ed. Oxford/New York: Oxford University Press.

Mills, Claudia. 2003. "The Child's Right to an Open Future?" *Journal of Social Philosophy* 34 (4): 499–509. doi:10.1111/1467-9833.00197.

Milne, Brian. 2013. *The History and Theory of Children's Citizenship in Contemporary Societies*. 1st ed. Dordrecht/New York: Springer. http://dx.doi.org/10.1007/978-94-007-6521-4.

Minujin, Alberto, Enrique Delamonica, Alejandra Davidziuk, and Edward D. Gonzalez. 2006. "The Definition of Child Poverty: A Discussion of Concepts and Measurements." *Environment and Urbanization* 18 (2): 481–500. doi:10.1177/0956247806069627.

Morgan, Craig, Tom Burns, Ray Fitzpatrick, Vanessa Pinfold, and Stefan Priebe. 2007. "Social Exclusion and Mental Health: Conceptual and Methodological Review." *British Journal of Psychiatry* 191 (December): 477–483. doi:10.1192/bjp.bp.106.034942.

Munoz-Darde, Veronique. 1999. "Is the Family to Be Abolished, Then?" *Proceedings of the Aristotelian Society* 99 (1): 37–56.
Najman, Jake M., Mohammad R. Hayatbakhsh, Alexandra Clavarino, William Bor, Michael J. O'Callaghan, and Gail M. Williams. 2010. "Family Poverty over the Early Life Course and Recurrent Adolescent and Young Adult Anxiety and Depression: A Longitudinal Study." *American Journal of Public Health* 100 (9): 1719–1723. doi:10.2105/AJPH.2009.180943.
Nandi, Arijit, M. Maria Glymour, Ichiro Kawachi, and Tyler J. VanderWeele. 2012. "Using Marginal Structural Models to Estimate the Direct Effect of Adverse Childhood Social Conditions on Onset of Heart Disease, Diabetes, and Stroke:" *Epidemiology* 23 (2): 223–232. doi:10.1097/EDE.0b013e31824570bd.
National Center on Family Homelessness. 2011. *America's Youngest Outcasts 2010*. Needham, MA: National Center on Family. http://www.homelesschildrenamerica.org/mediadocs/280.pdf (last accessed January 27, 2015).
Neuhäuser, Christian, and Julia Müller. 2011. "Relative Poverty." In *Humiliation, Degradation, Dehumanization: Human Dignity Violated*, edited by Paulus Kaufmann, Hannes Kuch, Christian Neuhäuser, and Elaine Webster, 1st ed., 159–172. Dordrecht/New York: Springer.
Nikulina, Valentina, Cathy Spatz Widom, and Sally Czaja. 2010. "The Role of Childhood Neglect and Childhood Poverty in Predicting Mental Health, Academic Achievement and Crime in Adulthood." *American Journal of Community Psychology* 48 (3–4): 309–321. doi:10.1007/s10464-010-9385-y.
Noggle, Robert. 2002. "Special Agents: Children's Autonomy and Parental Authority." In *The Moral and Political Status of Children*, edited by David Archard and Colin M. Macleod, 1st ed., 97–117. Oxford/New York: Oxford University Press.
Nolan, Brian, and Christopher T. Whelan. 2010. "Using Non-Monetary Deprivation Indicators to Analyze Poverty and Social Exclusion: Lessons from Europe?" *Journal of Policy Analysis and Management* 29 (2): 305–325. doi:10.1002/pam.20493.
Norris, Adele N., Anna Zajicek, and Yvette Murphy-Erby. 2010. "Intersectional Perspective and Rural Poverty Research: Benefits, Challenges and Policy Implications." *Journal of Poverty* 14 (1): 55–75. doi:10.1080/10875540903489413.
Norton, Andy. 2001. *A Rough Guide to PPAs: Participatory Poverty Assessment: An Introduction to Theory and Practice*. Edited by Overseas Development Institute (London). London: Centre for Aid and Public Expenditure Overseas Development Institute. http://info.worldbank.org/etools/docs/library/238411/ppa.pdf (last accessed January 27, 2015).
Nussbaum, Martha. 2000. *Women and Human Development – the Capabilities Approach*. 1st ed. Cambridge/New York: Cambridge University Press.
———. 2001. "Political Objectivity." *New Literary History* 32 (4): 883–906. doi:10.1353/nlh.2001.0056.
———. 2003. "Capabilities as Fundamental Entitlements: Sen and Social Justice." *Feminist Economics* 9 (2–3): 33–59. doi:10.1080/1354570022000077926.
———. 2006. *Frontiers of Justice: Disability, Nationality, Species Membership*. Cambridge/London: Belknap Press.
———. 2011. *Creating Capabilities: The Human Development Approach*. 1st ed. Cambridge/London: Belknap Press.

O'Connor, Alice. 2001. *Poverty Knowledge: Social Science, Social Policy, and the Poor in Twentieth-Century U.S. History*. 1st ed. Princeton: Princeton University Press.
Olsaretti, Serena. 2013. "Children as Public Goods?" *Philosophy and Public Affairs* 41 (3): 226–258. doi:10.1111/papa.12019.
O'Neill, Onora. 2001. "Agents of Justice." *Metaphilosophy* 32 (1–2): 180–195. doi:10.1111/1467-9973.00181.
Oosterlaken, Ilse. 2012. "Is Pogge a Capability Theorist in Disguise? A Critical Examination of Thomas Pogge's Defence of Rawlsian Resourcism." *Ethical Theory and Moral Practice* 16 (1): 205–215. doi:10.1007/s10677-012-9344-9.
Øyen, Else. 2009. "The Paradox of Poverty Research: Why Is Extreme Poverty Not in Focus?" In *Absolute Poverty and Global Justice: Empirical Data, Moral Theories, Initiatives*, edited by Elke Mack, Michael Schramm, Stephan Klasen, and Thomas Pogge, 1st ed., 259–271. Farnham/Burlington: Ashgate.
Page, Edward A. 2008. "Distributing the Burdens of Climate Change." *Environmental Politics* 17 (4): 556–575. doi:10.1080/09644010802193419.
———. 2012. "Give It Up for Climate Change: A Defence of the Beneficiary Pays Principle." *International Theory* 4 (02): 300–330. doi:10.1017/S175297191200005X.
Palloni, Alberto. 2006. "Reproducing Inequalities: Luck, Wallets, and the Enduring Effects of Childhood Health." *Demography* 43 (4): 587–615. doi:10.1353/dem.2006.0036.
Pascal, Christine, and Tony Bertram. 2009. "Listening to Young Citizens: The Struggle to Make Real a Participatory Paradigm in Research with Young Children." *European Early Childhood Education Research Journal* 17 (2): 249–262. doi:10.1080/13502930902951486.
Paul, Karsten I., and Bernad Batinic. 2009. "The Need for Work: Jahoda's Latent Functions of Employment in a Representative Sample of the German Population." *Journal of Organizational Behavior* 31 (1): 45–64. doi:10.1002/job.622.
Percy-Smith, Barry, and Nigel Thomas, eds. 2010. *A Handbook of Children and Young People's Participation: Perspectives from Theory and Practice*. London/New York: Routledge.
Phillips, Ben, Riyana Miranti, Yogi Vidyattama, and Rebecca Cassells. 2013. *Poverty, Social Exclusion and Disadvantage in Australia*. National Centre for Social and Economic Modelling, University of Canberra. www.natsem.canberra.edu.au/storage/Poverty-Social-Exclusion-and-Disadvantage.pdf (last accessed January 27, 2015).
Pichler, Florian, and Claire Wallace. 2008. "Social Capital and Social Class in Europe: The Role of Social Networks in Social Stratification." *European Sociological Review* 25 (3): 319–332. doi:10.1093/esr/jcn050.
Pierik, Roland, and Ingrid Robeyns. 2007. "Resources versus Capabilities: Social Endowments in Egalitarian Theory." *Political Studies* 55 (1): 133–152. doi:10.1111/j.1467-9248.2007.00646.x.
Pinderhughes, Ellen E., Robert Nix, E. Michael Foster, and Damon Jones. 2001. "Parenting in Context: Impact of Neighborhood Poverty, Residential Stability, Public Services, Social Networks, and Danger on Parental Behaviors." *Journal of Marriage and Family* 63 (4): 941–953. doi:10.1111/j.1741-3737.2001.00941.x.
Pizzi, Michael A., and Kerryellen Vroman. 2013. "Childhood Obesity: Effects on Children's Participation, Mental Health, and Psychosocial Development."

Occupational Therapy in Health Care 27(2): 99–112. doi:10.3109/07380577.201 3.784839.

Pogge, Thomas. 2002. "Can the Capability Approach Be Justified?" *Philosophical Topics* 30 (2): 167–228. doi:10.5840/philtopics200230216.

———, ed. 2007. *Freedom from Poverty as a Human Right: Who Owes What to the Very Poor?* 1st ed. Oxford/New York: Oxford University Press.

Prince, Martin, Vikram Patel, Shekhar Saxena, Mario Maj, Joanna Maselko, Michael R. Phillips, and Atif Rahman. 2007. "No Health without Mental Health." *Lancet* 370 (9590): 859–877. doi:10.1016/S0140-6736(07)61238-0.

Pritchard, Colin, and Richard Williams. 2011. "Poverty and Child (0–14 Years) Mortality in the USA and Other Western Countries as an Indicator of 'How Well a Country Meets the Needs of Its Children' (UNICEF)." *International Journal of Adolescent Medicine and Health* 23 (3): 251–255. doi: 10.1515/ijamh.2011.052.

Qvortrup, Jens. 1994. "Childhood Matters: An Introduction." In *Childhood Matters: Social Theory, Practice and Politics*, edited by Jens Qvortrup, Marjatta Bardy, Giovanni Sgritta, and Helmut Wintersberger, 1–24. Aldershot: Avebury Press.

———. 2004. "Editorial: The Waiting Child." *Childhood* 11 (3): 267–273. doi:10.1177/0907568204044884.

Raphael, Dennis. 2011. "Poverty in Childhood and Adverse Health Outcomes in Adulthood." *Maturitas* 69 (1): 22–26. doi:10.1016/j.maturitas.2011.02.011.

Rawls, John. 1971. *A Theory of Justice*. 1st ed. Cambridge/London: Harvard University Press.

———. 1982. "Social Unity and Primary Goods." In *Utilitarianism and Beyond*, edited by Amartya Sen and Bernard Williams, 1st ed., 159–186. Cambridge: Cambridge University Press.

———. 2005. *Political Liberalism*. Expanded ed. New York: Columbia University Press.

Reading, Richard. 1997. "Poverty and the Health of Children and Adolescents." *Archives of Disease in Childhood* 76 (5): 463–467. doi:10.1136/adc.76.5.463.

Reddy, Sanjay G., and Thomas Pogge. 2010. "How Not to Count the Poor." In *Debates on the Measurement of Global Poverty*, edited by Sudhir Anand, Paul D. Segal, and Joseph Eugene Stiglitz, 1st ed., 42–85. Oxford/New York: Oxford University Press.

Redecker, Christine, Miriam Leis, Matthijs Leendertse, Yves Punie, Govert Gijsbers, Paul Kirschner, Slavi Stoyanov, and Bert Hoogveld. 2011. *The Future of Learning: Preparing for Change*. 1st ed. Vol. 66836–2011. JRC. Luxembourg: Office for Official Publications of the European Communities. http://ftp.jrc.es/EURdoc/JRC66836.pdf (last accessed January 27, 2015).

Ridge, Tess. 2002. *Childhood Poverty and Social Exclusion: From a Child's Perspective*. 1st ed. Bristol: Policy Press.

———. 2009. *Living with Poverty: A Review of the Literature on Children's and Families' Experiences of Poverty*. Research Report No. 594. London: Department for Work and Pensions. http://www.bris.ac.uk/poverty/downloads/keyofficialdocuments/Child%20Poverty%20lit%20review%20DWP.pdf (last accessed January 27, 2015).

———. 2011. "The Everyday Costs of Poverty in Childhood: A Review of Qualitative Research Exploring the Lives and Experiences of Low-Income Children in the UK." *Children and Society* 25 (1): 73–84. doi:10.1111/j.1099-0860.2010.00345.x.

Robeyns, Ingrid. 2003. "Sen's Capability Approach and Gender Inequality: Selecting Relevant Capabilities." *Feminist Economics* 9 (2–3): 61–92. doi:10.10 80/1354570022000078024.

———. 2005. "The Capability Approach: A Theoretical Survey." *Journal of Human Development* 6 (1): 93–114. doi: 10.1080/146498805200034266.

———. 2006. "The Capability Approach in Practice." *Journal of Political Philosophy* 14 (3): 351–376. doi: 10.1111/j.1467-9760.2006.00263.x.

———. 2009. "Equality and Justice." In *An Introduction to the Human Development and Capability Approach: Freedom and Agency*, edited by Séverine Deneulin and Lila Shahani, 1st ed., 101–120. London/Sterling/Ottawa: Earthscan/International Development Research Centre.

Ruggeri Laderchi, Caterina, Ruhi Saith, and Frances Stewart. 2006. "Does It Matter That We Do Not Agree on the Definition of Poverty? A Comparison of Four Approaches." In *Understanding Human Well-Being*, edited by Mark McGillivray and Matthew Clarke, 1st ed., 19–53. Tokyo/New York: United Nations University Press.

Ruiz-Casares, Mónica, Cécile Rousseau, Ilse Derluyn, Charles Watters, and François Crépeau. 2010. "Right and Access to Healthcare for Undocumented Children: Addressing the Gap between International Conventions and Disparate Implementations in North America and Europe." *Social Science and Medicine* 70 (2): 329–336. doi:10.1016/j.socscimed.2009.10.013.

Russell, Mary, Barbara Harris, and Annemarie Gockel. 2008. "Parenting in Poverty: Perspectives of High-Risk Parents." *Journal of Children and Poverty* 14 (1): 83–98. doi:10.1080/10796120701871322.

Santiago, Catherine DeCarlo, Martha E. Wadsworth, and Jessica Stump. 2011. "Socioeconomic Status, Neighborhood Disadvantage, and Poverty-Related Stress: Prospective Effects on Psychological Syndromes among Diverse Low-Income Families." *Journal of Economic Psychology* 32 (2): 218–230. doi:10.1016/j.joep.2009.10.008.

Schoeman, Ferdinand. 1980. "Rights of Children, Rights of Parents, and the Moral Basis of the Family." *Ethics* 91 (1): 6–19.

Schweiger, Gottfried. 2012. "Philosophie und Armut: Überlegungen zu ihrem Zusammenhang." *Diskurs: Gesellschafts- und Geisteswissenschaftliche Interventionen* 8 (1): 66–87.

Sen, Amartya. 1980. "Equality of What?" In *The Tanner Lectures on Human Value*, edited by Sterling M. McMurrin, 1st ed., 195–220. Salt Lake City: University of Utah Press.

———. 1983. "Poor, Relatively Speaking." *Oxford Economic Papers* 35 (2): 153–169.

———. 1985. "Well-Being, Agency and Freedom: The Dewey Lectures 1984." *Journal of Philosophy* 82 (4): 169–221.

———. 1990. *On Ethics and Economics*. Oxford/Cambridge: Blackwell.

———. 1992. *Inequality Reexamined*. 1st ed. Cambridge/London: Harvard University Press.

———. 1993. "Capability and Well-Being." In *The Quality of Life*, edited by Martha Nussbaum and Amartya Sen, 1st ed., 30–53. Oxford: Clarendon Press.

———. 1999a. *Development as Freedom*. 1st ed. New York: Anchor Books.

———. 1999b. *Commodities and Capabilities*. 1st ed. Oxford/New York: Oxford University Press.

———. 2004a. "Elements of a Theory of Human Rights." *Philosophy and Public Affairs* 32 (4): 315–356.

———. 2004b. "Capabilities, Lists, and Public Reason: Continuing the Conversation." *Feminist Economics* 10 (3): 77–80. doi:10.1080/135457004200 0315163.

———. 2005. "Human Rights and Capabilities." *Journal of Human Development* 6 (2): 151–166. doi:10.1080/14649880500120491.

———. 2009. *The Idea of Justice*. 1st ed. London/New York: Allen Lane.

Sen, Amartya, and Bernard Williams. 1992. "Introduction: Utilitarianism and Beyond." In *Utilitarianism and Beyond*, edited by Amartya Sen and Bernard Williams, 1–21. Cambridge/New York: Cambridge University Press.

Shue, Henry. 1996. *Basic Rights: Subsistence, Affluence, and U.S. Foreign Policy*. 2nd ed. Princeton: Princeton University Press.

Sime, Daniela. 2008. "Ethical and Methodological Issues in Engaging Young People Living in Poverty with Participatory Research Methods." *Children's Geographies* 6 (1): 63–78. doi:10.1080/14733280701791926.

Spicker, Paul. 2007. "Definitions of Poverty: Twelve Clusters of Meaning." In *Poverty: An International Glossary*, edited by Paul Spicker, Sonia Alvarez Leguizamón, and David Gordon, 2nd ed., 229–243. London/New York: Zed Books.

Thompson, Ross A. 2007. "The Development of the Person: Social Understanding, Relationships, Conscience, Self." In *Handbook of Child Psychology*. Vol. 3: *Social, Emotional, and Personality Development*, edited by William Damon and Richard M. Lerner, 6th ed., 24–98. Hoboken: Wiley.

Townsend, Peter. 1979. *Poverty in the United Kingdom: A Survey of Household Resources and Standards of Living*. 1st ed. Berkeley: University of California Press.

UNICEF. 2005. *The State of World's Children 2005: Childhood under Threat*. 1st ed. New York: UNICEF. www.unicef.org/sowc05/english/sowc05.pdf (last accessed January 27, 2015).

———. 2007. *Children on the Brink: A Focused Situation Analysis of Vulnerable, Excluded and Discriminated Children in Romania*. Bucharest: UNICEF ROMANIA. www.unicef.org/ceecis/06-rom-sitan_En.pdf (last accessed January 27, 2015).

———. 2012. *Levels and Trends in Child Mortality*. Report 2012. New York: UNICEF. www.unicef.org/videoaudio/PDFs/UNICEF_2012_child_mortality_for_web_0904.pdf (last accessed January 27, 2015).

UNICEF IRC. 2012. *Measuring Child Poverty: New League Tables of Child Poverty in the World's Rich Countries*. Innocenti Report Card 10. Florence: UNICEF Innocenti Research Centre. http://www.unicef-irc.org/publications/pdf/rc10_Eng.pdf (last accessed January 27, 2015).

———. 2013. *Child Well-Being in Rich Countries: A Comparative Overview*. Innocenti Report Card 11. Florence: UNICEF Innocenti Research Centre. www.unicef.org/media/files/RC11-ENG-embargo.pdf (last accessed January 27, 2015).

Uprichard, Emma. 2008. "Children as 'Being and Becomings': Children, Childhood and Temporality." *Children and Society* 22 (4): 303–313. doi:10.1111/j.1099-0860.2007.00110.x.

Vallentyne, Peter. 2005. "Of Mice and Men: Equality and Animals." *Journal of Ethics* 9 (3–4): 403–433. doi:10.1007/s10892-005-3509-x.

Venkatapuram, Sridhar. 2011. *Health Justice*. 1st ed. Cambridge/Malden: Polity Press.

———. 2013. "Health, Vital Goals, and Central Human Capabilities." *Bioethics* 27 (5): 271–279. doi:10.1111/j.1467-8519.2011.01953.x.

Walker, Melanie, and Elaine Unterhalter, eds. 2010. *Amartya Sen's Capability Approach and Social Justice in Education*. 1st ed. Basingstoke: Palgrave Macmillan.

Walker, Robert, Grace Bantebya Kyomuhendo, Elaine Chase, Sohail Choudhry, Erika K. Gubrium, Jo Yongmie Nicola, Ivar LøDemel, et al. 2013. "Poverty in Global Perspective: Is Shame a Common Denominator?" *Journal of Social Policy* 42 (2): 215–233. doi:10.1017/S0047279412000979.

Weinreb, Linda, Cheryl Wehler, Jennifer Perloff, Richard Scott, David Hosmer, Linda Sagor, and Craig Gundersen. 2002. "Hunger: Its Impact on Children's Health and Mental Health." *Pediatrics* 110 (4): e41.

Welsh, Janet A., Robert L. Nix, Clancy Blair, Karen L. Bierman, and Keith E. Nelson. 2010. "The Development of Cognitive Skills and Gains in Academic School Readiness for Children from Low-Income Families." *Journal of Educational Psychology* 102 (1): 43–53. doi:10.1037/a0016738.

Widom, Cathy Spatz, Sally J. Czaja, Tyrone Bentley, and Mark S. Johnson. 2012. "A Prospective Investigation of Physical Health Outcomes in Abused and Neglected Children: New Findings from a 30-Year Follow-Up." *American Journal of Public Health* 102 (6): 1135–1144. doi:10.2105/AJPH.2011.300636.

Williams, David R., Michelle Sternthal, and Rosalind J. Wright. 2009. "Social Determinants: Taking the Social Context of Asthma Seriously." *Pediatrics* 123 (Supplement): S174–S184. doi:10.1542/peds.2008-2233H.

Williamson, Deanna L., and Jeff Carr. 2009. "Health as a Resource for Everyday Life: Advancing the Conceptualization." *Critical Public Health* 19 (March): 107–122. doi:10.1080/09581590802376234.

Williamson, Jeffrey G. 2011. *Trade and Poverty: When the Third World Fell Behind*. 1st ed. Cambridge: MIT Press.

Wilson, William J. 1997. *When Work Disappears: The World of the New Urban Poor*. 1st ed. New York: Vintage Books.

Wittchen, Hans-Ulrich, Frank Jacobi, Jürgen Rehm, Anders Gustavsson, Mikael Svensson, B. Jönsson, J. Olesen, et al. 2011. "The Size and Burden of Mental Disorders and Other Disorders of the Brain in Europe 2010." *European Neuropsychopharmacology: The Journal of the European College of Neuropsychopharmacology* 21 (9): 655–679. doi:10.1016/j.euroneuro.2011.07.018.

Wolff, Jonathan, and Avner de-Shalit. 2007. *Disadvantage*. 1st ed. Oxford Political Theory. Oxford/New York: Oxford University Press.

———. 2013. "On Fertile Functionings: A Response to Martha Nussbaum." *Journal of Human Development and Capabilities* 14 (1): 161–165. doi:10.1080/19452829.2013.762177.

Yoshikawa, Hirokazu, J. Lawrence Aber, and William R. Beardslee. 2012. "The Effects of Poverty on the Mental, Emotional, and Behavioral Health of Children and Youth: Implications for Prevention." *American Psychologist* 67 (4): 272–284. doi:10.1037/a0028015.

Young, Iris Marion. 2011. *Responsibility for Justice*. Oxford Political Philosophy. Oxford/New York: Oxford University Press.

Zavaleta Reyles, Diego. 2007. "The Ability to Go About without Shame: A Proposal for Internationally Comparable Indicators of Shame and Humiliation." *Oxford Development Studies* 35 (4): 405–430. doi:10.1080/13600810701701905.

Zhang, Ming. 2003. "Links between School Absenteeism and Child Poverty." *Pastoral Care in Education* 21 (1): 10–17. doi:10.1111/1468-0122.00249.

Index

adaptive preferences, 16–17, 46, 106, 132, 155
Alstott, Anne, 155–157
Anderson, Elizabeth, 104
Archard, David, 105–106, 150, 155

Biggeri, Mario, 8, 31–32, 35, 48–49, 68, 167–168
Brighouse, Harry, 8–9, 105–106, 149–150, 155

capabilities, 7–8, 12–13, 22–25, 36
 evolving capabilities, 28, 31–32, 35, 68
 selecting capabilities, 37–51
Capability Approach, 6–8, 15–66, 118–119, 149, 165–166
child poverty
 concepts of, 1–5, 70–85, 165–166
 in the EU, 5, 75–82, 84–85, 117, 120–121
 experience of, 46–47, 104–115, 143
 material deprivation, 71, 76–84
 in the USA, 5, 72–75, 83–85, 103, 116, 117, 153
children
 agency, 28–29, 31, 47, 131, 142
 autonomy, 36–37, 156
 nature of childhood, 26–31
 participation, 95, 105–107
 vulnerability and powerlessness, 26–28
 well-becoming, 7–11
 well-being, 7–11, 48–49, 82–84
conversion factors, 23–25, 32, 60, 170
corrosive disadvantage, 13, 33–35, 47, 62, 87–88, 101, 116, 158–159

De-Shalit, Anvar, 7, 9, 33–35
dignity, 37, 43–44, 60, 112
Dworkin, Roland, 19–21, 118

education, 67–69, 93–94, 98–104
equality of opportunity, 13, 56

functionings, 12–13, 15–16, 22–23, 28, 35–36
fertile functionings, 33–35, 62, 87, 93–94

health, 67–69, 85–93, 101, 102
humiliation, 111–115

justice
 agents of justice, 120–148
 currency of justice, 16–37
 equality, 19–21, 51–64, 104, 112–113, 159, 168–170
 global justice, 162–175
 priority, 47, 62–63, 159, 172
 social justice, 5–6
 sufficiency, 51–64

Macleod, Colin, 28

Nussbaum, Martha, 6–8, 29, 35–36, 39–40, 52–53, 62, 119, 166–168

responsibility
 ability to pay principle, 125–126
 beneficiary principle, 127–129
 family and parents, 122, 133–134, 142, 146, 148–160
 state, 143–144, 146, 148–160, 171–172
rights
 children, 27, 29, 105, 106, 107, 149, 156, 157
 parents, 132, 149, 150, 151, 156, 157

Sen, Amartya, 6–7, 16–19, 22–23, 37–39, 58, 71, 106, 167, 175
social exclusion, 67–69, 93–98

threshold, 15, 52, 53–66, 70–76, 94, 163–170

Wolff, Jonathan, 7, 9, 33–35

Young, Iris Marion, 13, 122–124, 127, 129, 130–135

The manufacturer's authorised representative in the EU is Springer Nature Customer Service Centre GmbH, Europaplatz 3, 69115 Heidelberg, Germany. If you have any concerns regarding our products, please contact ProductSafety@springernature.com

Printed and bound by CPI Group (UK) Ltd, Croydon, CR0 4YY
23/03/2026
02076458-0010